CHENG CHUNG
BOOK CO., LTD.

CHENG CHUNG
BOOK CO., LTD.

CHENG CHUNG
BOOK CO., LTD.

CHENG CHUNG
BOOK CO., LTD.

實用
視聽華語
2 上

PRACTICAL AUDIO-VISUAL CHINESE

主 編 者◎國立臺灣師範大學國語教學中心
編輯委員◎范慧貞・蕭美美・劉咪咪

正中書局

序

中國文化上下五千多年，歷史悠久，博大精深，是中國人在從漁獵採集社會到游牧農業社會一系列發展裡，所孕育出來的文明瑰寶，於世界文化史上，佔有無比重要的地位。時至十九、二十世紀，從一八四〇年鴉片戰爭至今一百五十多年間，中國文化受到了來自西方的工業社會及後工業社會的挑戰，開始因應變革、學習調適、檢討反省、轉化創新。

尤其是在二次世界大戰後的五十年間，中國人開始分裂成兩個實驗室，各自尋求因應轉化創新之道。第一個實驗室在大陸，可稱之為大陸型導向的中國文化實驗區；另一個在臺灣，可視之為海洋型導向的文化實驗區。任何人，如欲瞭解中國文化在二十世紀的最新發展，必須要對這兩個實驗區裡所產生的成果，細心考察、分析對比，缺一不可。

海洋型導向的中國文化，包括臺灣、香港、新加坡、……以及全世界有華人聚居的地方，最近十幾年來，尚可包括新進發展的廣州、深圳及大上海地區。總之，海洋型導向的中國文化，傾向自由、開放、多元化的思考模式，社會的發展也兼容並蓄，彈性十足；人們吸收新知快，應變能力強；尊重知識、提倡文教、發展科技、努力人文。相信在二十一世紀，這種文化風格，將推廣至所有華人居住的地方，並進一步產生新的成果，回饋西方社會。

而上述理想之實現，其最重要的手段與工具，便是中國語言的學習與推廣。師大國語文中心第六任主任李振清教授有鑑於此，早在民國七十八年，便著手新版國語文教材之策畫與編纂，此一浩大的工程，在國語文中心第七任葉德明教授手中，得以完全實現。由葉主任主編，陳惠玲執行編輯，在中心教師陳夜寧、王淑美、盧翠英、范慧貞、劉咪咪、蕭美美、張仲敏、韓英華、錢進明等的通力合作之下，於民國八十三年厚達千餘頁的《實用視聽華語》三巨冊，終於大功告成，是為當今學習中文的最佳教材。全書內容單元，體例清新，形式及題材充滿了創意，成績斐然，廣獲好評，是目前最受歡迎的華語讀本。

然葉主任及編輯群謙沖為懷，並沒有立即將全書正式出版，而以「試用本」的形式問世，希望通過實際教學，吸取各方專家意見，冀能將全書修訂得盡善盡美，以便嘉惠更多的學子。

如今，此一修訂本即將由正中書局正式製版付梓，李、葉兩位主任多年的努力，終於完全開花結果。我在此，除了向編者及書局道賀外，也希望藉由此書的正式發行，使海內外所有的專家學者，有機會瞭解此書、使用此書，並提出更進一步的改進之道。同時也希望世界上愛好中華文化的友人，通過此書，能更深刻的瞭解海洋型導向中國文化，並探索其與大陸型中國文化之間，複雜又奧妙的互動關係。

畢竟語文只是工具、只是鑰匙；文化才是材料，才是百寶箱，等待我們去不斷琢磨，去時時開啟。

1999年8月

編輯要旨

時代在進步，國際間的文化交流也日漸擴充，為了達到彼此間學術研究的目的，學習語文是必要的溝通工具。中華民國教育部有鑑於國內所出版的中文教材已不敷應用，而於一九九〇年九月委託國立臺灣師範大學國語教學中心編纂「實用視聽華語教材」。

本部教材共分《實用視聽華語》㈠、㈡、㈢等三套，每套包括課本、教師手冊、學生作業簿等三冊，每課均附有十分鐘的錄影帶。

本書在編寫之初曾邀請國內外專家學者舉行會議，商定編輯計畫、編寫之方式及各冊教材應包括之內容。

本書之教法強調以「溝通式」教學為主，因此配合視聽媒體，在每課之前讓學生先看一次錄影帶，引起動機後再進行教學。待學生對於生字、語法、課文、課室活動等全部熟悉後，再看一次錄影帶。此時學生應該對內容完全了解，並說出正確的語言。

《實用視聽華語㈠》課本二十五課，重點在訓練學生的基本發音語法及常用字彙，達到語言流利的目的。

《實用視聽華語㈡》課本二十八課，偏重大學校園活動和日常生活的話題，介紹文化差異，包括社會、歷史、地理等。語法配合情景介紹句子結構用法，並加上各種不同形式的手寫短文，增加學生識別手寫漢字的能力。

《實用視聽華語㈢》課本二十課，課文介紹中華文化之特質及風俗習慣，以短劇、敘述文及議論文等體裁為主，內容包括民俗文化、傳統戲劇、文字、醫藥、科技、環保、消費、消閒等，配合時代潮流，提高學生對目前各類話題討論的能力。

本書所有的生字與生詞注音係採用**國語注音符號與漢語拼音**並列，以收廣為使用之效。

《實用視聽華語㈠》課本共有生字六百一十四個、生詞八百八十五條；《實用視聽華語㈡》課本共有生字九百個，生詞共計一千三百條；《實用視聽華語㈢》課本生詞七百二十三條。

語法說明係參考耶魯大學教材系統，並按照實際句子情況解釋，在《實用視聽華語㈠》教材中偏重基本句型練習，共有八十九個；《實用視聽華語

㈡》教材則以連結結構為重點，共使用二百五十個句型；《實用視聽華語㈢》教材則以書面語之文法為主，介紹文章內所用之文法要點六十七個。

每冊教材所包括的內容大致如下：1.課文、對話；2.生字、生詞及用法；3.語法要點及句型練習；4.課室活動；5.短文；6.註釋。《實用視聽華語㈠》及《實用視聽華語㈡》漢字書寫均安排在學生作業中練習。《實用視聽華語㈢》課本中介紹成語及俗語，並附「閱讀與探討」、「佳文欣賞」等項目。

本書《實用視聽華語㈠》教材由陳夜寧、王淑美、盧翠英三位老師負責編纂工作；《實用視聽華語㈡》教材由范慧貞、劉咪咪、蕭美美老師等編寫；《實用視聽華語㈢》教材由錢進明、張仲敏、韓英華老師編寫。英文由Christian A. Terfloth, Robert Kinney; Laura Burian, Earl S. Tai, Michael Fahey, Robert Murphy; Norman Eisley 等人翻譯。插圖由林芳珠、吳昌昇、朱晏臨、吳佳謀、王翰賢、蘇菁瑛等六位畫家完成。

本書在編寫初稿完成後，曾邀請國內外學者專家進行審查，經過前後三次修正。審查委員如下：美國夏威夷大學李英哲教授、猶他大學齊德立教授、麻州大學鄧守信教授、柏克萊加州大學張洪年教授、印地安那大學嚴棉教授、麻州衛斯理學院馬靜恆教授、佛羅里達大學屈承熹教授、麻州威廉斯學院顧百里教授、清華大學曹逢甫教授、東海大學馮以堅教授、臺灣師大施玉惠教授、臺灣師大吳國賢教授、臺灣師大羅青哲教授、中華語文研習所何景賢博士。

本書之編纂工作費時三年，並進行半年試教及內容修正，感謝所有費心編輯及審核的作者及專家學者，使這部中文教材得以問世，在各位教學者使用後，敬請指示。

葉德明

1999年8月

目　錄

第一課

新室友

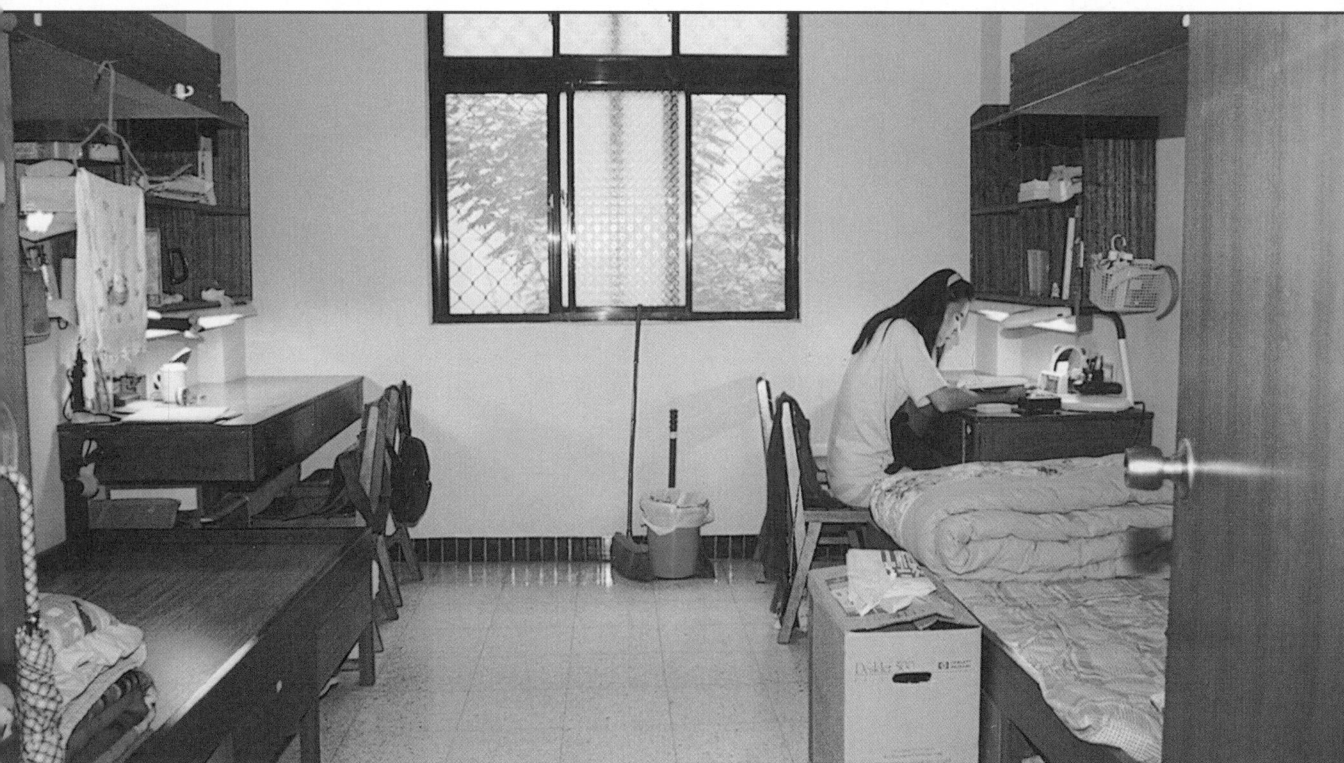

・臺灣的大學女生宿舍（吳俊銘攝）

（美國大學學生宿舍電梯門口，高偉立在等電梯。林建國跟爸爸、媽媽拿著行李走過去。）

建國：我的房間在五樓。（電梯門開了，四人走進去）

偉立：嗨！你們好。

媽媽：你會說中文啊？

偉立：我學過一點兒。我是中文系二年級的學生。

建國：我是新生。我叫林建國。你呢？

偉立：我是William。我的中文名字是高偉立。

建國：這是我爸媽。

偉立：林先生，林太太[1]，幸會，幸會[2]。

爸媽：你好！（出了電梯）

偉立：我也住五樓。你住幾號房？

建國：五〇六。

偉立：真的嗎？我也住五〇六。Great! **噢**，對了[3]。太棒了。

媽媽：是啊！真沒想到建國的室友會說中國話。（進了房間）

建國：這是我的床吧？（把東西放下，上下左右看一看）

嗯，看起來還不錯，**就是**舊了點兒。

媽媽：舊點兒**沒關係**，你自己弄乾淨**就好了**。（對偉立）

以後要麻煩你照顧他了。這是他第一次離開家。

建國：媽！我不是小孩子了。

媽媽：好，好，我知道。可是他是二年級，知道的**總是**多一點兒。

爸爸：我們做父母的**總是**不放心，怕孩子不會照顧自己。

偉立：我父母本來也一樣，後來我開始送報、幫忙做家事，因為我做得還不錯，他們慢慢兒地就放心了。

媽媽：難怪有人說西方小孩比東方小孩獨立。

建國：那是因為你們從來不讓我們獨立。

媽媽：我們覺得把書念好最重要[4]，所以沒叫你們做家事，也不希望你們去打工。好了[5]，**還是**先把箱子裡的東西拿出來**吧**！（打開箱子）

建國：你看，我說得沒錯吧！你又要幫我做了。

媽媽：對不起，我又忘了。好，好，你就自己**來**吧！

建國：你放心，沒問題。我們去吃飯吧！我餓了！

爸爸（對偉立）：要不要一起去？

偉立：謝謝，我吃過了。

媽媽：那[6]就走吧。別忘了鑰匙。

※ ※ ※ ※ ※ ※

（在宿舍裡，偉立正在看報）

偉立：回來**啦**[7]?! 你爸媽呢？

建國：回去了。

偉立：你家在哪兒？

建國：波士頓。你呢？

偉立：Buffalo，水牛城，在紐約州。你爸媽好像很關心你。

建國：是啊！可是我媽太嘮叨，有時候我真受不了。

偉立：那[6]你一定很高興可以住校了？可是大概過**不了幾**天，你**就**會想他們了。你們在家都說中文嗎？

建國：我十歲的時候，全家就從臺灣移民到美國來了。我爸媽怕我們把中文忘了，所以在家的時候，一定要我們說中文。你呢？你為什麼要學中文？

偉立：我幾年前在國家地理雜誌裡看到一篇文章，介紹中國的萬里長城，看了以後，就開始**對**中國**有興趣**了。

建國：你的中文說得不錯，口音不太重。你們中文課都學些什麼？有沒有意思？

偉立：說話跟寫字。我覺得很有意思。可是寫字比較難。

建國：我也不太會寫。那[6]我也去選你們的課，好不好？

偉立：好啊！

・大學女生宿舍門口（范慧貞提供）

生詞及例句

1. 室ㄕˋ友ㄧㄡˇ (shìyǒu)　*N*: **roommate, housemate**

　我們以前是室友，我現在不跟他住在一起了。

2. 宿ㄙㄨˋ舍ㄕㄜˋ (sùshè)　*N*: **dormitory**

3. 電ㄉㄧㄢˋ梯ㄊㄧ (diàntī)　*N*: **elevator, lift**（**M**：部）

　梯ㄊㄧ子˙ㄗ (tī·zi)　*N*: **ladder**

　樓ㄌㄡˊ梯ㄊㄧ (lóutī)　*N*: **stairs**

　東西太重了，別走樓梯，坐電梯吧！

4. 系ㄒㄧˋ (xì)　*N/M*: **department (in colleges)**

　張：你在大學念什麼系？

　王：我念中文系。

5. 新ㄒㄧㄣ生ㄕㄥ (xīnshēng)　*N*: **freshman, first-year student, new student**

　今年中文系有多少新生？

6. 幸ㄒㄧㄥˋ會ㄏㄨㄟˋ (xìnghuì)　*IE*: **It is a pleasure to meet you!**

　張：我來介紹一下，這是李先生。這是高先生。

　高：李先生，你好。

　李：幸會，幸會。

7. 棒ㄅㄤˋ (bàng)　*SV*: **good; fine; excellent, great!**

　那個學生的歌，唱得真棒！

8. 沒ㄇㄟˊ關ㄍㄨㄢ係˙ㄒㄧ (méi//guān·xì)

　IE/VO: **It's not important, It doesn't matter, It's nothing, It's all right /no trelated, no relationship to X**

　你不打電話給他也沒什麼關係，他已經知道了。

　關ㄍㄨㄢ係˙ㄒㄧ (guān·xì)　*N*: **relationship**

　⑴最近我們國家跟那個國家的關係不太好，你最好不要去旅行。

　⑵我們都姓陳，可是我們沒有什麼關係。

9. 照ㄓㄠˋ顧ㄍㄨˋ (zhàogù)　*V*: **to look after; to take care of**

(1)他的工作就是照顧病人。

(2)再見了，好好兒照顧自己。

10. 總ㄗㄨㄥˇ是ㄕˋ (zǒngshì) *A*: **always, invariably**

人總是會生病的。

11. 難ㄋㄢˊ怪ㄍㄨㄞˋ (nán'guài) *A*: **no wonder**

張：他在美國住了十年。

王：難怪英文說得那麼好。

12. 西ㄒㄧ方ㄈㄤ (xīfāng) *N*: **the West, Occident**

會說中國話的西方人多不多？

東ㄉㄨㄥ方ㄈㄤ (dōngfāng) *N*: **the East, Orient**

東方學生上課的時候不大喜歡問問題嗎？

13. 獨ㄉㄨˊ立ㄌㄧˋ (dúlì) *V/SV*: **independent, to be independent**

(1)美國是一七七六年獨立的。

(2)你什麼事都要別人替你做，怎麼能獨立呢？

14. 從ㄘㄨㄥˊ來ㄌㄞˊ不ㄅㄨˋ (cóngláibù) *A*: **never (habitual)**

張：你們喝不喝酒？

王：我從來不喝酒，謝謝你。

李：我從來沒喝過酒，可是今天想喝一點。

15. 打ㄉㄚˇ工ㄍㄨㄥ (dǎ//gōng) *VO*: **to work part-time or temporarily**

這個學生下了課，要去圖書館打兩小時的工。

16. 打ㄉㄚˇ開ㄎㄞ (dǎ//kāi) *RC*: **to open up**

這個窗戶壞了，我打不開。

17. 來ㄌㄞˊ (lái) *V*: **to do (something implied in the context)**

(1)你要吃什麼，自己來，不必客氣。

(2)張：我替你拿行李。

李：我來，我來。

18. 鑰ㄧㄠˋ匙˙ㄕ (yào·shi) *N*: **key（M：把）**

這把鑰匙是開哪個門的？

19. 州ㄓㄡ (zhōu) *N/M*: **state (section of a nation)**

美國一共有五十州。

20. 關ㄍㄨㄢ 心ㄒㄧㄣ (guānxīn)　*V/N*: **to be concerned about/concern**

(1) 他不太關心孩子的健康。

(2) 我已經好了，謝謝你的關心。

21. 嘮ㄌㄠˊ 叨ㄉㄠ (láodāo)

SV/V: **to be a nag, to be repetitive in speech/to nag at**

(1) 孩子常常覺得自己的父母很嘮叨。

(2) 不是你媽媽喜歡嘮叨你，你自己想想，她說了這麼多次，你聽了沒有？

22. 受ㄕㄡˋ 不ㄅㄨˋ 了ㄌㄧㄠˇ (shòu·bùliǎo)

RC: **cannot stand, cannot bear, unable to endure**

天氣這麼熱，誰受得了啊？

23. 會ㄏㄨㄟˋ (huì)　*AV*: **will, shall**

今天晚上會不會下雨？

24. 全ㄑㄩㄢˊ 家ㄐㄧㄚ (quánjiā)　*N*: **the entire family**

去年他們全家到加拿大去玩了兩個星期。

全ㄑㄩㄢˊ (quán)　*SV/A*: **entire, whole**

(1) 本來去年全年的國家地理雜誌我都有，現在小王拿走了一本就不全了。

(2) 我的錢全都給你了，我現在一毛錢也沒有了。

全ㄑㄩㄢˊ 國ㄍㄨㄛˊ (quán guó)　*N*: **the whole nation**

全ㄑㄩㄢˊ 校ㄒㄧㄠˋ (quán xiào)　*N*: **the whole school**

全ㄑㄩㄢˊ 世ㄕˋ 界ㄐㄧㄝˋ (quán shìjiè)　*N*: **the whole world**

完ㄨㄢˊ 全ㄑㄩㄢˊ (wánquán)

A: **completely, wholly, totally, fully, entirely**

我沒學過中文，他說的中國話，我完全不懂。

25. 移ㄧˊ 民ㄇㄧㄣˊ (yímín)　*V/N*: **to migrate/an immigrant**

(1) 王先生打算明年移民到加拿大去。

(2) 紐約這幾年有很多臺灣去的新移民。

26. 地ㄉㄧˋ 理ㄌㄧˇ (dìlǐ)　*N*: **geography**

地ㄉㄧˋ 圖ㄊㄨˊ (dìtú)　*N*: **map**（**M**：張）

27. 雜誌 (zázhì) *N*: **magazine（M：本）**

28. 篇 (piān) *M*: **[used for papers, literary articles, essays, etc.]**

29. 文章 (wénzhāng) *N*: **essay, literary article**

他那篇文章寫得真棒，你看了沒有？

30. 興趣 (xìngqù) *N*: **interest**

這幾年，他最大的興趣是學中文。

有興趣 (yǒu//xìngqù)

SV/VO: **interesting/to be interested, have an interest in**

(1)他最有興趣的功課是地理。

(2)你有沒有興趣跟我一起去看電影？

對(X)有興趣 (duì(X)yǒu//xìngqù)

PT: **to have an interest in (X), to be interested in (X)**

我對寫毛筆字很有興趣。

有趣 (yǒuqù)

SV: **interesting, fascinating, amusing**

他的話真有趣，大家聽了都笑了。

31. 口音 (kǒuyīn) *N*: **accent (for a spoken language)**

他的紐約口音不太好懂。

32. 選 (xuǎn) *V*: **to select, to choose**

這兩張畫，你選一張掛上吧！

歎詞跟語助詞 Interjections and Particles

1. 嗨 (hài) *I*: **Hi! [greeting]**

嗨！你好！

2. 噢 (òu) *I*: **Oh! [sudden realization]**

噢，我想起來了！

3. 呣 (ṁ) *P*: **mmm! [contentment]**

呣！你說得一點都不錯！

4. 啦 (·la)

P: **[combined sounds of "le" and "a", denoting exclamation or interrogation]**

吃飽啦？

專有名詞 Proper Names

1. 林建國 (Lín Jiàn'guó) Lin, Jianguo
2. 高偉立 (Gāo Wěilì) Gao, Weili
3. 波士頓 (Bōshìdùn) Boston
4. 水牛城 (Shuǐniú Chéng) Buffalo
5. 紐約州 (Niǔyuē Zhōu) State of New York
6. 臺灣 (Táiwān) Taiwan
7. 國家地理雜誌 (Guójiā Dìlǐ Zázhì) National Geographic Magazine
8. 萬里長城 (Wànlǐ Chángchéng) The Great Wall of China

注釋

1. 高偉立說："林先生，林太太……". In Chinese society, it is impolite to address friends' (peers') parents as ×先生 or ×太太. They should be called 伯父 (bófù) and 伯母 (bómǔ). 伯父 is one's father's elder brother. 伯母 is the wife of one's father's elder brother. Evolving from a long tradition, this custom helps to promote a feeling of cordial familiarity and makes one feel like part of an extended family. Now people in Taiwan often use other more informal terms── ×伯伯，×媽媽.（伯伯 means the same as 伯父）
2. "幸會，幸會。" is used when one is first introduced to somebody, but it is seldom used among the younger generation. Instead they usually say, "很

高興認識你。" or "你好。".

3. Here, 對了 does not mean "correct." It is similar to saying: "By the way......" or "Oh, yes, ..." as an introduction to a statement which the speaker suddenly thinks of or remembers.

4. "我們覺得把書念好最重要。" is a commonly held notion in Chinese society. In traditional China, people of learning , 士 (shì), occupied the highest class of the society. Only they could be officials who served the emperor after they had passed the government exams. Chinese people still believe that effective study will lead to a successful future, bringing honor to oneself and one's family. Therefore study is of primary importance.

5. "好了，還是先把箱子裡的……" This 好了 is used to suggest to others that they close the issue. It is similar to saying : " Okay, okay. Let's ......" .

6. "那就走吧。" If 那 or 那麼 is at the beginning of a sentence, serving as a way to connect the sentence to what was said earlier, it means "then" "in that case", or "So".

7. 回來啦 is a common form of greeting and functions in much the same way as "Hi, how are you doing ? " or "Hi, what's up ?" The most common Chinese greeting is " 吃過飯了沒有？" or " 吃飽了沒有？" Depending on the situation, simple and obvious facts are mentioned and used as greetings to start a conversation, such as:" 出去啊?!" ,"回家啦?!", "上街啊?!", "上哪兒去啊？" etc. The speaker does not necessarily expect an extended answer. Usually a simple " 是啊！"is considered satisfactory.

文法練習

（Ｉ）(topic) V 起來…… V as if, (looks as if, sounds as if, etc.)

⊙看起來還不錯，……

It looks as if it's not too bad......

用法說明：說話者對主題 (topic) 所做的評斷、估計或推測。「起來」的後面常是 SV，或描寫、修飾性的短句，主題可省略。

Explanation : This pattern is used to show the speaker's estimation or assessment of the topic. Following 起來 is often an adjective or a descriptive, modifying clause. The subject can be omitted.

練習：把下面各句改成「V 起來」的句子。

Exercise: Please rewrite the following sentences using V 起來.

1. 你穿這件衣服非常漂亮。

   You look very beautiful wearing this outfit.

   →這件衣服，你穿起來非常漂亮。

   You look very beautiful wearing this outfit.

2. 我媽媽嘮叨的時候，我真受不了。

   ....

3. 那件事說容易，做大概不容易。

   ....

4. 算一算他的年紀，已經六十歲了。

   ....

5. 這個盒子太大，恐怕不方便帶。

   ....

6. 照顧那麼多病人，一定很麻煩。

   ....

(II) (topic) 看起來……，就是……。

It looks............, one thing howev-

⊙看起來還不錯，就是舊了點。

It looks pretty good; however, it's a little old.

用法說明：前句是說話者對主題表面、正面的評斷，後句則是說話者對主題唯一不滿意之處。

Explanation: The first part of the sentence is the speaker's appraisal of the outward appearance of the subject. The latter part the sentence states a point which makes the speaker less than completely satisfied with the subject.

練習：用「看起來……，就是……。」及所給提示回答下面問題。

Exercise: Please use the "看起來……，就是……。" pattern to answer the following questions using the information provided.

1. 你覺得這個房子怎麼樣？（乾淨、不夠大）

   What do you think about this house? (clean, not big enough)

   →看起來很乾淨，就是不夠大。

   It appears to be very clean, but it's not big enough.

2. 那個盤子非常漂亮，你為什麼不買？（太貴了）

   ……………………………………………………………………

3. 你不喜歡我新買的汽車嗎？（很好、只有兩個門不方便）

   ……………………………………………………………………

4. 你剛剛吃的那個蛋糕好像很好吃，真的好吃嗎?（太甜了）

   ……………………………………………………………………

5. 我買的這個桌子好不好？（不錯、矮了點）

   ……………………………………………………………………

☞ 二 ……沒關係，……就好了。

It doesn't matter.....,......then it'll be fine.

⊙舊點沒關係，你自己弄乾淨就好了。

It doesn't matter that it's a little old. You clean it yourself, then it'll be fine.

用法說明：前句情況雖然不好，但問題不大，後句的辦法或情形就可以解決。有讓步的意思。

Explanation: Although the situation stated at the beginning of the sentence is a problem, it is not a big one. The latter portion of the sentence shows how the problem can be resolved. This pattern implies that one is making concession.

練習：請回答問題。（學生不會時，老師可給括弧中的提示）

Exercise: Please answer the following questions. (Teachers may provide hints when the students are having trouble.)

1. 書架壞了，怎麼辦？（再買一個）

   The bookcase is broken. What should we do? (buy another)

   →壞了沒關係，再買一個就好了。

   It doesn't matter if it's broken. Just buy another (and the problem will be resolved).

2. 今天沒買到肉，吃什麼？（有青菜）

   ....

3. 這兩個字，他寫錯了，沒關係吧？（改一改）

   ....

4. 我不去，行不行？（送份禮物）

   ....

5. 你穿這件，你男朋友不喜歡怎麼辦？（我自己喜歡）

   ....

☞ 三 總是 always / invariably

⊙他是二年級，知道的總是多一點。

He is a sophomore; he will invariably know a little more (than you).

⊙我們做父母的總是不放心，……

We parents never stop worrying, ...

用法說明：「總是」的用法有兩種：⑴跟「常常」的意思差不多，但事情發生的頻率更高。正、反兩面的情形都可用。⑵表示一定存在的事實。如果「總是」後面有助動詞，「是」可省略。句尾常有「的」，表示肯定。

Explanation: There are two uses for 總是: (1) It is similar to 常常 (often), but the rate of occurrence is higher (“very, very often,” “always”). It can be used in both positive and negative implications. (2) It indicates the invariability of a fact. If 總是 is followed by an auxiliary verb, then 是 can be omitted. 的 is often placed at the end of the sentence to express certainty.

練習：Exercises:

㈠請把「常常」換成「總是」，然後加一個句子說明頻率較高的原因。

Please replace 常常 with 總是, and then add a sentence to explain why the rate of occurrence is higher.

1. 他常常在那家飯館吃飯。

   He often eats at that restaurant.

   →他總是在那家飯館吃飯，因為飯館就在學校旁邊。

   He always eats at that restaurant because it's right next to the school.

2. 這個字，他常常寫錯。（很難寫）

   ....

3. 她常常很晚起來。（天天都睡得很晚）

   ....

4. 我常常打電話給他。（不喜歡寫信）

   ....

5. 老師說的話，他常常聽不懂。（中文不好）

   ....

㈡請用「總是」完成下面對話。

Please use 總是 to complete the dialogues below.

1. 張：我覺得我的孩子長得好慢，他什麼時候才會長大啊?!

   I think that my son is growing really slowly.When will he grow up?

   李：別急，孩子總是會長大的。

   Don't worry, children all grow up eventually.

2. 張：你為什麼一定要住在學校附近呢？郊區的房子便宜多了！

   李：住在學校附近 ____________，上課下課不必坐車，走路就到了。

3. 張：你怎麼帶這麼多錢出門？

李：我怕不夠，多帶些錢 ____________ 。

4. 張：我已經學了五百個中國字了，還不能看中文報嗎？

李：當然不行，想看中文報 ____________ 。

5. 張：我從來沒生過病，沒想到今天也感冒了。

李：人 ____________ ，身體好也得小心。

☞ 四 還是……吧！

(after considering the options) It's best to

⊙還是先把箱子裡的東西拿出來吧。

I think we should unpack the trunk first. (Though not explicitly stated, the option here is whether to continue debating or unpack the trunk first.)

用法說明：「還是……」是表示說話者比較主題之各種情況後，做出的結論，「吧」表示建議。

Explanation: 還是 indicates that the speaker has a conclusion after considering different sitvations. 吧 shows that the statement is a proposal or suggestion.

(1) 還是……

練習：用「還是……」完成下面各句。

Exercise: Please use "還是……" to complete the sentences below.

1. 夏天太熱，冬天太冷，還是秋天最舒服。

Summer is too hot and winter is too cold. Fall is still the most comfortable.

2. 用刀叉吃中國菜不方便，還是 ____________ 。（筷子）

3. 你這個辦法太好了，別人都想不出來，還是 ____________ 。（聰明）

4. 我病了，只有老王來看我，還是 ____________ 。（關心我）

5. 那個房子一百多萬，我們都買不起。他買了，還是 ____________ 。（有錢）

（II）還是……吧！

練習： 用「還是……吧」及所給提示回答下面各問題，需要的話並說明做此選擇之理由。

Exercise: Please use “還是……吧” to answer the following questions or statements using the information provided. Please provide additional explanation for your answers as necessary.

1. 你打算開車去，坐飛機去？（開車太累、坐飛機）
   Do you plan to go by car or by plane?
   →開車去太累，還是坐飛機去吧！
   It's too tiring to drive. I think it's better to fly.
2. 我們去游泳，怎麼樣？（天氣這麼冷、跳舞）
   ……………………………………………………………………………………
3. 這個橘子太酸了！（吃蘋果）
   ……………………………………………………………………………………
4. 我想看電影，可是沒錢！（在家看電視）
   ……………………………………………………………………………………
5. 吃飯的時間到了，我這封信還沒寫完，怎麼辦？（菜冷了就不好吃了、先吃飯）
   ……………………………………………………………………………………

☞ 五 來 to do

⊙好，好，你就自己來吧。 Okay, okay, then just do it yourself.

用法說明：「來」可以表示「做」某件事，但這「某件事」必需是雙方都知道所指為何的某件事。

Explanation: 來 can be used to mean “to do” some action, and the action referred to by 來 must be understood by both the speaker and the listener.

練習： 請用「來」完成下面對話。

Exercise: Please use 來 to complete the dialogues below.

1. 姐姐：媽媽不在家，我又要做飯，又要洗碗，真麻煩！
   Elder sister: Mom isn't home. I have to cook, and I have to wash the

dishes, too. What a pain!

妹妹：你做飯吧！洗碗，我來。

Younger sister: You cook. I'll do the dishwashing.

2. 張：這麼重的箱子，你一個人搬得動嗎？

李：當然搬不動，__________。

3. 張：謝謝你給我們準備了這麼多好吃的東西。

李：沒什麼，別客氣！想吃什麼，__________。

4. 小兒子：每次都是哥哥開車，今天讓我開，好不好？

爸爸：不行，你剛學會，那條路又不好走，還是__________。

5. 太太：有人來了，我去開門。

先生：__________，你看電視吧！

☞ 六

(Ⅰ)(S)V 不了幾 M(N)，(S) 就……

before a few M (N) occurs, (S) will............

⊙……大概過不了幾天，你就會想他們了。

............before long, you'll probably be missing them .

用法說明： 本句是由 RC「V 不了」跟「不／沒 V+幾(QW)+M+N」兩個句型合成的。意思是前句情況不會維持很久或動作次數不會太多，就會發生後句的情況。

Explanation: This sentence pattern is a combination of the RC pattern "V 不了" and the pattern "不／沒 V+幾(QW)+M+N". It means that the situation presented in the first clause will not be completed before the situation in the second clause occurs.

練習： 請用本句型改寫下面各句。

Exercise: Please use this sentence pattern to rewrite the sentences below.

1. 李小姐常常只走三、五分鐘就累了。

Miss Lee often gets tired after just three or five minutes of walking.

→李小姐走不了幾分鐘，就累了。

Miss Lee can't even walk for a few minutes without getting tired.

2. 他妹妹總是只吃一兩口東西就不吃了。

....

3. 也許只能穿幾次，這件衣服就不能穿了。

....

4. 我弟弟每天念書只念兩三頁，就想出去玩 。

....

5. 他很忙，每次來，說兩三句話就要走。

....

(II) (S) 沒 V 幾 M(N),(S) 就……了

用法説明：如果是已經發生的實際情況，就得用這個句型。

Explanation: If the sentence is describing an actual situation that has already occurred, then this pattern must be used.

練習：請把下面各句改成「沒 V 幾 M (N) (S) 就……了」，並說明兩句的分別。

Exercise: Please rewrite the sentences below using the "沒 V 幾 M(N)(S) 就……了" pattern, and explain the differences between the original and the rewritten sentences.

1. 李小姐走不了幾分鐘，就累了。

Miss Lee can't even walk for a few minutes without getting tired.

→李小姐沒走幾分鐘，就累了。

Miss Lee hadn't even walked for a few minutes before she got tired.

2. 他妹妹吃不了幾口就不吃了。

....

3. 也許穿不了幾次，這件衣服就不能穿了。

....

4. 我弟弟每天念書，念不了幾頁就想出去玩。

....

5. 他很忙，每次來，說不了幾句話就要走。

....

☞ 七 S 對……有興趣 S is interested

⊙我以前在國家地理雜誌裡看到一篇文章……，看了以後就開始對中國有興趣了。

I once saw an article in National geographic Magazine............ . After I saw it I started to be interested in China.

用法說明：在中文裡，當事者有興趣的對象、事物應在「有興趣」之前。「對」是「對於」的意思。

Explanation: In Chinese, the thing that the subject is interested in should be placed before 有興趣. 對 means "concerning, toward, in".

練習：請改寫下面各句。

Exercise: Please rewrite the following sentences.

1. 跳舞，他非常有興趣。

   Dancing? He is very interested in this.

   →他對跳舞非常有興趣。

   He is very interested in dancing.

2. 照像，我有很大的興趣。

   ....

3. 打網球，我爸爸越來越有興趣了。

   ....

4. 什麼運動，他妹妹都沒有興趣。

   ....

5. 做家事，我女朋友一點興趣都沒有。

   ....

☞ 八 歎詞跟語助詞的用法

The use of Interjections & Modal Particles

(I)歎詞 Interjections

歎詞通常位於句首，每個歎詞包含一定的意義，與後面句子的意思有關聯。但歎詞沒有確切的詞彙意義，聲調高低長短不同時，意思也不同。

Interjections are usually placed at the beginning of sentences and do not always have concrete, translatable definitions. However, they always express a specific tone related to the sentence that follows. As the pitch and length of the interjection varies, so does its implication.

(一)噢

⊙噢，對了！

Oh! Right! or Oh! Yes! (I remember!)

用法說明：表示醒悟、領會，語調低而短。

Explanation: This indicates realization or understanding. The tone is low and short.

練習：在句首加上「噢」，並注意說時之語調。

Exercise: Please place the word 噢 at the beginning of each of the following sentences, paying particular attention to the tone of voice when speaking.

1. 我懂了。

   I understand.

   →噢，我懂了。

   Oh! I understand.

2. 你就是張先生的弟弟。

   ....

3. 我想起來了。

   ....

4. 你不喜歡吃肉。

   ....

(二)呣

⊙呣，看起來還不錯，……

Mmm, it looks pretty good,............

用法說明： 語調低降，表示滿意、讚許。

Explanation: The pitch is low and falling, indicating satisfaction or approval.

練習： 在句首加上「嘸」，注意說時之語調。

Exercise: Please add the word 嘸 to the beginning of each of the following sentences, paying particular attention to the tone of voice when speaking.

1. 這件衣服真好看。

   This article of clothing is really nice.

   →嘸，這件衣服真好看。

   Mmm, this article of clothing is really nice.

2. 還是你說得對。

   ....

3. 你媽做的菜好吃多了。

   ....

4. 這樣做就對了。

   ....

(II) 語助詞　(modal) particles

語助詞一般位於句末，讀作輕聲，所表示的語氣由其語調和語言環境來決定。現僅介紹與課文相同之用法。

Particles are usually placed at the end of sentences and read in neutral tone. Its implications are determined by the tone of voice and context. Though particles can have many uses, here, only explanations for their use in the text are given.

㈠啦

⊙回來啦?!

You're back?!

用法說明： 「啦」是「了」跟「啊」的合音，用於打招呼，語調較低。「了」表示完成、改變或即將發生，「啊」在此表示疑問，或不確定的意思。

Explanation: 啦 is the combined sound of 了 and 啊, and it is used as a greeting and spoken with a slightly low tone. 了 indicates completion, change, or the imminence of an action, while 啊 indicates doubt or uncertainty.

練習：根據所給情況及提示，用「啦」打招呼。

Exercise: Please use 啦 to form a greeting in the following situations.

A. 完成　showing completion

1. 看見朋友從飯館出來。（吃）

   You see some friends come out from a restaurant. (eat)

   →吃飽啦?!　或：吃過啦?!

   You're finished eating? or: You've eaten?

2. 下午五點多，看見朋友從公司出來。（下班）

   ....

3. 早上看見家裡的客人從房間出來。（起來）

   ....

B. 改變　showing change

1. 朋友病了一個禮拜以後，第一次來上課。

   This is the first time your friend comes to class after a week of illness.

   →你好啦?!

   You're well now?

2. 看見朋友開著一輛新車來上班。（買新車）

   ....

3. 一進門看見弟弟的朋友要回家。（不坐）

   ....

C. 即將發生（常跟「要」連用）　showing the imminence of an action or situation

1. 看見朋友把他家裡的桌子、椅子搬上車。

   You see your friend moving the table and chairs from his

house to his car.

→你們要搬家啦?!

You're moving?

2. 看見同學拿著行李要上車。(走)

....

3. 下班以後在車站看見朋友在等車。(回家)

....

課室活動

Divide the students into pairs. As the course has just begun, it is assumed they do not know one another. Give them a couple of minutes to get acquainted by asking one another questions in Chinese. Then ask each student to take turns introducing his/her partner to the class . If time is limited, just select a few students.

Some suggested getting-acquainted questions include:

1. 你姓什麼?叫什麼?
2. 你家在哪裡?
3. 你住哪裡?
4. 你父母做什麼工作?
5. 你是哪一系的學生?
6. 沒有課的時候,你喜歡做什麼?
7. 你為什麼要學中文?

短文

高偉立的日記

八月三十一日 星期日 晴

太棒了！我的室友是中國人，他們全家是八年前從台灣移民來的。我跟他們都說中國話，這好像是我第一次說那麼多中文。

林建國瘦瘦的，不怎麼高，很像他爸爸。他看起來人很好，我們大概過不了多久，就可以是好朋友了。他住校，他媽媽好像比他還緊張，總是想幫他做這個、做那個。他爸爸很少說話，可是對我很客氣。記得去年爸媽送我來的時候，也告訴我要好好兒地照顧自己，可是不像林建國的父母那樣——什麼都不放心。

林建國也要選中文系的課，他一定學得比較快、比較好，我得更用功才行。以後有什麼不懂的地方，就可以問他了。

Vocabulary:

*日記 (rìjì)：diary

第二課

吃什麼好

・四菜一湯（吳俊銘攝）

（在中國飯館）

服務生：請進。幾位？

偉立：兩個。（對建國）生意真好，快客滿了。

服務生：請跟我來。（到一個沒人的桌子前面）請坐。這是菜單，你們先看看。

偉立：我們吃特餐吧！比較快，也比較便宜。

建國：什麼好吃？

偉立：我最喜歡他們的七號木須肉。十四號青豆蝦仁[1]也不錯。要是你喜歡吃辣的，可以試試十三號宮保雞丁。

建國：說得我更餓了。我就要宮保雞丁吧！

偉立：我還是吃木須雞肉。

服務生：兩位想點什麼？決定了嗎？

偉立：我們吃特餐，一個七號，一個十三號。

服務生：喝什麼湯呢？我們有酸辣湯和蛋花湯。

偉立：我要酸辣湯，你呢？

建國：我也要酸辣湯。

服務生：哪位點木須雞肉？兩張餅夠不夠[2]？

偉立：可不可以再加兩張？我餓得不得了！

服務生：可以。謝謝，馬上就來。

（服務生把他們點的東西送來）

偉立：請你給我們筷子，好不好？

服務生：沒問題。（服務生走開）

服務生（把筷子拿來）：請慢用[3]。

（偉立要建國看旁邊那一桌）

偉立：欸！你看她們吃的是什麼？

建國：我也不知道，有青花菜，胡蘿蔔，還有肉。她們說的好像是中國話，你敢不敢問她們？

偉立：怎麼不敢？怕什麼？！（轉頭對那一桌的女孩兒）對不起，你們是中國人吧？

美真：是啊！

偉立：請問你們吃的是什麼菜？

美真：我吃的是芥蘭牛肉[4]。她吃的是銀芽豬肉[5]。

偉立：銀芽是什麼？

台麗：就是這個，本來叫豆芽，你沒吃過嗎？

建國：我媽很喜歡，我們家常吃。你們是臺灣來的嗎？

美真：是啊！上個月才來的。我叫謝美真。

台麗：我叫陳台麗，也是上個月來的。我們都是來留學的。

建國：我叫林建國，他是我室友高偉立。

偉立：很高興認識你們！怎麼樣？這裡的菜味道好不好？

美真：**算是**不錯的，可是跟我們平常吃的不一樣。也許美國人喜歡這樣的口味。**對**中國人**來說**，每個菜吃起來都差不多。

台麗：**就是嘛**！而且你看，你們先喝湯，我們中國人先吃飯。還有，我們的木須肉也不是跟餅一起吃的。

美真：對啊！這就叫「中菜西吃」[6]。不過總是比學校餐廳好。學校餐廳的大鍋菜，吃**來**吃**去**就那幾樣。真膩！

偉立：所以我們有時候得出來換換口味。

台麗：想我們在臺灣的時候，要吃**什麼就**有**什麼**。**連**半夜**都**找得到地方吃。臺灣小吃、美國速食、法國大餐，什麼都有。

美真：要是你去臺灣住幾個月，你一定會胖**得**上不了飛機[7]。麥當勞、炸雞、水餃、北京烤鴨、廣東點心，（叫服務生算賬）**只要**你想得出來，**就**吃得到。

偉立：真的啊？

建國：上次我姑姑[8]來，也這麼說。有機會我也要回去看看。

（服務生送來兩個籤餅[9]跟賬單）

美真：（拿起賬單）對不起，我們還有課，先走了。籤餅給你們吃吧。我們沒有飯後吃甜點的習慣。再見。

飯湯免費請自助，最低消費每人一道菜

桌號：　　請先付款

價目	品　名	數量	價目	品　名	數量
60	招牌快餐		120元	糖醋里肌	
60	焢肉快餐			梅干扣肉	
60	豬腳快餐			杏菜銀魚	
70	魚排快餐		130元	白切雞	
70	肉排快餐			糖醋花枝	
80	雞腿快餐			宮保花枝	
80	牛腩快餐			宮保魷魚	
50元	炒青菜			紅燒魚	
	炸豆腐			五更腸旺	
			140元	蔥油雞	
60元	豆干肉絲			宮保雞丁	
	蘿蔔煎蛋			蝦仁角瓜	
	蔥花煎蛋			炒青蚵	
	麻婆豆腐			鹽酥青蚵	
	肉醬豆腐			紅燒鱈魚	
70元	開洋白菜			糖醋鱈魚	
	蕃茄炒蛋			紅燒牛腩	
	紅燒肉			青椒雞丁	
	桂竹筍肉絲			糖醋雞丁	
	雪菜肉絲		150元	蝦仁豆腐	
	芙蓉煎蛋			清炒蝦仁	
70元	滷豬腳			宮保蝦仁	
	回鍋肉			糖醋蝦仁	
	苦瓜肉絲			蔥燒鮮蚵	
	魚香茄子			薑絲大腸	
	肉醬茄子			脆皮大腸	
100元	洋蔥牛肉			紅燒獅子頭	
	青嫩牛肉		200元	豆瓣魚	
	蔥爆牛肉			鹽酥虱目魚	
	京醬肉絲			鐵板蝦仁豆腐	
	蒜泥白肉		時價	清蒸鱈魚	
	培根高麗菜			豆酥鱈魚	
120元	鐵板豆腐			清蒸鯧魚	
	蛤仔魚瓜			豆酥鯧魚	
	筍絲大腸			鹽酥鯧魚	
	焢肉筍絲		時菜		
	炒三鮮				
	炒花枝		總計		
	炒蛤仔				

・菜單（范慧貞提供）

偉立、建國：謝啦。再見。

生詞及例句

1. 服ㄈㄨˊ務ㄨˋ生ㄕㄥ (fúwùshēng)

   N: **attendant, service person, waiter**

   服ㄈㄨˊ務ㄨˋ (fúwù) *N/V*: **service / to serve, give service to**

2. 客ㄎㄜˋ滿ㄇㄢˇ (kèmǎn) *IE*: **full house, sold out, no vacancy**

   那家旅館常常客滿，去晚了就沒有房間了。

   滿ㄇㄢˇ (mǎn) *SV/RE*: **to be full**

   瓶子裡水已經滿了，別再裝了。

3. 菜ㄘㄞˋ單ㄉㄢ (càidān) *N*: **menu**

   這個菜單上的菜，我差不多都吃過。

   名ㄇㄧㄥˊ單ㄉㄢ (míngdān) *N*: **roster of names, name list**

   通ㄊㄨㄥ知ㄓ單ㄉㄢ (tōngzhīdān) *N*: **notification, notice slip**

   單ㄉㄢ子˙ㄗ (dān.zi) *N*: **a list**

4. 辣ㄌㄚˋ (là) *SV*: **to be hot, spicy**

   這個湯又酸又辣，叫酸辣湯。

5. 敢ㄍㄢˇ (gǎn) *AV*: **to dare**

   外面太黑了，她不敢一個人出去。

6. 留ㄌㄧㄡˊ學ㄒㄩㄝˊ (liúxué) *V*: **to study abroad**

   我姐姐打算畢業以後，到英國去留學。

   留ㄌㄧㄡˊ學ㄒㄩㄝˊ生ㄕㄥ (liúxuéshēng) *N*: **student studying abroad**

   留ㄌㄧㄡˊ (liú) *V*: **to remain, to stay; to keep, reserve; to detain**

   (1)他還沒回來，我們給他留些飯菜吧！

   (2)我留他吃飯，可是他一定要走。

   留ㄌㄧㄡˊ起ㄑㄧˇ來ㄌㄞˊ (liúqǐ·lái)

   RC: **to save, to put away for later use.**

這些紙別扔了，留起來下次用吧！

7. 算是 (suànshì) *V*: **to be considered as**

要是你的頭不疼了，你的病就算是好了。

8. 口味 (kǒuwèi) *N*: **taste, flavor**（**M**：種）

我們兩個人的口味不一樣，他喜歡吃甜的，我愛吃鹹的。

9. 而且 (érqiě)

CONJ: **moreover, in addition, furthermore**

我要準備明天的功課，而且我很累，不想出去。

10. 不過 (búguò) *CONJ/A*: **but, however / only, merely**

(1)烤肉的味道不錯，不過我更喜歡炸雞。

(2)他不過是個孩子，你不必跟他生氣。

11. 餐廳 (cāntīng)

N: **dining hall; restaurant**（**M**：個／家）

這家餐廳的菜又便宜又好吃。

12. 膩 (nì) *SV/RE*: **to be bored with, tired of**

(1)天天吃一樣的東西，一定會覺得很膩。

(2)這個歌越聽越好聽，聽了這麼多次，我還沒聽膩。

13. 半夜 (bànyè) *N*: **midnight, in the middle of the night**

他昨天晚上玩到半夜兩點才回家。

14. 算帳（賬） (suàn//zhàng)

VO: **to settle accounts, figure out a bill**

(1)小姐，算帳！一共多少錢？

(2)那個小姐算了半天的帳了，還沒算出來。

帳單 (zhàngdān)

N: **a bill (at a restaurant, shop, etc.)**

15. 姑姑 (gū·gu) *N*: **aunt, father's sister**

16. 機會 (jīhuì) *N*: **chance, opportunity**

有機會我想到法國去旅行。

17. 習慣 (xíguàn)

V/N: **to get used to, to be accustomed to / habit**

(1)我習慣看著報吃早飯。

(2)壞習慣總是很難改的。

18.特ㄊㄜˋ餐ㄘㄢ (tècān)

N: **a special dish of a restaurant, a special dish of the day**

19.青ㄑㄧㄥ豆ㄉㄡˋ (qīngdòu) *N*: **green peas**

20.蝦ㄒㄧㄚ仁ㄖㄣˊ (xiārén) *N*: **shelled shrimp**

蝦ㄒㄧㄚ (xiā) *N*: **shrimp**

21.餅ㄅㄧㄥˇ (bǐng) *N*: **baked or fried flat cake**（**M**：張／個）

22.青ㄑㄧㄥ花ㄏㄨㄚ菜ㄘㄞˋ (qīnghuācài) *N*: **broccoli**

23.胡ㄏㄨˊ蘿ㄌㄨㄛˊ蔔˙ㄅㄛ（紅ㄏㄨㄥˊ蘿ㄌㄨㄛˊ蔔˙ㄅㄛ）(húluó·b) (hóngluó·b)

N: **carrot**

蘿ㄌㄨㄛˊ蔔˙ㄅㄛ (luó·bo) *N*: **radish, turnip**

24.豆ㄉㄡˋ芽ㄧㄚˊ (dòuyá) *N*: **bean sprouts**

銀ㄧㄣˊ芽ㄧㄚˊ (yínyá)

N: **silvery sprouts, fancy name for bean sprouts**

銀ㄧㄣˊ色ㄙㄜˋ (yínsè) *AT*: **silver color**

他的新汽車是銀色的。

25.豬ㄓㄨ肉ㄖㄡˋ (zhūròu) *N*: **pork meat**

豬ㄓㄨ (zhū) *N*: **pig, hog, swine**

26.大ㄉㄚˋ鍋ㄍㄨㄛ菜ㄘㄞˋ (dàguōcài)

N: **food prepared in a big pot, institutional food (made in mass quantities)**

請你嚐嚐我們公司餐廳的大鍋菜。

鍋ㄍㄨㄛ (guō)

N/M: **cooking pot (container used for cooking food) / Measure for cooked food.**

我上次去看我男朋友，想做一鍋湯給他吃，可是找不到大一點兒的鍋。

27.連ㄌㄧㄢˊ…… 都ㄉㄡ (lián……dōu) *PT*: **even**

他什麼都忘了，連自己的名字都忘了。

28. 小ㄒㄧㄠˇ吃ㄔ (xiǎochī)

N: **food served at a night market stall, a street stall, a small diner, etc., which can be eaten as a meal, a snack, or a side dish**

29. 速ㄙㄨˋ食ㄕˊ (sùshí) *N*: **"fast food"**

速ㄙㄨˋ食ㄕˊ麵ㄇㄧㄢˋ (sùshímiàn) *N*: **instant noodles**

30. 大ㄉㄚˋ餐ㄘㄢ (dàcān)

N: **an abundant meal on special occasions**

今天是他的生日，他要請我們吃大餐。

31. 水ㄕㄨㄟˇ餃ㄐㄧㄠˇ (shuǐjiǎo) *N*: **boiled Chinese dumplings**

餃ㄐㄧㄠˇ子˙ㄗ (jiǎo·zi)

N: **Chinese dumpling made of various fillings stuffed in a dough wrapper**

32. 烤ㄎㄠˇ鴨ㄧㄚ (kǎoyā) *N*: **roast duck**

鴨ㄧㄚ子˙ㄗ (yā·zi) *N*: **duck**

33. 甜ㄊㄧㄢˊ點ㄉㄧㄢˇ (tiándiǎn) *N*: **dessert**

歎詞跟語助詞 Interjections and Particle

1. 欸（ㄟˋ, ㄟˊ, ㄟˇ）(èi, éi, ěi) *I:* **[to attract attention or express surprise]**

(1)欸，把那封信拿給我。

(2)欸？他怎麼還沒來？

(3)欸？你怎麼可以站在床上？

2. 嘛˙ㄇㄚ (·ma)

P: **[used at end of a sentence implying that what precedes it is obvious]**

張：他的中文怎麼那麼棒？

李：他是中國人嘛！

專有名詞和特殊名詞 Proper Names & special Names

1. 謝美真 (Xiè Měizhēn) Xie, Meizhen
2. 陳台麗 (Chén Táilì) Chen, Taili
3. 木須肉 (mùxū ròu) Mooshoo pork or chicken
4. 宮保雞丁 (gōngbǎo jīdīng) Kongbao chicken
5. 芥蘭牛肉 (jièlán niúròu) beef and kale
6. 酸辣湯 (suānlà tāng) hot and sour soup
7. 蛋花湯 (dànhuā tāng) egg drop soup
8. 麥當勞 (Màidāngláo) McDonald's
9. 北京 (Běijīng) Beijing
10. 廣東 (Guǎngdōng) Canton
11. 籤餅 (qiānbǐng) fortune cookies

注釋

1. "……七號木須肉。十四號青豆蝦仁……" Usually there are no numbers for dishes on restaurant menus in Taiwan.
2. "哪位吃木須肉？兩張餅夠不夠？" In Taiwan 木須肉 is usually eaten without thin pancakes. Like other dishes, it is eaten with rice. The original characters for 木須 were 木樨 , but not many people recognize this form today.
3. 請慢用 is said by a person (perhaps a host or waiter) who has just served a dish. It literally means "Take your time to eat it" and is equivalent to the Western expression , "Enjoy your meal."
4. 芥蘭牛肉, 芥蘭 is Chinese kale. It is hard to find this vegetable in the United States, so most Chinese restaurants there use broccoli as a substitute. However they still name the dish "kale." That is why in the text 建國 said there were broccoli, carrots and meat in the girl's plate .

5. 銀芽豬肉 is bean sprouts with pork. 銀芽 is 豆芽. Chinese like to create auspicious names for dishes, because they think it will bring them good luck and fortune. Sometimes they also give poetic names to the vegetables they use. 銀芽 is one example. 銀 means silver. Silver sprouts are named for the silvery translucence of sauted bean sprouts and sound tastier than just plain bean sprouts.
6. 中菜西吃 means to eat Chinese food in a Western fashion. It can be done in several different ways. Some examples are having the soup course first, changing some of the ingredients and eating a dish without rice. Chinese use chopsticks to take food from communal dishes placed in the center of the table to their individual rice bowls. The meat or vegetable is placed on top of the rice, the entire bowl is raised to the mouth, and then the food is transferred into the mouth using chopsticks. Some people have adopted the Western custom of using plates rather than bowls and of using serving utensils for communal dishes. Sometimes the dishes are also passed around rather than left in the center of the table for the entire meal.
7. "你一定會胖得上不了飛機" means "You will certainly become too fat to get on the plane." This exaggeration is meant as a joke. In general, Chinese are not very sensitive to being fat. While being skinny is in fashion among many younger people, the older generation still think being a little fat is good. It is a symbol of being able to afford a good life.
8. 姑姑 is one's father's sister. If she is married, she may be called 姑媽. Mother's sister is called 阿姨 (āyí) or 姨媽 (yímā). The name given the wife of one's father's younger brother is 嬸嬸 (shěn·shen), while the wife of one's mother's brother is known as 舅媽 (jiùmā).
9. 籤餅 means fortune cookie. It is also called 幸運餅. They are complementary in Chinese restaurants in the States. You will not find these in Chinese restaurants in Taiwan. Chinese eat fruit and/ or drink tea after a meal. There are usually no sweet desserts at normal meals, although they are sometimes served at formal banquets.

文法練習

一 V/SV 得 N/PN ……N/PN V/SV 得 ……

V/SV to the point that N/PN. . . . . .

⊙說得我更餓了。 As you say that, I feel even hungrier.

⊙你一定會胖得上不了飛機。

You'll certainly become too fat to get on the plane.

用法說明：「得」前面的動詞或 SV 常是原因，「得」後面的補語表示結果和程度。即某動作或狀態使當事者出現某種情態。而且該結果和程度多半是誇張的或不好的。當事者可在句首，亦可在「得」之後。當事者在「得」之後時，有被動的感覺。

Explanation: The verb or SV preceding 得 is often a cause or reason, while the information after 得 is a resulting outcome or level of completion. This outcome or level of completion is often exaggerated for emphasis or effect, and usually has a negative tone. The subject being spoken about can be placed at the beginning of the sentence or after 得. When it is placed after 得, the sentence has a passive tone.

練習：Exercises:

(I) V 得 ……

㈠請用「V 得 N/PN……」改寫下面各句。

Please rewrite the following sentences using the "V 得 N/PN……" pattern.

1. 王先生吃了很多，所以走不動了。

   Mr. Wang ate a lot, so he can't walk.

   →王先生吃了很多，吃得他走不動了。

   Mr. Wang ate so much that he can't walk.

2. 我打了四個小時的球，累極了。

....

3. 他喝了太多酒，不會走路了。

....

4. 我們談了很久，就忘了吃午飯了。

....

5. 書上的字太小，他看了以後就頭疼了。

....

㈡請把下面各句改成「N/PN + V 得……」句子，如果當事者相同，第二個主語應該省略。

Please rewrite the following sentences using the "N/PN + V 得……" pattern. If the subject being spoken about is the same, it should be omitted the second time .

1. 王先生吃了很多，吃得他走不動了。

   Mr. Wang ate so much that he can't walk.

   →王先生吃了很多，吃得走不動了。

   Mr. Wang ate so much that he can't walk.

2. 我打了四個小時的球，打得我累極了。

....

3. 他喝了太多酒，喝得他不會走路了。

....

4. 我們談了很久，談得我們忘了吃午飯了。

....

5. 書上的字太小，看得他頭疼了。

....

(II) SV 得……

㈠請用「SV 得 N/PN……」完成下面各句。

Please use "SV 得 N/PN……" to complete the sentences below.

1. 我走了一天的路，累得我一坐下就睡著了。

I walked for a full day, and was so tired that I fell asleep as soon as I sat down.

2. 他越來越胖，胖得他＿＿＿＿＿＿＿＿＿＿。
3. 昨天晚上太冷，冷得我媽媽＿＿＿＿＿＿＿＿＿＿。
4. 火車快開了，他還沒來，急得他女朋友＿＿＿＿＿＿＿＿＿＿。
5. 這個橘子真酸，酸得我＿＿＿＿＿＿＿＿＿＿。

㈡請用「N/PN＋SV 得……」及提示回答下面各題。

Please use the "N/PN＋SV 得……" pattern and the provided information to answer the questions below.

1. 聽說你弟弟很高興，他有多高興？

I heard that your little brother is very happy. How happy is he?

→他高興得跳起來了。

He's so happy that he jumped for joy.

2. 他有多餓？（可以吃下一頭牛）

……………………………………………………………………

3. 你爸爸非常忙嗎？（沒有時間吃飯）

……………………………………………………………………

4. 李先生真的很氣嗎？（說不出話來）

……………………………………………………………………

5. 你為什麼不喜歡很香的花呢？（受不了）

……………………………………………………………………

☞ 三 算是 to be considered as

⊙算是不錯的。

Not bad. (literally: "It could be regarded as something that's not too bad.")

用法說明：「算是」的意思是「可以說是」，語氣較不肯定，後面可以是名詞或修飾語，如果是SV，最好加「的」，表示一種狀態或情況。

Explanation: 算是 means "one could say that it is..." and carries a slight tone of uncertainty. 算是 can be followed by a noun or a modifier. If 算是 is followed by an SV, it is best to add a 的， which acts as a nominalizer.

練習：用「算是」完成句子。

Exercise: Complete the sentences below using 算是.

1. 他在德國住了二十年，可以算是德國人了。

   He has lived in Germany for twenty years, so could be considered a German now.
2. 你的頭不疼了，病就算是＿＿＿＿＿＿＿＿＿＿＿＿。
3. 我家離學校六公里，算是＿＿＿＿＿＿＿＿＿＿＿＿。
4. 他們念的書都很難，這本算是＿＿＿＿＿＿＿＿＿＿＿＿。
5. 張小姐念中學的時候有一百七十公分，在女同學當中算是＿＿＿＿＿＿＿＿＿＿＿＿。

☞ 三 對 NP 來說……　As far as NP is concerned

⊙對中國人來說，每個菜吃起來都差不多。

For Chinese people, every dish tastes about the same.

用法說明：「對」後面的是當事者，本句型是站在當事者立場，表示意見或看法。

Explanation: Following 對 is a person or group. This sentence pattern speaks from this person or group's point of view, expressing their opinions or thoughts.

練習：請用「對……來說……」回答問題。

Exercise: Please use the "對……來說……" pattern to answer to the following questions.

1. 日本人說中國字不難寫，你們美國人呢？

   Japanese say that Chinese characters aren't difficult to write. What about you Americans?

   →對我們美國人來說，中國字很難寫。

   So far as Americans are concerned, Chinese characters are very difficult to write.

2. 你覺得宮保雞丁好吃嗎？

....

3. 一年級的新生每星期上二十個小時的課，多不多？

....

4. 學校的學生太少，好不好？

....

5. 一件衣服一千塊，貴不貴？

....

☞ 四 就是嘛！ That's right! Indeed!

⊙美真：……對中國人來說，每個菜吃起來都差不多。

台麗：就是嘛！

Meizhen: For Chinese , every dish tastes about the same.

Taili: Indeed!

（１）嘛

用法說明：「嘛」是語助詞 (P)，放在句子後面，語調低，對顯而易見的事情表示肯定的語氣，有「本來就是這樣，本來就應該這樣」的意思。因為「嘛」前的句子是敘述一顯而易見的事，沒有「嘛」就沒有「你應該知道」的含義。

Explanation: 嘛 is a particle. It is placed at the end of a sentence and pronounced with a low pitch, indicating definite affirmation of a preceding statement. The connotation is that "this is invariable and is fitting and appropriate". The statement preceding 嘛 describes an obvious matter, and 嘛 implies that "one ought to know this."

練習：Exercises:

(一)用「嘛」完成下面對話。

Please complete the following dialogues using 嘛 .

1. 李：他什麼都不會，什麼都不懂。

Lee: He can't do anything , and he doesn't understand anything.

張：他還是個孩子嘛！

Chang: C'mon, he's still a child!

2. 李：他的中文說得真好。

張：________________________________！

3. 李：這一課，我有很多地方都不懂，怎麼辦？

張：________________________________！

4. 李：王小姐為什麼還沒來？

張：________________________________！

5. 李：你為什麼不坐電梯？

張：________________________________！

㈡把下面句中的「嘛」去掉，並比較兩句的不同。（可用英文）

Please remove 嘛 from the sentences below and compare the two sentences, explaining the difference(s). (English may be used as necessary.)

1. 累了就休息嘛！

If you're tired, just take a rest then! (Implies: It's obvious! You ought to know that!)

→累了就休息。

If you're tired, then take a rest. (No implication of: "It's obvious! You ought to know that !")

2. 你覺得冷就多穿點衣服嘛！

....

3. 他這麼嘮叨，誰受得了嘛！

....

4. 用筷子吃飯是中國人的習慣嘛！

....

5. 我們是好朋友，我幫你是應該的嘛！

....

（II）就是嘛！ Indeed!

用法説明： 表示完全同意對方的觀點、說法或意見。意思是「事情就是你說的那樣」。

Explanation: This indicates that you totally agree with another's point of view, opinion, or statement. It means "the situation is exactly as you stated".

練習： 用「就是嘛」完成下面對話。

Exercise: Complete the dialogues below using 就是嘛 .

1. 張：不準備，當然考不好啊！

   Chang: If you don't prepare, of course you'll do poorly on the test!

   王：就是嘛！

   Wang: I couldn't agree more.

2. 張：身體不健康，有錢有什麼用?!

   王：________________________！

3. 張：現在是冬天，可是熱得跟夏天一樣！

   王：________________________！

4. 張：住得近比住得遠方便，他為什麼要搬家?!

   王：________________________！

5. 張：這家餐廳的菜這麼難吃，怎麼會客滿?!

   王：________________________！

☞ 五 V來V去

⊙學校餐廳的大鍋菜，吃來吃去就那幾樣。

After repeatedly eating the school cafeteria's mass-produced food, one still just finds those same few dishes.

用法説明： 強調不斷重覆某一動作，由於動詞不同，而有兩種不同意思：(A) 不停地往返來回不同的地方。(B) 某個動作被重覆多次以後，說話者或當事者得到某種看法或感想。「V 來 V 去」後不可再加賓語 (O)。

Explanation: This pattern shows that an action is continually repeated. Depending on what verb is used, there are two possible meanings: (A) Continual movement between two different locations. (B) Repetition of an action upon many different objects which leads the speaker or person involved to develop a conclusion . An object cannot be placed after "V 來 V 去" .

練習：請改寫下面各句。

Exercises: Please rewrite the sentences below.

A. Different locations

1. 林太太急得在屋子裡從這邊走到那邊，從那邊走到這邊。

   Mrs. Lin was so anxious she walked from here to there and there to here in the house.

   →林太太急得在屋子裡走來走去。

   Mrs. Lin was so anxious she paced back and forth in the house.

2. 小孩子不應該在街上從這裡跑到那裡，從那裡跑到這裡。

   ....

3. 她的工作就是每天從這個城市飛到那個城市，從那個城市飛到這個城市。

   ....

4. 他把這張桌子從這裡搬到那裡，又從那裡搬到這裡，怎麼放都覺得不好。

   ....

5. 這些書，你每天從家裡帶到學校，又從學校帶回家，不麻煩嗎？

   ....

B. Repeated action upon different object

1. 他聽過很多歌，還是覺得這首歌最好聽。

   He's listened to many songs, but still thinks that this song is the best.

   →他聽來聽去還是覺得這首歌最好聽。

   He's repeatedly listened to many songs, but still thinks that this song is the best.

2. 他要買生日禮物給女朋友，想了半天，才決定買一本書。

……………………………………………………………………………………

3. 說了那麼多，大家都覺得是你的錯。

……………………………………………………………………………………

4. 穿了這麼多家公司的鞋，還是這家的最舒服。

……………………………………………………………………………………

5. 這條褲子他比了半天，都覺得不夠長。

……………………………………………………………………………………

☞ 六

(I) …… QW …… 就 …… QW ……

⊙在臺灣要吃什麼就有什麼。

In Taiwan, whatever you'd want to eat is readily available.

用法說明：疑問代詞 (QW) 表示任指，前後兩個疑問代詞指的是同一事物。意思是「隨便，都可以，只要合乎『就』前面的希望、要求或需求，沒有特別的限制」。如果 QW 是「誰」，第二個「誰」也可以放在「就」的前面。

Explanation: Both QWs in this pattern represent the same desired object. This pattern shows that anything which fits the conditions described before 就 is easily available, without any special restrictions. If the QW is 誰, the second 誰 can also be placed in front of 就 .

練習：請用「...... QW ......就...... QW ......」回答下面問題。

Exercise: Please Use the pattern "...... QW ......就...... QW ......" to answer the following questions.

1. 張：我坐哪兒？

   Chang: Where should I sit?

   李：你想坐哪兒就坐哪兒。

   Lee: Sit wherever you want.

2. 張：誰去買票？

   李：……………………………………………………………………

3. 張：你要借多少錢？

李：……………………………………………………………………

4. 張：這件事應該怎麼辦？

李：……………………………………………………………………

5. 張：我什麼時候去你家比較好？

李：……………………………………………………………………

(II) QW + SV 就 V + QW & 怎麼 SV 就怎麼 V

用法說明：用法與 I 一樣，但意思是：只要合乎「就」前面的條件即可。「多少」、「幾」，不適用本句型。而「誰」和「什麼時候」則應在 V 前面。

Explanation: The usage here is similar to (I) above. However, this pattern means that whatever fits the conditions described before 就 is acceptable. 多少 and 幾 should not be used with this pattern. And 誰 or 什麼時候 must be placed before, not after, the verb.

練習：用「QW + SV 就 V + QW」或「怎麼 SV 就怎麼 V」回答下面問題。

Exercise: Please answer the questions below using "QW + SV 就 V + QW" or "怎麼 SV 就怎麼 V"。

1. 張：你要買哪個？

Chang: Which one do you want to buy?

李：哪個便宜，我就買哪個。

Lee: Whichever one is cheaper, that's the one I'll buy.

2. 張：去哪裡吃飯比較好？

李：＿＿＿＿＿＿＿＿＿＿＿＿＿＿＿＿＿＿＿＿＿＿＿＿ 3.

3. 張：我們兩個誰先休息？

李：＿＿＿＿＿＿＿＿＿＿＿＿＿＿＿＿＿＿＿＿＿＿＿＿ 4.

4. 張：我什麼時候可以告訴他這件事？

李：＿＿＿＿＿＿＿＿＿＿＿＿＿＿＿＿＿＿＿＿＿＿＿＿ 5.

5. 張：你想玩什麼？

李：＿＿＿＿＿＿＿＿＿＿＿＿＿＿＿＿＿＿＿＿＿＿＿＿ 6.

6. 張：我們怎麼去紐約？

李：____

☞ 七 連……都／也……　　even......

⊙連半夜都找得到地方吃。

Even in the middle of the night you can find a place to eat.

用法說明： 說話者認為「連」後面的情況是不平常的，有強調的意思。N、SV、V、VO、S-V，或短句都可放在連的後面。

Explanation: The speaker thinks that the situation mentioned after 連 is unusual or worthy of note and thus uses this pattern for emphasis. N, SV, V, VO, S-V or a simple sentence all can be placed after 連.

練習： 用「連……都／也……」改寫下面各句。

Exercise: Please rewrite the following sentences using the "連……都／也……" pattern.

㈠連 N/NP 都／也……

1. 我太忙，沒時間吃飯。

   I'm too busy. I don't have time to eat.

   →我太忙，連飯都沒時間吃。

   I'm too busy. I don't even have time to eat.

   or →我太忙，連吃飯的時間都沒有。

   I'm too busy. I don't even have the time to eat.

2. 這件事太容易了，小孩子也會做。

   ....

3. 他真有錢，他買得起飛機。

   ....

㈡連 VO 都／也……

1. 我太忙，沒時間吃飯。

   I'm too busy. I don't have time to eat.

   →我太忙，連吃飯都沒時間。

   I'm too busy. I don't even have time to eat.

2. 你今天怎麼了？看電影也沒興趣了嗎？

…………………………………………………………………………………………

3. 他什麼都不會，打電話也不會。

…………………………………………………………………………………………

㈢連 S-V 都／也……

1. 這件衣服太小，我最小的弟弟也穿不下。

This article of clothing is too small. My youngest brother can't get it on either.

→這件衣服太小，連我最小的弟弟穿都穿不下。

This piece of clothing is too small; even my youngest brother can't get it on.

2. 那個菜很辣，墨西哥 (Mòxīgē, Mexico) 人都受不了。

…………………………………………………………………………………………

3. 這個字真難寫，老師也寫不好。

…………………………………………………………………………………………

㈣連 clause（短句）都／也……

1. 老師請客，你不去，不太好吧？

The teacher invited us. It would be a bad idea for you not to show up, don't you think?

→連老師請客你也不去，不太好吧？

Even with the teacher inviting us you're not going to show up. That's not too good, don't you think?

2. 你真奇怪！為什麼不許我睡覺？

…………………………………………………………………………………………

3. 媽媽太緊張了，爸爸做事她也不放心。

…………………………………………………………………………………………

㈤連 V 都／也不／沒 V……

1. 他接到我的信，沒看就扔了。

He received my letter and threw it away without reading it.

→他接到我的信，連看都沒看就扔了。

He received my letter and threw it away without even reading it.

2. 我去借錢，他什麼都沒想就說不行。

....

3. 我弟弟病了，今天不想玩了。

....

4. 我吃得太飽了，站不起來了。

....

㈥連 SV 都／也 不／沒 SV

1. 這個東西一點都不甜，怎麼能叫糖呢？

This thing isn't sweet at all. How can it be called candy?

→這個東西連甜都不甜，怎麼能叫糖呢？

This thing isn't even sweet. How can it be called candy?

2. 這杯茶不熱了，真難喝。

....

3. 他說錯了話，大家都看著他，可是他的臉一點也沒紅。

....

☞ 八 只要……，就……　As long as ......(then)......

⊙只要你想得出來，就吃得到。

Whatever you can think of to eat is available.

用法說明：「只要」後面是假設的唯一條件，如果合於此條件就有「就」後面的結果。只能用於一般或未來的情況，已經發生的則不適用。因為只有一個條件，感覺上不太難做到。

Explanation: Following 只要 is a single hypothetical stipulation. As long as this stipulation is met, then the situation after 就 will result, since the condition is relatively simple and easy to satisfy. This pattern can only be used to describe habitual or future situations. It cannot be used for an action which has already occurred.

練習：用「只要……，就……。」回答下面問題。

Exercise: Please use “只要……，就……” to answer the questions below.

1. 你願意搬到那兒去住嗎？

   Are you willing to move there?

   →只要去學校方便，我就願意。

   As long as it's convenient to go to school from there, I'm willing.

2. 我們明年都可以畢業嗎？

   ……………………………………………………………………

3. 你的車，今天晚上可以借我嗎？

   ……………………………………………………………………

4. 我們什麼時候去野餐？

   ……………………………………………………………………

5. 我越來越胖，怎麼辦？

   ……………………………………………………………………

☞ 九 歎詞「欸」的用法 The use of “欸” Interjection

⊙欸，你看，她們吃的是什麼？

Hey, look! What is it that they are eating?

用法說明：語調高降（第四聲）表示招呼並提醒別人注意，或答應別人的叫喚。語調高揚（第二聲）表示驚訝，或忽然想起。語調曲折（第三聲）表示不太同意。用於較熟的朋友之間。

Explanation: When the tone starts high and descends (fourth tone), this indicates a greeting that is meant to get another's attention or answer another's call. When the tone starts fairly high and ascends (second tone), this indicates that one is surprised or has suddenly thought of something. When the tone drops and then rises (third tone), this indicates that one disagrees. This interjection is very informal and is used in more casual settings.

練習：Exercises:

㈠根據所給情況及提示，用「欸」(èi) 招呼並提醒對方注意。

Please use "欸(èi)" to express a greeting or warning in accordance with the provided hints.

1. 看見同學沒拿書就走了。

You see a classmate leaving without taking his/her book.

→欸，你忘了拿書了！

Hey! You forgot to take your book!

2. 上課的時間到了，可是室友還在看報。

....

3. 弟弟的女朋友進來，可是弟弟在寫功課，沒看見。

....

㈡用「欸」(èi) 答應別人的叫喚。

Please respond to others' callings using "欸(èi)".

1. 建國！建國！你快來！

Jian Guo! Jian Guo! Come here quickly!

→欸！來了！

Ok, I'm coming!

2. 張小姐！

....

㈢用「欸」(éi) 表示驚訝。

1. Please use "欸(éi)" to show surprise.

(1) 已經十點了，看見哥哥還沒去上班。

It's already ten o'clock, and you see that your brother hasn't gone to work yet.

→欸，你怎麼還在家？

Huh? Why are you still home?

(2) 覺得朋友今天來得比平常早。

....

(3) 服務生送來一個你沒點的菜。

....

㈣用「欸」(éi) 表示忽然想起。

Please use "欸(éi)" to indicate that you have suddenly thought of something.

1. 聽到別人說要寄信，想起寫好的信也還沒寄。

You hear someone say they are going to mail a letter and (suddenly) remember that you still haven't mailed a letter that you finished writing (either).

→欸，我的信也還沒寄。

Oh! I still haven't mailed my letter yet either!

2. 要去開車的時候，找不到鑰匙。

....

3. 打工的時候忙得不得了，餓了才想起來忘了吃午飯。

....

㈤用「欸」(ěi) 表示不太同意。

Please use "欸(ěi)" to show your disagreement.

1. 你聽見弟弟對他同學說話不太客氣，你覺得這樣不對。

You hear your little brother impolitely talking to his classmate. You feel that it is not proper to talk in this way.

→欸，對同學說話怎麼這麼不客氣!?

Hey, how come you are so impolite to your classmate?

2. 你看見室友把髒東西扔到窗戶外面去。

....

3. 你看見好朋友的小孩吃飯的時候玩筷子。

....

課室活動

Role Playing: Ask for three volunteers. Two of them act as friends going to a Chinese restaurant. The third acts as their waiter. The two friends first place their order. After being served, one of them is appalled to find a hair（一根頭髮 yìgēn tóufǎ）in a dish. What would they do in this situation? Have the students speak and act out their reactions. Give them two minutes to prepare. A fourth role may be added–that of the owner of the restaurant , the 老闆 (lǎobǎn) or the manager（經理）.

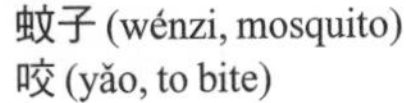
蚊子 (wénzi, mosquito)
咬 (yǎo, to bite)

牠 (tā, it)

短文

建國給父母的信

爸
媽：

你們好！上課已經一個多禮拜了，我在這裏一切都好，請放心。姐姐怎麼樣？我還沒給她打電話。你們一定沒想到我會用中文寫信吧？這學期我選了中文系的課，應該多練習寫字。

昨天我跟高偉立去市區一家中國飯館吃飯，那裏的菜都是美國人的口味，吃起來不怎麼樣，還是媽媽做的好吃。不過高偉立常去，他特別喜歡那裏的木須肉。如果他吃過媽媽做的宮保雞丁，就一定不會再想去那家飯館了。

我們在吃飯的時候，認識了兩個剛來的女留學生。她們在我們學校念研究所。聽她們說在台灣要吃什麼，就有什麼，說得高偉立對台灣更有興趣了。

我的信寫得不錯吧？希望爸爸看了會高興得給我多寄點錢來。先謝謝了！我要去上課了，有空再給你們寫信，

敬祝

健康、快樂！

兒建國敬上
九月十日

AEROGRAMME•VIA AIRMAIL•PAR AVION

Vocabulary:

1. 敬 (jìng) means to respect. 敬上 means to respectfully offer to a superior . When one writes a letter to his / her elders, one should place 敬上 after his/her signature.

第三課

我想去臺灣

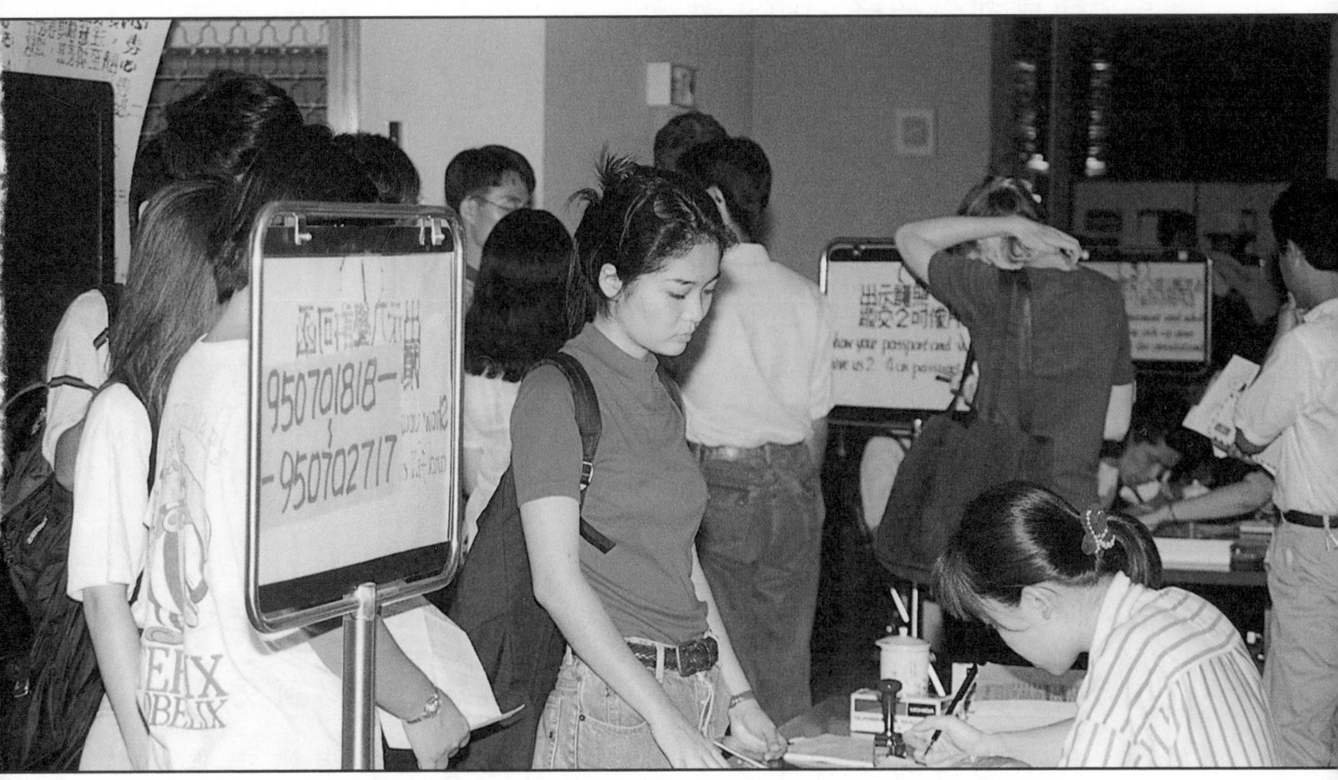

・學生註冊情形（吳俊銘攝）

（高偉立敲辦公室的門）

教授：請進。

偉立：張老師，您好！我來請教幾個問題，昨天已經跟您約好了。

教授：好的[1]，請坐。有什麼問題？有什麼需要我幫忙的？

偉立：謝謝。我覺得這兒沒有說中文的環境，我想得去臺灣或中國大陸**才**能把中文學好。**不知道**我們跟那邊的學校有沒有交換計畫？

教授：有。你打算什麼時候去？

偉立：**要是**可能的**話**，明年就去。

教授：很好。我們跟臺灣的大學、大陸的大學都有交換計畫。有一年的，也有兩三個月的暑期班。申請表我這兒都有，要不要拿一份兒去看看？

偉立：好。容不容易申請？申請的人多不多？

教授：這**要看**你的成績了。你**先**填申請表，**再**寫一份兒學習計畫。

偉立：然後呢？

教授：你還得申請成績單，再請老師寫一封推薦信。把這些東西一起交給系辦公室。記得要在二月一號以前交來！

偉立：我還想請問學費要多少？機票貴不貴？我大概需要準備多少錢？

教授：學費每個學校不一樣。**等**你決定去哪兒以後，我**再**告訴你。機票**嘛**，當然是越早訂越便宜。

偉立：有沒有我可以申請的獎學金？

教授：當然有。要是申請不到，你也可以去補習班[2]教一點英文。在臺灣有不少外國學生**一邊**學中文，**一邊**教英文[3]。要是真的還有困難，我們也可以想辦法補助。

國立臺灣師範大學國語教學中心

入學申請表

APPLICATION FOR ADMISSION

Mandarin Training Center
NATIONAL TAIWAN NORMAL UNIVERSITY
162 Hoping East Road, Section 1
Taipei 10610, Taiwan
Republic of China

INSTRUCTIONS: Type or Print clearly. Complete both sides of this form. 本表正反兩面，請以正楷填寫清楚

①英文姓名 ENGLISH NAME
Last: Wildrick
First: Robert
Middle: Michael

②中文姓名 CHINESE NAME: 李安其

③國　籍 NATIONALITY: U.S.A.

④出生日期 DATE OF BIRTH: 11/19/71

⑤性　別 SEX: ☒男Male ☐女Female

⑥現任職務 PRESENT OCCUPATION: Graduate Student

⑦永久地址 HOME ADDRESS
226 Connecticut Ave — no. and street
Washington, D.C. — city — state (or province)
U.S.A. — country — 20013 — postal (zip)code

⑧通訊地址 MAILING ADDRESS (Complete only if different from home address)
右列日期以後，請寄至永久地址 Send mail to home address after ____ month ____ day ____ year
no. and street
city — state (or province)
country — postal (zip)code

⑨希望何時開始上課 WHICH PERIOD OF STUDY ARE YOU APPLYING FOR?
☐第一期1st Quarter (Sep.1－Nov.23) ☐第三期3rd Quarter (Mar.1－May.24) ☒暑期班Summer Session (Jul.1－Aug.24)
☐第二期2nd Quarter (Dec.1－Feb.28) ☐第四期4th Quarter (Jun.1－Aug.24)

＊入學申請截止時間爲每學期開始上課之前三個月，請申請人特別注意此一期限。
The application deadline is always exactly three months before the start of the quarter (or session) for which you want to apply.

⑩預計上課多久 APPROXIMATELY HOW LONG DO YOU PLAN TO STUDY AT THE MTC?
☐一期1 Three-month Quarter ☐暑期班2 Months (Summer Session only) ☒一期以上Other (Specify no. of quarters: 2)

⑪是否曾在本中心申請過 HAVE YOU EVER APPLIED TO THE MTC BEFORE? ☐是Yes ☒否No

若是舊生，請寫下以前的學生證號碼：
If you have studied at the MTC before, what was your student number? ☐☐☐☐☐☐☐☐☐－☐

⑫教育背景EDUCATIONAL BACKGROUND (List high school only if you did not attend university.)

	高中 High School	大學 University	碩士班 Graduate School	博士班 Post-Graduate School
學校名稱 Name of School	Johnston High	Emory University	U.C.L.A.	
所在地(國名、城市) City and Country	Johnston, Iowa	Atlanta, GA, USA	Los Angeles, LA, USA	
學位及畢業日期 Degree and Date	High School Diploma '89	B.A. '93		
主修 Major		English		
副修 Minor				
平均成績 Overall Grade Average	3.42	3.58		

本欄請勿填寫（辦公室用）FOR OFFICE USE ONLY

收件 年 月 日	護照	簽證	來台 年 月 日	電話
期別 今年 ☐1 ☐2 ☐3 ☐4 ☐S		明年 ☐1 ☐2 ☐3 ☐4 ☐S		程度

入籍學號 ☐☐☐☐☐☐☐☐☐

☐ ☐✓ ☐2N
☐ ☐× ☐N
☐ ☐CC

・學生入學申請表（范慧貞提供）

偉立：那麼學分怎麼算呢？

教授：**要看**你在那邊念了什麼書，念了多少時間以後才能決定。

偉立：聽說有的學校跟我們沒有交換計畫，可是也不錯，能不能給我介紹幾個？

教授：好啊。資料我這兒都有，你需要**的話**，隨時歡迎你來拿。都聽明白了吧？

偉立：明白了。謝謝您。

※ ※ ※ ※ ※ ※

（教室外面）

偉立：嗨！美真，你好。很高興又碰見你了。

美真：你好，高偉立[4]。你去哪裡啊[5]？

偉立：圖書館，你呢？

美真：我剛下課，想到美容院去剪頭髮[6]。

偉立：我想問你幾個問題，你有時間嗎？

美真：沒關係。我還有半個鐘頭。

偉立：明年我想到臺灣去學中文。不知道臺灣的物價怎麼樣？生活容易不容易？

美真：這兩年物價比較高。不過你會說英文，在臺灣找工作不難，生活應該沒有問題。

偉立：住呢？房子好不好找？房租貴不貴？

美真：學校附近有很多分租給學生的房間，也可以幾個學生合租一個公寓。有些外國學生住在中國人家裡，**要是**願意教房東英文**的話**，房租可以少算一點，**有時候還**可以不必付房租。市區的房租比郊區的貴，當然也**得看**是什麼樣的房子。

偉立：那交通方便嗎？需不需要自己有車？

美真：在臺灣坐公車最方便，沒有車不是問題。**哎喲**[7]！我得走了，要不然就來不及了，我們下次再談吧！

偉立：好啊！你快走吧！謝謝你啦！

美真：哪裡[8]，別客氣。

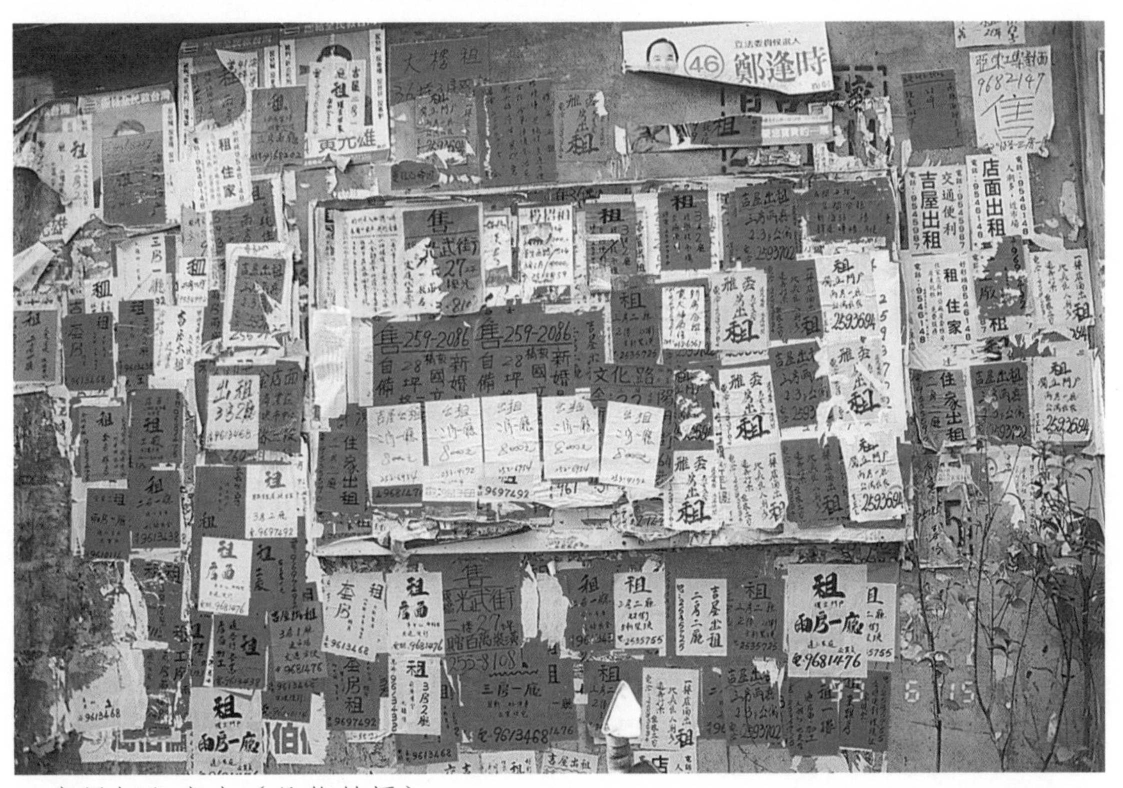

・房屋招租廣告（吳俊銘攝）

生詞及例句

1. 敲ㄑㄧㄠ (qiāo) *V*: **to knock; to beat; to tap; to pound**

吃飯的時候，不可以用筷子敲碗。

2. 辦ㄅㄢˋ公ㄍㄨㄥ室ㄕˋ (bàngōngshì) *N*: **office（M：間）**

教ㄐㄧㄠˋ室ㄕˋ (jiàoshì) *N*: **classroom**

3. 教ㄐㄧㄠˋ授ㄕㄡˋ (jiàoshòu) *N*: **professor（M：位）**

張教授的辦公室是不是在樓上？

4. 約ㄩㄝ (yuē)

V/N: **make an appointment / appointment, engagement**

(1)我打電話約他今天晚上去看電影。

(2)我今晚已經有約了，明天再跟你去吃飯，好不好？

約ㄩㄝ會ㄏㄨㄟˋ (yuēhuì) *V/N*: **to have a date / date**

你今天穿得這麼漂亮，跟誰約會啊？

5. 請ㄑㄧㄥˇ教ㄐㄧㄠˋ (qǐngjiào) *V*: **to ask advice, to consult with**

(1)高先生，有一件事我不太清楚，想跟您請教請教。

(2)要是你有不懂的問題，應該去請教老師。

6. 環ㄏㄨㄢˊ境ㄐㄧㄥˋ (huánjìng)

N: **environment, surroundings, financial conditions (of a family)**

(1)他家附近的環境真不好，又髒又亂。

(2)他家環境很好，所以他從來不必打工。

7. 交ㄐㄧㄠ換ㄏㄨㄢˋ (jiāohuàn) *V*: **to exchange, swap**

明天舞會完了以後，大家要交換禮物。

交ㄐㄧㄠ (jiāo) *V*: **to hand in, give to, pass on to**

請你替我把這張名單交給謝老師。

交ㄐㄧㄠ朋ㄆㄥˊ友ㄧㄡˇ (jiāo//péngyǒu) *VO*: **to make a friend**

他最近交了幾個中國朋友，所以常常有機會說中文。

8. 計ㄐㄧˋ畫ㄏㄨㄚˋ (jìhuà)

V/N: **to plan, to map out / plan, project, program**

(1)我計畫明年夏天到臺灣去學兩個月中文。

(2)這個計畫不錯，不過你得先跟你父母談談。

9. 暑ㄕㄨˇ期ㄑㄧˊ班ㄅㄢ (shǔqíbān) *N*: **summer school, summer session**

去年夏天他在那所學校念了兩個月的暑期班。

10. 申ㄕㄣ請ㄑㄧㄥˇ表ㄅㄧㄠˇ (shēnqǐngbiǎo) *N*: **application form（M：張）**

申ㄕㄣ請ㄑㄧㄥˇ (shēnqǐng) *V*: **to apply for**

很多人都想申請那個電腦公司的工作。

表ㄅㄧㄠˇ (biǎo) *N*: **table, form, list**

11. 填ㄊㄧㄢˊ (tián) *V*: **to fill in; to stuff**

我的申請表只填了姓名、地址，忘了填電話號碼。

12. 成ㄔㄥˊ績ㄐㄧ (chéngjī)

N: **grade (at school), academic record, achievement**

他這學期特別用功，所以成績很好。

成ㄔㄥˊ績ㄐㄧ單ㄉㄢ (chéngjīdān) *N*: **report card, transcript**

13. 推ㄊㄨㄟ薦ㄐㄧㄢˋ信ㄒㄧㄣˋ (tuījiànxìn) *N*: **letter of recommendation**

現在找工作，大概都需要有推薦信。

推ㄊㄨㄟ薦ㄐㄧㄢˋ (tuījiàn) *V*: **to recommend**

他一畢業，老師就推薦他去一家銀行工作了。

14. 學ㄒㄩㄝˊ習ㄒㄧˊ (xuéxí) *V*: **to study; to learn**

住校是一個學習獨立的好機會。

15. 學ㄒㄩㄝˊ費ㄈㄟˋ (xuéfèi) *N*: **school tuition fees**

這個大學的學費很貴，沒有錢的人念不起。

水ㄕㄨㄟˇ費ㄈㄟˋ (shuǐfèi) *N*: **water bill**

電ㄉㄧㄢˋ費ㄈㄟˋ (diànfèi) *N*: **electricity bill**

電ㄉㄧㄢˋ話ㄏㄨㄚˋ費ㄈㄟˋ (diànhuàfèi) *N*: **telephone bill**

旅ㄌㄩˇ費ㄈㄟˋ(lǚfèi) *N*: **travel costs**

16. 訂ㄉㄧㄥˋ (dìng)

V: **to conclude, draw up(a treaty, an agreement, etc.); to order, subscribe to; to book, make reservations (in a hotel, restaurant, theater, etc.)**

我們下個星期去旅行，旅館房間已經訂好了。

17. 獎ㄐㄧㄤˇ學ㄒㄩㄝˊ金ㄐㄧㄣ (jiǎngxuéjīn) *N*: **scholarship, fellowship**

他申請了那個大學中文研究所的獎學金。

金ㄐㄧㄣ子˙ㄗ (jīn·zi) *N*: **gold（M：塊）**

18. 補ㄅㄨˇ習ㄒㄧˊ班ㄅㄢ (bǔxíbān)

N: **tutorial school (a private institution that offers tutoring in various subjects), cram school（M：家）**

我媽覺得我的成績不夠好，所以我下了課還要去補習班上課。

補ㄅㄨˇ習ㄒㄧˊ (bǔxí) *V*: **to receive tutoring**

他想來美國，可是英文不好，所以得先補習。

補ㄅㄨˇ助ㄓㄨˋ (bǔzhù)

V/N: **to subsidize / a subsidy, allowance**

(1)你買車的錢不夠，公司可以補助你一點。

(2)家裡環境不好的學生，可以跟學校申請補助。

補ㄅㄨˇ課ㄎㄜˋ (bǔ//kè)

VO: **to have / to give a make up lesson**

張老師說他今天不舒服，不能來上課，下禮拜一給你們補課。

19. 困ㄎㄨㄣˋ難ㄋㄢˊ (kùnnán) *N/SV*: **difficulty / to be difficult, hard**

(1)你要是有什麼困難，找他幫忙一定沒問題。

(2)他病了，好像說話都很困難。

20. 學ㄒㄩㄝˊ分ㄈㄣ (xuéfēn) *N*: **academic credits**

暑期班的中文課，可以算幾個學分？

21. 資ㄗ料ㄌㄧㄠˋ (zīliào) *N*: **materials; data, information**

你寫這篇文章需要的資料，圖書館都有。

22. 明ㄇㄧㄥˊ白ㄅㄞˊ (míng·bái)

V/SV: **to understand, realize, know/ to be clear**

你要是還不明白，可以請他再說一次。

23. 碰ㄆㄥˋ見ㄐㄧㄢˋ／碰ㄆㄥˋ到ㄉㄠˋ (pèng//jiàn/pèng//dào)

RC: **to meet unexpectedly, to run into, to chance upon**

(1)昨天我在街上碰見一個好久不見的老朋友。

(2)明天星期六沒課，我恐怕碰不見他。

碰ㄆㄥˋ (pèng) *V*: **to touch, bump**

這種杯子很容易破，你最好別碰。

碰ㄆㄥˋ上ㄕㄤˋ (pèng·shàng)

RC: **to run up against, to come across**

他沒有工作，又生病了，要是你碰上這樣的事，你怎麼辦？

24. 美ㄇㄟˇ容ㄖㄨㄥˊ院ㄩㄢˋ (měiróngyuàn) *N*: **beauty parlor（M：家）**

理ㄌㄧˇ髮ㄈㄚˇ廳ㄊㄧㄥ (lǐfǎtīng) *N*: **barber shop**

這條街上有幾家美容院，只有一家理髮廳。

25. 剪ㄐㄧㄢˇ頭ㄊㄡˊ髮ㄈㄚˇ (jiǎn //tóu·fǎ) *VO*: **to give / get a haircut**

我小時候媽媽常給我剪頭髮。

剪ㄐㄧㄢˇ (jiǎn) *V*: **to cut (with scissors), to clip, to trim**

他覺得那條褲子太長，就剪短了一點。

頭ㄊㄡˊ髮ㄈㄚˇ (tóu·fǎ) *N*: **hair (on the human head)**

26. 物ㄨˋ價ㄐㄧㄚˋ (wùjià) *N*: **price of goods**

日本的物價高，我什麼都買不起。

房ㄈㄤˊ價ㄐㄧㄚˋ (fángjià) *N*: **housing prices**

菜ㄘㄞˋ價ㄐㄧㄚˋ (càijià) *N*: **vegetable prices ; food prices**

這裡的菜價很便宜，可是房價越來越高。住比吃貴多了。

價ㄐㄧㄚˋ錢ㄑㄧㄢˊ (jiàqián) *N*: **price; cost**

這本書的價錢不貴，只要五塊錢。

27. 生ㄕㄥ活ㄏㄨㄛˊ (shēnghuó) *N/V*: **life / to live**

(1)這幾年他在外國的生活怎麼樣？

(2)這裡的物價這麼高，怎麼生活？

活ㄏㄨㄛˊ (huó) *SV/V*: **to be alive, living / to live**

(1)這條魚還是活的。

(2)人活著就得吃飯。

生ㄕㄥ活ㄏㄨㄛˊ費ㄈㄟˋ (shēnghuófèi)

N: **living expenses, cost of living**

你父親每個月給你多少生活費？

28. 房ㄈㄤˊ租ㄗㄨ (fángzū) *N*: **rent**

這個房子很舊，所以房租比較便宜。

租ㄗㄨ (zū) *V*: **to rent**

我沒車，打算租輛車去東部旅行。

分ㄈㄣ租ㄗㄨ (fēnzū) *V*: **to sublet, to rent separately**

這個房間我們不用，分租給別人吧。

合ㄏㄜˊ租ㄗㄨ (hézū)

V: **to jointly rent, rent together, share rental**

我們四個人在學校附近合租了一個大房子。

出ㄔㄨ租ㄗㄨ (chūzū)

V: **to be for rent; offer for rent; rent to others**

租ㄗㄨ出ㄔㄨ去ㄑㄩˋ (zū//chū·qù) *RC*: **to rent out**

張：請問，你有房間出租嗎？

李：對不起，已經租出去了。

29. 公ㄍㄨㄥ寓ㄩˋ (gōngyù)

N: **apartment building, multi-story multi-family dwelling（M：棟 dòng／間）**

30. 房ㄈㄤˊ東ㄉㄨㄥ (fángdōng) *N*: **landlord**

二ㄦˋ房ㄈㄤˊ東ㄉㄨㄥ (èrfángdōng) *N*: **subleasor**

張小姐把她租的公寓分租一個房間給我，所以她是我的二房東。

房ㄈㄤˊ客ㄎㄜˋ (fángkè) *N*: **tenant**

31. 付ㄈㄨˋ (fù) *V*: **to pay**

今天我請你吃飯，當然應該我付錢。

32. 交ㄐㄧㄠ通ㄊㄨㄥ (jiāotōng) *N*: **traffic; transportation**

這裡公共汽車很多，交通很方便。

通ㄊㄨㄥ (tōng)

V/SV/RE: **to go, move or flow unobstructed; to communicate / open, passable / unobstructed**

(1)我很久沒跟他通信了，他好嗎？
(2)他鼻子不通，大概感冒了。
(3)這個電話壞了，我打了很多次，都打不通。

33.來ㄌㄞˊ不ㄅㄨˋ及ㄐㄧˊ (lái·bùjí)
RC: **to have insufficient time, to be too late (to do something)**
飛機三點起飛，現在才一點，還來得及。

歎詞 Interjection

1.哎ㄞ喲ㄧㄛ (āiyō) *I*: **[indicating surprise or discontent]**
哎喲，我的頭好疼啊！

專有名詞 Proper Names

1.中ㄓㄨㄥ國ㄍㄨㄛˊ大ㄉㄚˋ陸ㄌㄨˋ（大陸）(Zhōngguó Dàlù) mainland China

注釋

1. 好的 means "Yes." This 的 is a particle, indicating certainty and making the tone of 好的 polite and gentle. 是的 functions the same way.
2. 補習班 means "tutorial school". There are many different kinds of 補習班 in Taiwan, most of which are privately run. People go to 補習班 for special tutoring in a vast array of subjects. Although the most popular courses are review courses to prepare for various examinations (college entrance exams, TOEFL, civil service exams, etc.), there are also programs for such things as learning languages, driving, cooking, playing musical instruments, etc.
3. "……教英文". English teaching positions are governed by R.O.C.'s Foreign Labor Lows. Students desiring more information on teaching

English in Taiwan should contact the nearest local representative agency.

4. “你好，高偉立。” The Chinese student called William by his full Chinese name, not only the first name. Chinese students at school address one another using their full names, as does the teacher. In other circumstances such as at work, however, it is not polite to address peers using their full names unless they are friends. The first name is used alone only by family and close friends. Younger people should not address older people by their first name nor their full name, but instead should address them by their surname plus a title or by the name of their relationship.

5. “你去哪裡啊？” is a greeting. See Note 5 of Lesson 1. It is the same as asking “上哪兒去啊？”. It is not necessary to describe one’s destination in detail. An appropriate reply might be “出去。”, “上街。”, or “去買東西。” etc.

6. “去美容院剪頭髮。” means to go to the beauty parlor to have one’s hair cut. It is not necessary to make an appointment to have one’s hair done in Taiwan. In the United States, however, sometimes one has to make an appointment before going to a barbershop or a beauty parlor. This is why in the text 美真 says she has a half hour.

7. 哎喲 is used when something unexpected or unpleasant happens. This interjection is spoken mostly by women.

8. Here, 哪裡 does not mean “where?” It is used when one receives praise or gratitude from other people. It is similar to saying: “It’s really nothing.”

文法練習

☞ 一 才 only if

⊙我想去臺灣或中國大陸才能把中文學好。

I think that only by going to Taiwan or Mainland China can one be proficient in Chinese.

用法說明：前句是後句的必要條件，如果不具備前句的條件，絕不可能達成後句的情況。第二課的「只要……，就……」是假設性的狀況，而「才」不但可以用在一般及未來的情況，已發生的也適用，語氣也強許多。

Explanation: The first clause of the sentence describes requirements for the second clause. If the requirements are not met, it is impossible to achieve the situation described in the second clause. This pattern is different from "只要……，就……" (see Ch. 2). 才 describes the relative difficulty of a situation and means "only if this requirement is met can one. . . . . .," "只要……，就……" on the other hand describes the relative ease of a situation and means "all must do is meet this requirement."

練習：Exercises:

㈠請用「才」回答下面各問題。

Please use 才 to answer the questions below.

1. 你明天要去游泳嗎？

   Do you want to go swimming tomorrow?

   →天氣好，我才去。

   I'll only go if the weather is nice.

2. 他姐姐願意租這個房子嗎？

   ……………………………………………………………………………………

3. 你的照像機可以借我用一天嗎？

   ……………………………………………………………………………………

4. 你說你不喜歡他，你昨天為什麼要跟他出去呢？

……………………………………………………………………………………

5. 他的病怎麼好得那麼快？

……………………………………………………………………………………

6. 沒有人知道這件事，你是怎麼知道的？

……………………………………………………………………………………

7. 大學生都可以喝酒嗎？

……………………………………………………………………………………

8. 你每天晚上都看電視嗎？

……………………………………………………………………………………

9. 你常在那個中國飯館吃飯嗎？

……………………………………………………………………………………

㈡請把下面各句改成「才」的句子，並比較兩句的不同。

Please rewrite the sentences below using 才 and compare the differences between the two sentences.

1. 只要你會說英文，就可以做這個工作。

As long as you can speak English, you can do this job

→你會說英文，才可以做這個工作。

You can only do this job if you can speak English.

2. 只要你去，我就去。

……………………………………………………………………………………

3. 只要明天不下雨，我就參加。

……………………………………………………………………………………

4. 只要你對別人好，別人就會對你好。

……………………………………………………………………………………

5. 只要你好好念書，就能畢業。

……………………………………………………………………………………

㈢請改正下面各句，必要時可請學生說明原因。

Please correct the sentences below and, if necessary, explain the reasons for your corrections.

1. 只要我問他，他就告訴我了。(sic.)

→只 要我問他，他就會告訴我。

All I have to do is ask him, and he will tell me.

→我問他，他才告訴我的。

He told me only after I asked him.

2.只要你給錢，他就賣給你了。

....

3. 只要你寫完功課，我就讓你看電視了。

....

☞ 二 不知道…… I wonder.......

⊙不知道我們跟那邊的學校有沒有交換計畫？

I wonder if we have an exchange program with schools there?

⊙不知道臺灣的物價怎麼樣？

I wonder how prices are in Taiwan?

用法說明：「不知道」表示疑問，前面的主語 (S)「我」省略了。有時是婉轉提出問題，希望對方回答。

Explanation: The subject, 我 normally placed before 不知道 has been omitted. This pattern indicates doubt and is sometimes a subtle way to propose a question in the hope that the other will answer.

練習：Exercises:

㈠請按提示用「不知道」發問，再請另一學生回答。

One student asks a question using 不知道 and the information provided. Another student answers the question.

1. 跟一個同學談王老師的病，想知道他現在怎麼樣了。

Discuss Teacher Wang's illness with a classmate. You'd like to know how he is now.

→不知道他的病好了沒有？

答：聽說好多了。

A: I wonder if Teacher Wang has recovered from his illness?

B: I heard he's feeling much better .

2. 跟一個室友談到一部電影，想約他一起去看。

....

3. 跟老師談到一本有名的書，希望老師借給你看。

....

4. 跟朋友談到現在租的房子不好，想搬家，希望朋友幫忙找。

....

5. 跟同學談學校的交換計畫，想知道高偉立參加不參加。

....

㈡請按提示用「不知道」表示疑問，並不期待對方回答。

Please use 不知道 to indicate doubt in the situations below. Note that these questions do not anticipate a reply.

1. 明天要去旅行，今天天氣不好，怕明天會跟今天一樣。

You're going on a trip tomorrow. Today's weather is not very good, and you're afraid it will be the same tomorrow.

→不知道明天的天氣怎麼樣？

I wonder what the weather will be like tomorrow.

2. 要去看一個同學，怕他不在家。

....

3. 買了一個禮物要送給女朋友，希望她喜歡。

....

4. 覺得餓了，希望媽媽已經把飯做好了。

....

5. 快要考試了，怕考試太難，自己考不好。

....

☞ 三 （要是）……的話 if......

⊙要是可能的話，明年就去。

If it is possible, then I will go next year.

⊙你需要的話，隨時歡迎你來拿。

If you need it, you are welcome to come over and get it anytime.

⊙要是願意教房東英文的話，房租可以少算一點。

If you are willing to teach English to the landlord, then the rent can be made a little cheaper.

用法說明：這個句型跟「要是……」完全一樣。「要是」與「的話」可以並用，也可以省略其一。

Explanation: This sentence pattern is exactly the same as 要是 . Both 要是 and 的話 can either be used together or alone.

練習：請用「（要是）……的話」把兩個句子合成一個。

Exercise: Please use the pattern “（要是）……的話” to link together each of the two sentences below.

1. 他吃膩了，我們換換口味吧。

   He’s sick of eating this. Let’s change flavors.

   →要是他吃膩了的話，我們就換換口味吧。

   If he’s sick of eating this, then let’s change flavors.

2. 你關心我。你就不應該離開我。

   ....

3. 你喜歡吃這種口味。你可以點宮保雞丁。

   ....

4. 王太太有空。我們今天就請她照顧這個孩子。

   ....

5. 他還是不明白。他最好去請教張老師。

   ....

☞ 四 要／得看…… depends on......

⊙這要看你的成績了。

This depends on your academic performance.

⊙要看你在那邊念了什麼書，……

That depends on what books you study there, ...

⊙當然也得看是什麼樣的房子。

Of course it also depends on what kind of room it is.

用法說明：所談的事情由「看」後面的情況決定。「看」後面的短句可能包括：a.疑問詞 (QW)、b. 選擇式 (A / notA)、c.兩個相對的單音節、d. 如果語言環境清楚，前三種亦都可省略。

Explanation: The matter being discussed depends upon the situation stated after 看 . 看 can be followed by a clause with: a. a question word, b. a choice type question, c. a two opposite single-syllable stative verb. If the context is obvious, then nothing needs to follow 看 .

練習：請用「要／得看……」回答下面各問題。

Exercise: Please answer the questions below using "要／得看……" .

1.你明天一定要去嗎？

Will you definitely go tomorrow?

→a. 不一定，要看天氣怎麼樣。

No, not necessarily. It depends on what the weather is like.

→b. 要看天氣好不好。

It depends on whether the weather is good.

→c. 要看天氣好壞。

It depends on whether the weather is good (or bad).

→d. 要看天氣。

It depends on the weather.

2. 他想走路去，還是坐車去？

....

3. 你要不要買那個照像機？

....

4. 這本書多久可以看完？

....

5. 你什麼點心都喜歡吃嗎？

....

☞ 五 先……，再…… first.......then.......

⊙你先填表，再寫一份學習計畫。

First fill out the form, and then write out your study plans.

用法說明：說出做事的先後順序，做幾件事，則數量不拘。

Explanation: This pattern is used to explain the order of one or more actions. There is no limit on the number of actions.

練習：請用「先……，再……」回答下面各問題。

Exercise: Please answer the questions below using "先……，再……".

1. 下課以後，你想做什麼？

   What do you want to do after class?

   →我先去剪頭髮、買東西，再去吃飯、看電影。

   First I'm going to get my hair cut and go shopping, then I'm going to eat and watch a movie.

2. 你畢業以後，有什麼打算？

   ....

3. 炸雞怎麼做？

   ....

4. 我現在去找他，不知道方便不方便？

   ....

5. 我點了三個菜了，還要再點嗎？

   ....

☞ 六 等……再…… after...... then......

⊙等你決定去哪兒以後，我再告訴你。

I will tell you (more information) after you have decided where to go.

用法說明：當事者等某(些)情況發生，或某(些)動作完成以後，再做其他的事。

Explanation: The party involved will wait for a certain situation or action to occur before performing the action stated at the end of the sentence.

練習：Exercises:

㈠請用「等……，再……」回答下面各問題。

Please answer the questions below using "等……，再……".

1.我們現在可以走了嗎？

Can we go now?

→等吃完飯、洗好碗再走吧！

Let's go after we finish eating and washing the dishes.

2. 你搬家已經好幾天了，哪一天買床啊？

....

3. 這個消息，我什麼時候可以告訴他？

....

4. 下個星期要考試，這個週末你還回家嗎？

....

5. 天這麼黑，我們怎麼去找他呢？

....

㈡請改正下面各句，必要時可請學生說明原因。

Please correct the sentences below. Please explain your corrections when necessary.

1. 先雨停了以後，我再回家。(sic.)

→等雨停了以後，我再回家。

I will go home after the rain has stopped.

2. 你先大了，再搬到外頭住。

....

3. 現在太貴，先便宜了再買吧。

....

4. 爸爸先回來，我們再吃飯。

....

5. 先病好了，再出去玩。

....

☞ 七 嘛

⊙機票嘛，當然是越早訂越便宜。

Plane tickets...... Of course, the earlier you reserve them, the cheaper they are.

用法說明：「嘛」亦可寫作「麼」，語調低而緩，在句中表示停頓，大部分是說話者為了考慮下面的話該怎麼說，有時是為了喚起聽者的注意。

Explanation: 嘛 could also be written as 麼 . The tone is low and extended, marking a pause in the middle of the sentence. It is usually used when the speaker wants to think about his/her following statement. Sometimes it is used to summon the listener's attention.

練習：請完成下面對話。

Exercise: Please complete the dialogues below.

1. 張：游泳、跳舞，你都喜歡嗎？
   Chang: Do you like both swimming and dancing?
   李：游泳，我很喜歡，跳舞嘛，我一點興趣都沒有。
   Lee: Swimming, I like very much. Dancing, I am not interested in at all.
2. 張：一天三餐，你都吃得這麼多嗎？
   李：早飯、晚飯，我吃得比較多，午飯嘛，＿＿＿＿＿＿＿＿＿＿。
3. 張：這次考試難不難？
   李：大家都說很難，我嘛，＿＿＿＿＿＿＿＿＿＿＿＿＿＿。
4. 張：你要不要參加下星期的舞會？
   李：我還沒決定。參加嘛，怕沒時間準備考試；不參加嘛，＿＿＿＿＿＿＿＿＿＿＿＿＿＿。
5. 張：這學期學的功課都很容易。
   李：這學期很容易，下學期嘛，＿＿＿＿＿＿＿＿＿＿＿＿＿＿。

☞ 八 一邊……，一邊……

simultaneously v1 and v2 ; v1 and v2 at the same time

⊙在臺灣，有不少外國學生一邊學中文，一邊教英文。

In Taiwan many foreign students study Chinese and teach English at the same time.

用法說明：同時做兩件事情。這兩件事必需是實際的動作，而不是情況或狀態。

Explanation: Two actions are performed at the same time. The two items must be actions, not situations or circumstances.

練習：Exercises:

㈠請用「一邊……，一邊……」改寫下面各句。

Please rewrite the sentences below using "一邊……，一邊……".

1. 我明年要念大學，也要工作。

   Next year I will go to college, and I will also work.

   →我明年要一邊念大學，一邊工作。

   Next year I will both go to college and work at the same time.

2. 大家一起唱歌、跳舞，非常熱鬧。

   ……………………………………………………………………………………

3. 我哥哥總是在吃早飯的時候看報紙。

   ……………………………………………………………………………………

4. 他好像很急，走進門的時候就開始脫衣服了。

   ……………………………………………………………………………………

5. 很多人開車的時候，也跟旁邊的人談話。

   ……………………………………………………………………………………

㈡請改正下面各句，並說明原因。

Please correct the sentences below and explain the source of error.

1. 他一邊生病，還一邊工作。

   He is both sick and still working (sic.) [生病 is not an action and thus not be used with this pattern.]

   →他生病了還工作。

   He is sick, and yet he's still working.

2. 張先生總是一邊坐飛機，一邊看書。

....

3. 我喜歡一邊休息，一邊喝咖啡。

....

4. 昨天晚上我妹妹一個人在家，一邊怕，一邊哭。

....

5. 我一邊想，一邊生氣。

....

九 ……，有時候還…… sometimes.......even.......

⊙……房租可以少算一點，有時候還可以不必付房租。

......the rent can be made a little cheaper, in some cases you don't even have to pay rent at all.

用法說明：這個「還」有「程度更進一步」的意思。

Explanation: This 還 means that the intensity or degree is one level stronger.

練習：請完成下面各句。

Exercise: Please complete the sentences below.

1. 他一生氣就哭，有時候還丟東西打人。

   As soon as he gets angry he cries, and sometimes he even throws things at people.
2. 我哥哥常玩到很晚才回家，有時候還 ________________ 。
3. 他每個月的錢都不夠用，有時候還 ________________________ 。
4. 我爸爸年紀很大，可是每天慢跑，有時候還 ________________ 。
5. 這個學生很少做功課，有時候還 ________________________ 。

十 歎詞「哎喲」的用法 The use of Interjection "哎喲"

⊙哎喲！我得走了，要不然就來不及了，……

Oh no! I have to go; otherwise I won't make it,......

用法說明：「哎喲」，語調低降，放在句首，表示驚訝、驚喜、驚懼、焦急的叫聲，有時也是疼痛時的呻吟。為女性比較常用之歎詞。

Explanation: The tone of 哎喲 starts low and descends. Placed at the beginning of a sentence, it shows amazement, pleasant surprise or sudden fright. It can also be a cry of despair or pain. This interjection is often used by females.

練習：請根據下面情況用「哎喲」表示驚訝、驚喜、驚懼、焦急跟疼痛。

Exercise: Please use 哎喲 in the following situations to express the appropriate emotion.

1. 你的頭疼得不得了。

   You have an unbearable headache.

   → 哎喲，我的頭好疼啊！

   Ow! My head really hurts!

2. 你坐在窗戶前面看書，有人丟球，把你的窗戶打破了。

   ……………………………………………………

3. 走在街上，有人從後面搶走了你的錢包。

   ……………………………………………………

4. 跟朋友約好三點見，三點二十五分了他還沒來，你還有別的事情，三點半一定得走。

   ……………………………………………………

5. 有人敲門，開門一看，是多年不見的老朋友。

   ……………………………………………………

課室活動

Role Playing:

1. Select two of the students or ask for volunteers. One is looking for a place to rent, while the other is the landlord. The renter goes to see a place and engages the landlord in conversation. They can talk about 房租，水費，電費，電話費，and rules of the house. Give them two minutes to prepare.

2. Ask for another two volunteers. One is the landlord（房東），the other is a poor tenant（房客）who has not paid rent for two months. It is the day the tenant should pay the rent, so the landlord comes. Their conversation is about how to solve the problem of the unpaid rent. Give them two minutes to prepare. Some helpful supplementary words are: 借 (jiè, to loan), 利息 (lìxí, interest), 求 (qiú, to ask; to beg).

短文

廣告[1]

學中文的同學們：

想把中文學得更好嗎？有興趣參加我們的交換計畫到台灣去嗎？想不想在一個完全用中文的環境裡學習中文呢？

我們這裡有最好的中文老師，上課方法又新又有趣。我們用的書又有意思又有用。上過我們的課，要不了幾個月，就可以用中國話跟朋友討論[2]問題了。

你可以跟中國學生同住大學宿舍，也可以租房子，住在中國人家裡，自己看看中國人的生活習慣。宿舍有餐廳，學校附近有不少小飯館，可以試試很多口味的菜。學校就在市區，交通方便，去哪裡都很容易。

每年分兩個學期，每班最多五人，每週上課十小時。暑期班兩個月，每週上課二十小時，學期當中學校會帶學生出去旅行兩次。

要是想知道得更清楚，請來信或電話，我們就寄資料給你。

XX大學中文系
地址：………
電話：………

Vocabulary:

1.廣告 (guǎnggào): advertisement

2.討論 (tǎolùn): to discuss

第四課

談談地理吧

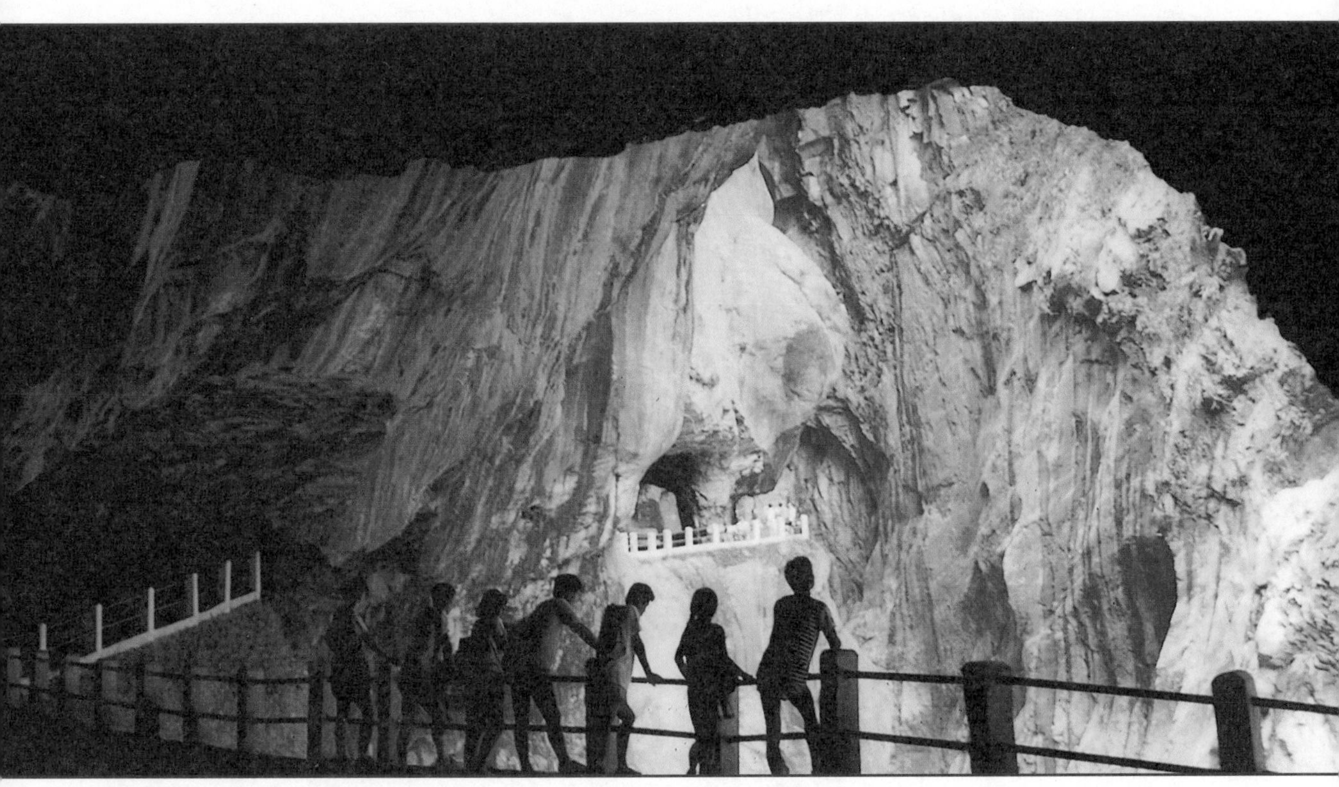

・臺灣風景：中部橫貫公路上的九曲洞（新聞局提供）

（郵局門口，李平拿著信走出來）

偉立：嗨！李平[1]，有信啊[2]？

李平：**嗯**，我女朋友寄來的。

偉立：難怪這麼高興，原來是接到了情書。（李平笑笑）**哇**！

好漂亮**的**郵票！臺灣的嗎？

李平（李平指著郵票）：這是我們故宮博物院[3]裡的東西。

偉立：故宮博物院？

李平：是臺灣最大的博物館。裡面的東西又多又好。外國人到了臺灣，都一定會去參觀。

偉立：這個博物館在哪兒？

李平：在臺北郊區。臺北在臺灣北部，是我們最大的城市。欸，臺灣在哪裡，你知道吧？

偉立：當然知道！別以為我什麼都不懂，好不好？臺灣是一個島，在亞洲，在中國大陸東南方。

李平：對！臺灣離大陸一百多公里，坐飛機到日本只要三個小時。

偉立：噢，對了，臺灣有多大[4]？

李平：差不多有康州、麻州**加起來**那麼大。

偉立：那很小嘛！

李平：是很小。**除了**海邊有一些平原**以外**，中部**都**是山。臺灣有兩千萬人口，大部分都住在西部。

偉立：為什麼？東部不好嗎？

李平：東部很好啊！只是平原比較小，颱風、地震比較多。而且從大陸過來的人[5]，都是先到西部。

偉立：嗯，這跟美國正相反。我們東部、西部有山，當中有平原。從歐洲來的移民，都是先到東部。

李平：臺灣東部發展比較慢，是因為中部山太多，交通不方

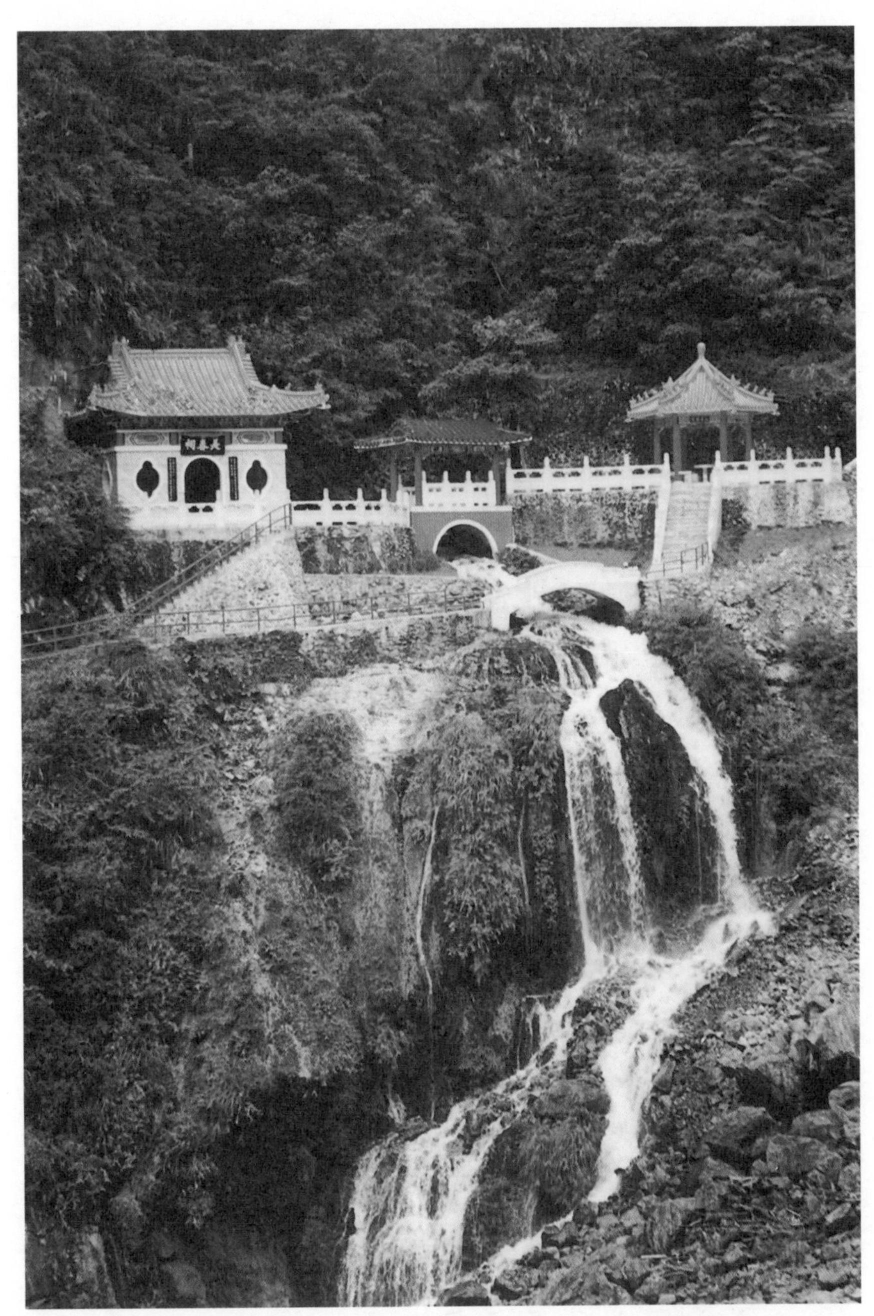

・臺灣風景：
花蓮長春祠
（新聞局提供）

便。你們中部是平原，為什麼很晚才往西發展呢？

偉立：因為從中西部越往西走越高，有高山，有高原，還有沙漠，都不適合人住。後來政府鼓勵年輕人到西部去，西部才發展**起來**。

李平：臺灣是在中部橫貫公路[6]開好以後，去東部的人才多**起來**的。

偉立：開這條路一定很辛苦吧？

李平：**雖然**很辛苦，**可是**值得。有了這條路，**不但**東部開始發展，大家**也**有機會欣賞到漂亮的風景。走過這條路的人，**沒有一個不**說好**的**。

偉立：真的？有這麼好的風景，我一定要去看看。不知道**跟**我們的大峽谷**比起來**怎麼樣？

李平：不一樣，**各有各的**美。你去看了就知道了。

偉立：除了這條路以外，從西部到東部沒有河嗎？

李平：我們的河都是從山區往東或往西流到海裡，而且都不長，對交通沒有什麼幫助。

偉立：山區的河大概都這樣。我們平原上有一條從北往南流的密西西比河，對我們的農業有很大的幫助。

李平：對了，你喜歡游泳，那你到臺灣去的時候，一定要去墾丁。墾丁在臺灣最南邊，是臺灣第一個國家公園[7]。那裡的海灘又漂亮又乾淨，連冬天都可以游泳。

偉立：去這些地方交通方便嗎？

李平：臺灣的交通方便極了，除了公路、鐵路跟飛機以外，另外還有高速公路。你什麼時候去？要是我不在臺灣，我可以請家人帶你去。

偉立：那太好了！

・臺北故宮博物院（吳俊銘攝影）

生詞及例句

1.郵ㄧㄡˊ局ㄐㄩˊ (yóujú)　　*N*: **post office**

郵ㄧㄡˊ票ㄆㄧㄠˋ (yóupiào)　　*N*: **postage stamp（M：張）**

我要買十張兩毛五分的郵票。

2.原ㄩㄢˊ來ㄌㄞˊ (yuánlái)

A: **originally, formerly, at first; (indicating discovery of the truth) it turns out that......**

⑴他原來住在紐約，現在搬到波士頓去了。

⑵原來他是中國人，難怪他的中文這麼好。

3.情ㄑㄧㄥˊ書ㄕㄨ (qíngshū)　　*N*: **love letter（M：封）**

情ㄑㄧㄥˊ人ㄖㄣˊ (qíngrén)　　*N*: **lover, sweetheart**

4.指ㄓˇ (zhǐ)　　*V*: **to point at, to point to, to point out**

請你指給我們看，哪輛車是你的？

5. 博ㄅㄛˊ物ㄨˋ館ㄍㄨㄢˇ (bówùguǎn)　　*N*: **museum**

6. 參ㄘㄢ觀ㄍㄨㄢ (cān'guān)　　*V*: **to visit (a place, exhibition, etc.)**

你們上課，我們能不能參觀？

7. 以ㄧˇ為ㄨㄟˊ (yǐwéi)　　*V*: **to think, assume (incorrectly)**

我以為他是坐飛機去的，原來他自己開車去了。

8. 島ㄉㄠˇ (dǎo)　　*N*: **island（M：個）**

日本是一個島國，北邊有很多小島。

9. 除ㄔㄨˊ了ㄌㄜ˙……以ㄧˇ外ㄨㄞˋ (chú·le......yǐwài)　　*PT*: **besides, except for**

(1) 除了你以外，人人都知道明天要考試。

(2) 除了中文以外，他還會說法文。

除ㄔㄨˊ (÷) (chú)　　*V*: **to divide**

除ㄔㄨˊ法ㄈㄚˇ (chúfǎ)　　*N*: **division (in mathematics)**

他才念小學一年級，只學過加法，還沒學除法。

10. 平ㄆㄧㄥˊ原ㄩㄢˊ (píngyuán)　　*N*: **plains, flat lands**

美國中西部是一個大平原。

高ㄍㄠ原ㄩㄢˊ (gāoyuán)　　*N*: **plateau.**

11. 人ㄖㄣˊ口ㄎㄡˇ (rénkǒu)　　*N*: **population**

世界上的人口越來越多了。

口ㄎㄡˇ (kǒu)

N/M: **mouth / M for family members, wells; mouthful**

他家一共有五口人。

12. 大ㄉㄚˋ部ㄅㄨˋ分ㄈㄣˋ (dàbù·fèn)　　*N/A/AT*: **major part, greater part**

來這個飯館吃飯的，大部分是外國人。

部ㄅㄨˋ分ㄈㄣˋ (bù·fèn)　　*N/M*: **part, section, share**

(1) 我們明天的考試只考文法部分。

(2) 你們剛剛說的話，有一部分我沒聽懂。

部ㄅㄨˋ (bù)

M: **(used for films, machine, multi-volume work of literature)**

看了那部中國電影以後，大家都想去中國看看。

13.颱ㄊㄞˊ風ㄈㄥ (táifēng)　　*N*: **typhoon**

臺灣每年夏天都有颱風。

14.地ㄉㄧˋ震ㄓㄣˋ (dìzhèn)　　*N*: **earthquake**

我媽不願在這裡買房子，因為地震太多。

15.相ㄒㄧㄤ反ㄈㄢˇ (xiāngfǎn)

V/N: **to be the opposite, to be contrary / the opposite**

(1)我喜歡大家一起玩，他跟我相反，他喜歡一個人去玩。

(2)「冷」的相反是「熱」

16.發ㄈㄚ展ㄓㄢˇ (fāzhǎn)

V/N: **to develop, expand / development, expansion**

(1)這裡交通方便，所以發展得很快。

(2)你不用功念書，以後能有什麼發展？

17.沙ㄕㄚ漠ㄇㄛˋ (shāmò)　　*N*: **desert（M：片）**

沙ㄕㄚ (shā)　　*N*: **sand**

18.適ㄕˋ合ㄏㄜˊ (shìhé)　　*V/SV*: **to be suited to, suitable for......(X)**

(1)那樣的衣服適合運動的時候穿。

(2)那樣的衣服運動的時候穿比較適合。

合ㄏㄜˊ適ㄕˋ (héshì)　　*SV*: **to be suitable, appropriate**

我想這個工作對你不合適，因為你不喜歡早起。

合ㄏㄜˊ (hé)　　*V*: **to suit, agree with**

這個公寓太小，不合我們的需要。

19.政ㄓㄥˋ府ㄈㄨˇ (zhèngfǔ)　　*N*: **government**

20.鼓ㄍㄨˇ勵ㄌㄧˋ (gǔlì)　　*V/N*: **to encourage, urge / encouragement**

(1)老師常常鼓勵我們要多念書，多問問題。

(2)孩子都需要父母的鼓勵。

21.年ㄋㄧㄢˊ輕ㄑㄧㄥ人ㄖㄣˊ (niánqīngrén)　　*N*: **young person, young people**

年紀大的人常常不懂年輕人做的事。

年ㄋㄧㄢˊ輕ㄑㄧㄥ (niánqīng)　　*SV*: **to be young**

我年輕的時候很喜歡跳舞。

輕ㄑㄧㄥ (qīng)　　*SV*: **to be light (in weight)**

箱子裡沒什麼東西，很輕。

22. 開ㄎㄞ 路ㄌㄨˋ (kāi//lù)　*VO*: **to open up a new road**

要是這裡開一條路，對大家都方便。

23. 辛ㄒㄧㄣ 苦ㄎㄨˇ (xīnkǔ)

SV: **to be difficult, hard, painful, exhausting; to experience difficulty, hardship, pain, exhaustion**

他每天教五個小時的書非常辛苦。

苦ㄎㄨˇ (kǔ)

SV/N: **to be toilsome, hard; sad; bitter / toil, hardship**

(1) 這次醫生給我的藥，真苦。

(2) 他這幾年都沒有工作，生活很苦。

(3) 先生離開我了，我一個人又要工作，又要照顧孩子，沒有人知道我心裡的苦。

24. 雖ㄙㄨㄟ 然ㄖㄢˊ (suīrán)　*A*: **though, although**

雖然坐電梯很快，可是走樓梯對身體比較好。

25. 值ㄓˊ 得ㄉㄜˊ (zhí·dé)

SV/A: **to be worthwhile, worth (doing something)**

(1) 做這件事用了很多時間，可是學到不少東西，非常值得。

(2) 那部電影很不錯，值得看。

值ㄓˊ (zhí)　*V*: **to be worth (time, money, effort)**

這棟公寓我買的時候只要十萬，現在值三十萬了。

值ㄓˊ 錢ㄑㄧㄢˊ (zhí//qián)　*SV/VO*: **to be valuable, costly**

(1) 沒關係，小偷偷走的都是不值錢的東西。

(2) 五百塊太貴了，這個照像機不值那麼多錢！

26. 不ㄅㄨˊ 但ㄉㄢˋ (búdàn)　*A*: **not only**

(1) 他不但去過歐洲，也去過亞洲。

(2) 這件衣服不但大，而且長，你穿不適合。

但ㄉㄢˋ 是ㄕˋ (dànshì)　*CONJ*: **but, still, however**

雖然他的成績不錯，但是不一定申請得到獎學金。

27. 欣ㄒㄧㄣ 賞ㄕㄤˇ (xīnshǎng)　*V*: **to appreciate, to admire**

(1)我很不欣賞那個人，因為他太隨便。

(2)我沒學過中國字，所以不懂怎麼欣賞毛筆字。

28.風景 (fēngjǐng) *N*: **scenery, landscape**

我常去鄉下欣賞美麗的風景。

29.各 (gè) *DEM*: **various, each, every**

(1)這兩個菜都是牛肉做的，可是各有各的味道。

(2)各位同學，現在請你們把功課交給我。

30.流 (liú) *V*: **to flow**

這條河是從山區流過來的。

河流 (héliú) *N*: **river**

地圖上的河流都是藍色的。

31.幫助 (bāngzhù) *V/N*: **to help, assist, aid / assistance, aid**

(1)有錢的人應該幫助沒錢的人。

(2)運動對健康有很大的幫助。

32.農業 (nóngyè) *N*: **agriculture, farming**

這個地方有很多高山，不能發展農業。

農人 (nóngrén) *N*: **farmer**

農民 (nóngmín) *N*: **peasant, peasantry**

33.國家公園 (guójiā gōngyuán) *N*: **national park**

34.海灘 (hǎitān) *N*: **seashore, beach**

夏天的時候，很多人去海邊玩，海灘上躺滿了人。

沙灘 (shātān) *N*: **beach**

35.高速公路 (gāosùgōnglù) *N*: **expressway, freeway（M：條）**

公路 (gōnglù) *N*: **highway（M：條）**

馬路 (mǎlù) *N*: **road, street, avenue（M：條）**

36.鐵路 (tiělù) *N*: **railway, railroad（M：條）**

鐵 (tiě) *N*: **iron（M：塊）**

37.另外 (lìngwài)

DEM/A: **another, the other / in addition, additionally**

(1)我有兩位中文老師，一位姓王，另外一位姓張。

(2)我給他打了電話，另外還給他寫了一封信。

歎詞跟語助詞 Interjections and Particle

1. 嗯˙ㄣ (·en) *I*: **[used to indicate agreement]**

嗯，你說得很對。

2. 哇˙ㄨㄚ (·wa)

I/P: **[used to indicate surprise, approval. 啊 is replaced by 哇 if the final word in a sentence ends with "ao", or "ou".]**

(1)哇！你們家的房子好大啊！

(2)您今天真早哇！

專有名詞 Proper Names

1. 李ㄌㄧˇ平ㄆㄧㄥˊ (Lǐ Píng) Li, Ping
2. 故ㄍㄨˋ宮ㄍㄨㄥ博ㄅㄛˊ物ㄨˋ院ㄩㄢˋ (Gùgōng Bówùyuàn) National Palace Museum
3. 亞ㄧㄚˋ洲ㄓㄡ (Yà Zhōu) Asia
4. 麻ㄇㄚˊ州ㄓㄡ (Má Zhōu) Massachusetts
5. 康ㄎㄤ州ㄓㄡ (Kāng Zhōu) Connecticut
6. 歐ㄡ洲ㄓㄡ (Ōu Zhōu) Europe
7. 中ㄓㄨㄥ部ㄅㄨˋ橫ㄏㄥˊ貫ㄍㄨㄢˋ公ㄍㄨㄥ路ㄌㄨˋ (Zhōngbù Héngguàn Gōnglù) the Central Trans-island Highway
8. 大ㄉㄚˋ峽ㄒㄧㄚˊ谷ㄍㄨˇ (Dàxiágǔ) Grand Canyon
9. 密ㄇㄧˋ西ㄒㄧ西ㄒㄧ比ㄅㄧˇ河ㄏㄜˊ (Mìxīxībǐ Hé) Mississippi River
10. 墾ㄎㄣˇ丁ㄉㄧㄥ (Kěndīng) Kenting

注釋

1. 李平 is a person's name. 李 is the surname and 平 is the first name. First names normally consist of two syllables, but sometimes people have single syllable names. One syllable first names are known as 單名. One can tell parents' expectations for their children from the names they give them. For example, the parents of 林建國 probably hope that he will one day contribute to the development of the country.
2. "有信啊？" is a greeting. See Note 5 of Lesson 1.
3. 故宮博物院, the National Palace Museum , stands on a scenic hillside setting in the northern suburbs of Taipei. The museum collection is the result of a successive Chinese imperial collection which was started by a Sung Dynasty emperor over a thousand years ago. This collection was passed down and added to from one generation to the next and from one dynasty to the next. In 1925, one year after the last emperor moved out of the Imperial Palace, the National Palace Museum was established, making the greatest collection of Chinese art in the world accessible to the public. During the 1930s and 40s the collection was transferred to various locations in mainland China to protect it from damage during the Sino-Japanese War and the Chinese Civil War. The collection was brought to Taiwan in 1949, and it was opened to the public at its present site in 1965. The Museum's collection now stands at close to 700,000 pieces.
4. "臺灣有多大？" The area of Taiwan, not including the small islands that surround it, is 35,824 square kilometers. By comparison, 麻州, the short name for 麻塞諸塞州 (Másàizhūsài Zhōu), the State of Massachusetts, has an area of 21, 456 square kilometers, and 康州, the short name for 康乃狄克州 (Kāngnǎidíkè Zhōu), the State of Connecticut, has an area of 12,997 square kilometers.
5. "而且從大陸過來的人……" Before 鄭成功 (Zhèng Chénggōng) and his troops drove the Dutch off of Taiwan island in December 1661, the

Dutch had controlled Taiwan for thirty-eight years. Emperor 康熙 (Kāngxī) of the Ching Dynasty proclaimed in 1684 that Taiwan was a territory of China. People from the southeastern coast of China started to move to Taiwan in large groups about three hundred years ago. They settled on plains along the west coast. In addition to descendants of the people who came from mainland China, Taiwan is also home to descendants of aborigine tribes which were already on the island before the new settlers arrived. Today there are altogether nine aboriginal tribes on Taiwan, numbering approximately 350,000 persons, which accounts for less than two percent of the total population.

6. 中部橫貫公路, the Central Trans-Island Highway, consists of a main road with two branches. The main road is from 東勢 (Dōngshì), on the west side, to 太魯閣 (Tàilǔgé), on the east side. Construction started in July 1956 and was completed in April 1960. The total length of the highway is 194.2 km. Along the road there are many high mountains, precipices, cliffs and virgin forests. The Central Trans-Island Highway was very difficult to construct. Frequent typhoons and earthquakes caused temporary setbacks. (The Northern Trans-Island Highway was completed in 1966, while the Southern Trans-Island Highway was finished in 1972.) The area along the Central Trans-Island Highway comprises the main part of 太魯閣國家公園, Taroko National Park, established in November 1986 as the fourth national park on Taiwan. The park, known for its high mountains and marble gorges, is a natural museum of geology.

7. 墾丁國家公園 Kenting National Park, the first national park established on Taiwan, is on the southern most tip of Taiwan. Established in September 1982, it ranges from the Pacific Ocean to the Taiwan Strait, from the Pashih Channel to the north side of Mount Nanjen（南仁山）. With a total area of 32,631 hectares (80,632 acres), it is the only national park in the tropical region of Taiwan. Within the park are hills, flatlands, lakes, grasslands, forests, beaches, coral reefs and many other landforms.

文法練習

☞ 一 好 SV 的 N！ What a SV N！

⊙好漂亮的郵票！

What a pretty stamp!

用法說明：「好」在這個句型中是副詞 (A)，有「非常、這麼」的意思。是感歎的語氣。也可以用「DEM-M-N 好 SV」的型式，如「這張郵票好漂亮」，但僅有敘述的意味。

Explanation: 好 is an adverb in this sentence pattern, meaning “very”, “what a ......”, or “such a......”. It has an exclamatory tone. 好 can also be used as an adverb in the pattern “DEM-M-N 好 SV”, as in “這張郵票好漂亮”, but in this pattern it is merely descriptive and carries no exclamatory tone.

練習：根據所給情況，用「好 SV 的 N！」表示感歎。

Exercise: Please use “好 SV 的 N！” in following situations to express exclamation.

1. 看到一個五歲的孩子在用電腦畫畫兒。
   You see a five-year old child drawing pictures on a computer.
   →好聰明的孩子！
   What a smart child!
2. 朋友說他的照像機是五百塊買的。
   ....
3. 朋友告訴你他上次去的那個地方夏天有五個月。
   ....
4. 走進弟弟的房間，看見報紙在地上，書在床上，衣服在桌子上。
   ....
5. 同學的媽媽只有三十六歲，看起來像他姐姐。
   ....

☞ 二 加起來　put together / added together

⊙差不多有康州、麻州加起來那麼大。

It's about as big as Connecticut and Massachusetts put together.

用法說明：「加起來」意思是「加在一起」，跟第一課的「看起來」、第二課的「吃起來」用法不同。

Explanation: 加起來 means "put together" or "added together". This usage is not the same as 看起來 (Ch.1) or 吃起來 (Ch.2).

練習：請用「加起來……」回答下面問題。

Exercise: Please use "加起來……" to answer the following questions.

1. 你們兩個人的錢買這本書，夠不夠？
   Do you (plural) have enough money to buy this book?
   →我們兩個人的錢加起來才夠。
   We only have enough if we put our money together.
   →我們兩個人的錢加起來還不夠。
   We don't have enough even when we put our money together.
2. 這個學期一共有幾天假？
   ……………………………………………………
3. 你們兩個加起來有他那麼重嗎？
   ……………………………………………………
4. 這個學期中文系有多少學生？
   ……………………………………………………
5. 你們家的客廳跟廚房加起來，比這間教室還大嗎？
   ……………………………………………………

☞ 三

(1)除了……以外／之外，都……

Except for / other than... all the others.....

⊙除了海邊有一些平原以外，中部都是山。

Except for some plains along the coast, the central part (of Taiwan) is all mountains.

(II)除了……以外／之外，還……

other than / besides......there is......

⊙臺灣的交通方便極了，除了公路、鐵路跟飛機以外，另外還有高速公路。

Taiwan's transportation is extremely convenient: besides public roads, railways, and airways, there's also the freeway.

用法說明：「除了」表示「不算在裡面」。後面可用名詞、動詞、SV 或短句。(I) (Ⅱ) 用法不完全相同：(I)不算特殊的，說明相同的，所以第二個短句常用「都」或「全」。(Ⅱ) 不算已經知道的，說明其他的，所以第二短句中，常有「還」或「也」等字。這個句型可以只說「……以外」，也可以只說「除了……」。主語可以放在第一個短句前，也可以放在第二個短句前。

Explanation: 除了 expresses exclusiveness. Following 除了 is a noun, a verb, a stative verb, or an entire clause. The usage in patterns (I) and (II), however, is not entirely identical: (I) The first clause indicates an exception to the norm, and either 都 or 全 is placed in the second clause. (II) The first clause shows part of a sequence, and 還 or 也 is used in the second clause to complete the sequence. In this pattern, "除了……" and "……以外" can each be used together or alone. The subject can be placed at the beginning of either the first clause or the second clause.

練習：Exercises:

(一)請用「除了……以外，都……」改寫下面各句。

Please use "除了……以外，都……" to rewrite the sentences below.

1. 他只會做生意，別的事情都不會。

He can only manage business affairs; he is incapable of doing anything else.

→他除了做生意以外，別的事情都不會。

Other than manage business affairs, he can't do anything else.

2. 他們家每個人都很矮，只有他比較高。

....

3. 那家餐廳週末一定客滿，平常沒什麼客人。

....

4. 我什麼水果都喜歡吃，就是不喜歡吃李子。

....

5. 他只有上課的時候不在家。

....

㈡請用「除了……以外，還……」回答下面問題。

Please use "除了……以外，還……" to answer the questions below.

1. 他買了西瓜，還買了什麼？

He bought watermelon. What else did he buy?

→除了西瓜以外，他還買了蘋果。

Besides watermelon, he also bought apples.

2. 你的生日要怎麼慶祝？

....

3. 你們去過哪些國家？

....

4. 你媽媽哪裡不舒服？

....

5. 你爸爸生氣的時候會怎麼樣？

....

☞ 四　V/SV 起來　start + to V/become SV

⊙……政府鼓勵年輕人到西部去，西部才發展起來。

The government encouraged young people to go the West; only then did the West begin to develop.

⊙……中部橫貫公路開好了後，去東部的人才多起來的。

Only after the Central Trans-Island Highway opened did the number of people who went to the East start to increase.

用法説明： 這個「起來」表示一個動作或一種狀態「開始」並持續下去，所描述的多為非常態的情況。這種用法「起來」常放在句尾，後面沒有修飾性的SV或短語，且多以RC的actual type肯定型式出現，偶爾也可以potential type表示。如有賓語，應該插在「起來」中間，成為「V起O來」。

Explanation: This 起來 indicates that an action or situation starts and continues. Usually, what is being described is an abnormal situation. This use of 起來 is often found at the end of a sentence and is not followed by a SV or clause. It is usually used as a positive form resultative compound in actual type form; occasionally it is used in potential type form. If there is an object, this object should be inserted between 起 and 來, so it becomes "V起O來".

練習：Exercises:

㈠請用「V起來」改寫下面各句。

Please rewrite the sentences below using "V起來".

1. 那個故事說到一半，她就開始哭了。

   She started crying halfway into the story.

   →那個故事說到一半，她就哭起來了。

   She came to tears halfway into the story.

2. 這個孩子疼得開始叫了。

   ……………………………………………………………………………

3. 我覺得他的話很有趣就笑了。

………………………………………………………………………………………………

4. 還沒說兩句話，張先生就開始打李先生了。

………………………………………………………………………………………………

5. 老師還沒叫他念書，他就開始念了。

………………………………………………………………………………………………

㈡請用「SV 起來」改寫下面各句。

Please rewrite the following sentences using "SV 起來".

1. 老師一說要考試，我們就開始緊張了。

As soon as the teacher said we would have a test, we started to feel anxious.

→老師一說要考試，我們就緊張起來了。

As soon as the teacher said we would have a test, we became anxious.

2. 他病了好久，可是現在慢慢地好了。

………………………………………………………………………………………………

3. 還沒到六月，天氣已經開始熱了。

………………………………………………………………………………………………

4. 這條街上的店一多，就會越來越熱鬧了。

………………………………………………………………………………………………

5. 大部分的人到了四十歲就開始胖了。

………………………………………………………………………………………………

㈢請用「V 起 O 來」回答問題。

Please answer the following questions with "V 起 O 來".

1. 今天早上的天氣很好。現在是下午。下雨了。這時候你會說什麼？

The weather was good this morning. It is in the afternoon. It's raining. What will you say in this situation?

答：今天早上天氣很好，怎麼下午下起雨來了?!

Answer: The weather was nice this morning. Why is it raining in the afternoon?!

2. 現在是下午三點，你看見媽媽開始做晚飯了。你會跟媽媽說什麼？

答：現在才三點，＿＿＿＿＿＿＿＿＿＿＿＿＿＿＿＿＿＿＿＿?!

3. 你室友從來不喝酒，可是你現在看見他在喝酒，你會跟他說什麼？

答：你從前不喝酒的，＿＿＿＿＿＿＿＿＿＿＿＿＿＿＿＿＿?!

4. 你朋友告訴你他現在在學中文，可是你記得他以前說中文很難聽，很奇怪。這時候你會說什麼？

答：你從前說中文很難聽，＿＿＿＿＿＿＿＿＿＿＿＿＿＿＿?!

5. 你弟弟非常不喜歡寫信，可是你今天看見他在給女朋友寫情書。這個事情你可以怎麼說？

答：我從來沒看過我弟弟寫信，＿＿＿＿＿＿＿＿＿＿＿＿＿?!

☞ 五 雖然……，可是 …… Although……,

⊙雖然很辛苦，可是值得。

Although it's very hard work, it's worth it.

用法說明： 本句型表示讓步，承認「雖然」後的短句是事實，但「可是」後的短句並不因此而不成立。「雖然」可省略，一般不省略「可是」，但如後半句中有「還是」，例如：「雖然他常送我禮物，（可是）我還是不喜歡他。」，此「可是」可以省略。請注意，只有「可是」，沒有「雖然」的句子，僅表示語氣轉折，與「雖然……可是……」的句子，語境並不相同。

Explanation: This sentence pattern shows that one concedes or admits that the phrase following 雖然 is true, but the phrase following 可是 is unaffected by this fact. "雖然" can be omitted, but "可是" usually cannot be omitted. If "還是" is placed in the second clause, then "可是" can be omitted, e.g. 雖然他常送我禮物，（可是）我還是不喜歡他。Be aware that sentences with only 可是, and no 雖然, indicate a change in tone. Their context is different from sentences with the "雖然……可是……" pattern.

練習： 請用「雖然……，可是……」完成下面對話。

Exercise: Please complete the following dialogues using "雖然……，可是……".

1. 張：你為什麼要學中文？我聽說中國字非常難寫。

Chang: Why do you want to study Chinese? I heard that Chinese characters are difficult to write.

李：寫中國字雖然麻煩，可是很有意思。

Lee: Although writing Chinese characters is tedious, it's very interesting.

2. 張：小王昨天就感冒了，沒想到今天還來上課。
   李：______________________。
3. 張：這件衣服價錢不算便宜，你真的要買嗎？
   李：______________________。
4. 張：你怎麼不認識他？你們不都是去年從紐約大學畢業的嗎？
   李：______________________。
5. 張：你那麼有錢，給他一點，有什麼關係嘛！
   李：______________________。

☞ 六 不但……，也／而且（也）／並且（也）……
not only...... but also

⊙不但東部開始發展，大家也有機會欣賞到漂亮的風景。

Not only did the East begin to develop, but everybody also got an opportunity to see the beautiful scenery.

用法說明：「不但……也……」表示不只是「不但」後面的情況，還有「也」後面的情況。如果前後兩短句的主語相同，主語在「不但」前面。如果兩主語不同，主語在「不但」的後面，及「也」的前面。（如前面例句）此句型與「又……又……」語境不同——兩個「又」後面的短語表示的情況同等重要。例如：1.張：你為什麼要租這個房子？李：因為這裡又便宜又乾淨。2.張：你租這個房子是因為房租很便宜嗎？李：對啊，這裡不但房租便宜，房間也很乾淨。

Explanation: "不但……也……" means "not only...... but also...... 'If the subject of the two clauses is the same, it should be placed before "不但". If the subjects are different, one should be placed after "不但", and the other should be placed before 也. Its context is different from the one of "又……又……" ——the two situations indicated by the phrases after 又

are equally important. Please refer to the following examples: 1.張：你為什麼要租這個房子？李：因為這裡又便宜又乾淨。2.張：你租這個房子是因為房租很便宜嗎？李：對啊，這裡房租不但便宜，房間也很乾淨。

練習：請用「不但……，也……」改寫下面各句。

Exercise: Please use "不但……，也……" to rewrite the following sentences.

1. 除了西瓜以外，他也買了蘋果。

   Other than watermelons, he also bought apples.

   →他不但買了西瓜，也買了蘋果。

   He not only bought watermelons; he also bought apples.

2. 她的生日，除了要請人吃飯以外，還要開舞會。

   ………………………………………………………………

3. 他媽媽又年輕又漂亮。

   ………………………………………………………………

4. 這個地方又有颱風又有地震。

   ………………………………………………………………

5. 王老師去過歐洲，也去過亞洲。

   ………………………………………………………………

6. 這次旅行，小張要去，小王也要去。

   ………………………………………………………………

7. 我現在租的房子房租貴，交通也不夠方便，所以我要搬家。

   ………………………………………………………………

☞ 七 沒有一 M (N) 不／沒……的
every, everyone (not a single N is not)

⊙走過這條路的人，沒有一個不說好的。

Everyone who has been on this road says it is good. (literally:"Of the people who have been on this road, there is not a single one who doesn't say it is good.")

用法說明：兩個否定就變肯定，強調沒有一個例外，語氣比直接肯定更強，句子較富變化。句末的「的」表示肯定。

Explanation: Two negatives form a positive. Emphasizing that there are no exceptions, this pattern carries a stronger tone than the simple positive form and adds variation to the sentence. The 的 at the end of the sentence expresses certainty.

練習：請用「沒有一M(N)不／沒……的」改寫下面各句。

Exercise: Please rewrite the sentences below using "沒有一 M (N) 不／沒……的".

1. 那些人，每一個我都認識。

   I know every one of those people.

   →那些人，沒有一個我不認識的。

   I know every one of those people (literally: Of those people, there isn't one that I don't know).

2. 我剛剛說的話都是真的。

   ……………………………………………………………………

3. 這個人真聰明，什麼事情都會做。

   ……………………………………………………………………

4. 他住校以後，天天都想家。

   ……………………………………………………………………

5. 張老師寫的書，我都看過了。

   ……………………………………………………………………

八 N_1 / NP_1 跟 N_2 / NP_2 比起來……　comparing N_1 with N_2

⊙不知跟我們的大峽谷比起來怎麼樣？

I wonder how it compares to our Grand Canyon?

用法說明：把 N_1 跟 N_2 或 NP_1 跟 NP_2 比較一下，做一評斷，評斷的句子要有描寫程度的副詞，如多了、一點或比較等。語言環境清楚時，N_1 / NP_1 可以省略。

Explanation: When you compare N_1 with N_2 or NP_1 with NP_2 and reach a judgment, the sentence with the comparison needs to have an adverb of degree, such as 多了, 一點, or 比較. When N_1 / NP_1 is clear from context, it may be omitted.

練習：請用「N_1 / NP_1 跟 N_2 / NP_2 比起來」回答下面問題。

Exercise: Please answer the questions below using "N_1 / NP_1 跟 N_2 / NP_2 比起來".

1. 你覺得你媽嘮叨還是我媽嘮叨？

   Who do you think is more of a nag, your mom my mom?

   →我媽跟你媽比起來，我媽嘮叨多了。

   Comparing my mom and your mom, my mom is much more of a nag.

2. 這家餐廳的菜比那家便宜嗎？

   ....

3. 這兩種獎學金，哪一種容易申請？

   ....

4. 美國人口多還是加拿大人口多？

   ....

5. 教書很辛苦，寫書呢？

   ....

☞ 九

(Ⅰ) 各有各的 N　　each has its own......

⊙各有各的美。

Each has its own beauty.

用法說明：「各」表示「每一個」，指某個範圍內的每一個體，人、地、事、物都可以。

Explanation: 各 means 每一個 ("every single") person, place, thing, or event in a specific and understood setting.

練習：請用「各有各的N」，改寫下面各句。

Exercise: Please rewrite the sentences below using "各有各的N".

1. 這些菜雖然都是牛肉做的，但是每一個都有不同的味道。

   Although all of these dishes are made with beef, every one of them has a distinct flavor.

   →這些菜雖然都是牛肉做的，但是各有各的味道。

Although all of these dishes are made with beef, each one has its own distinct flavor.

2. 我想這幾家公司以後每一家都會有不同的發展。

....

3. 他們每個人的困難都不一樣，我真不知道怎麼幫助他們。

....

4. 孩子們現在都大了，都有他們自己的家了。

....

5. 畢業以後大家的計畫都不一樣，有的人還想念書，有的人只想找工作。

....

(II) 各V各的　each V...... own......

用法說明：表示所做的事雖然相同，但每個人是分別做的。

Explanation: Indicates that, although each action undertaken is identical, each person performs it individually.

練習：請用「各V各的」完成下面對話。

Exercise: Please complete the following dialogues using "各V各的".

1. 張：你剛剛跟王小姐吃飯，是你請的客嗎？

   Chang: When you just ate with Miss Wang, was it you that treated?

   李：不，我們各付各的。

   Lee: No, we each paid our own bill.

2. 張：你跟你的室友常一起出去玩嗎？

   李：我們興趣不同，所以都是 ________________ 。

3. 張：你可以穿你姐姐的衣服吧？

   李：我們都是 ________________ ，她的衣服樣子我都不喜歡。

4. 張：你已經吃過了？你不等你弟弟嗎？

   李：他不一定什麼時候下班，所以我們 ________________ 。

5. 張：你跟你哥哥一起做生意嗎？

   李：他賣水果，我賣衣服，我們 ________________ 。

☞ 十 歎詞及語助詞用法
The use of Interjections & Modal Particles

(一) 嗯

⊙嗯，我女朋友寄來的。

Uh huh, it is from my girlfriend.

用法說明：「嗯」為歎詞，語調低降，用於回應，表示肯定對方的說法。「嗯」的後面大多有補充說明，也可免掉。

Explanation: 嗯 is an exclamation which has a low and descending tone. It is used to affirm something the other party has said. 嗯 is usually followed by a supplementary explanation, but this explanation may be omitted.

練習：用「嗯」完成下面對話。

Exercise: Please complete the following dialogues using 嗯.

1. 張：你下了課就回家嗎？
   Chang: Are you going home right after class?
   李：嗯，下了課就走。
   Lee: Uh huh, I'm going right after class.
2. 張：一邊念書，一邊工作很辛苦吧？
   李：____。
3. 張：你打算明天去參觀博物館嗎？
   李：____。
4. 張：這部電影真值得看。
   李：____。
5. 張：高速公路對城市的發展很有幫助。
   李：____。

(二) 哇

⊙哇！好漂亮的郵票！

Wow! What a beautiful stamp!

用法說明：「哇」用在句首做歎詞時，語調降，當面高聲表示稱讚、羨慕、驚喜或訝異。這種用法年輕人用得較多。如放在句尾做語助詞，是 u, ou, ao 跟「啊」的合音。

Explanation: When 哇 is used as an interjection at the beginning of a sentence with a high and falling tone, it indicates praise, admiration, pleasant surprise, or astonishment. This usage is more common amongst young people. If 哇 is used as a particle at the end of a sentence, it is the combined sound of "u", "ou", "ao" and "啊 (a)".

練習：Exercises:

㈠根據所給情況，用「哇」表示稱讚、羨慕、驚喜或訝異。

Please use 哇 to show praise, admiration, pleasant surprise or astonishment in the following situations.

1. 一開門看見女朋友穿了一件漂亮的新衣服。

   As soon as you open the door, you see your girlfriend wearing a beautiful new outfit .

   →哇！你今天好漂亮！

   Wow! You look gorgeous today!

2. 走進廚房，看見媽媽做了很多好菜。

   ………………………………………………………………………………

3. 朋友告訴你他爸爸送他一輛汽車。

   ………………………………………………………………………………

4. 累了，躺在床上，覺得非常舒服。

   ………………………………………………………………………………

5. 吃了朋友買的葡萄，味道好極了。

   ………………………………………………………………………………

㈡請念下面各句，並注意句尾「啊」的變音。

Please read the sentences below, paying special attention to the change of sound from 啊 to 哇 at the end of the sentence.

1. 你早啊！

Good morning.

→你早哇！

Good morning!

2. 那個人好高啊！

....

3. 走啊！你還等什麼？

....

4. 她為什麼哭啊？

....

5. 好啊，就這麼辦。

....

課室活動

1. Play the game 接詞, "connecting words." It is better to have the students sit in a circle. The instructor starts the game by saying a two or three syllable word. The teacher then asks a student to form a new word which begins with the last syllable (or one of the syllables if the last is too difficult) of the previous word, e.g., 同學→學生→生氣→汽水→水果→(Homophones are permitted.)

2. As a penalty, those who fail to keep the "merry-go-round" moving has to give a short summary of his/her hometown to the class. The summary should include

the following information: 在哪裡?有多大?有多少人口?什麼最有名?風景怎麼樣?

短文

簡介[1]臺灣(一)

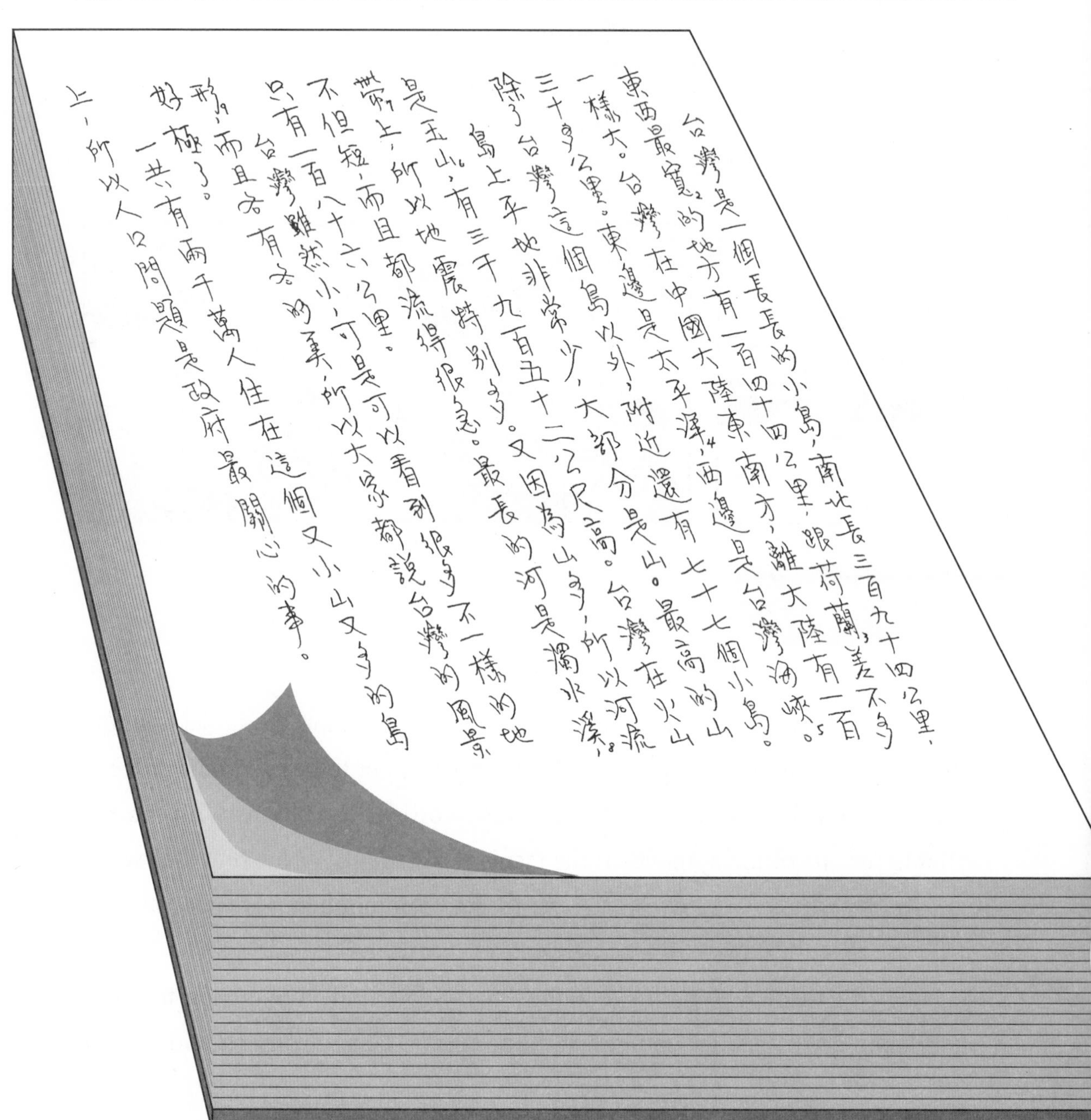

台灣是一個長長的小島，南北長三百九十四公里，東西最寬[2]的地方有一百四十四公里，跟荷蘭[3]差不多一樣大。台灣在中國大陸東南方，離大陸有一百三十多公里。東邊是太平洋，[4]西邊是台灣海峽。[5]除了台灣這個島以外，附近還有七十七個小島。
島上平地非常少，大部分是山。最高的山是玉山，[6]有三千九百五十二公尺高。台灣在火山帶[7]上，所以地震特別多。又因為山多，所以河流不但短，而且都流得很急。最長的河是濁水溪，[8]只有一百八十六公里。
台灣雖然小，可是可以看到很多不一樣的地形，[9]而且各有各的美，所以大家都說台灣的風景好極了。
一共有兩千萬人住在這個又小山又多的島上，所以人口問題是政府最關心的事。

Vocabulary:

1. 簡介 (jiǎnjiè)：brief introduction

2. 寬 (kuān)：wide

3. 荷蘭 (Hélán)：the Netherlands

4. 太平洋 (Tàipíng Yáng)：Pacific Ocean

5. 海峽 (hǎixiá)：strait

6. 玉山 (Yù Shān)：Jade Mountain

7. 火山帶 (huǒshāndài)：volcanic range

8. 濁水溪 (Zhuóshuǐ Xī)：Zhuoshui River

9. 地形 (dìxíng)：topography

第五課

氣候跟出產

・稻米（范慧貞提供）

（公共汽車站）

偉立：奇怪！今天**怎麼回事**？等了這麼久，都沒有車來。

台麗：是啊！平常都很準時的。（咳嗽）

偉立：你病啦？我剛剛就覺得你的聲音不太對。

台麗：已經一個多星期了，我**以為**只是小感冒，**沒想到**咳了這麼久。

偉立：吃藥了沒有？

台麗：我吃了一些家裡帶來的藥，可是沒什麼用。天氣這麼冷，我的身體還不能適應。

偉立：臺灣現在還很暖和嗎？

台麗：臺灣熱的時間很長，這時候大概還有三十度，就是華氏八十多度。

偉立：啊？差那麼多！難怪你會生病。那冬天也不冷嗎？

台麗：冬天差不多是你們的六十度。**再**冷**也**不會到零下[1]。因為臺灣北部常下雨，而且我們屋裡大部分不裝暖氣，所以覺得比較冷。**一般來說**，南部晴天的時候多，比北部暖和[2]。聽說臺灣的天氣跟你們的佛羅里達州差不多。

偉立：那麼，一年四季都很舒服吧？

台麗：也不一定，夏天又濕又熱，**並不**舒服。春天秋天的氣溫變化很大[3]，很容易感冒。

偉立：我們春秋天早晚的氣溫也差很多。冬天很冷，常常下雪，尤其是颳**起**風**來**，真是冷得受不了。

台麗：那我怎麼辦？

偉立：別怕，車裡、屋裡都有暖氣，不要在外面太久，就沒問題了。冬天穿的衣服、鞋子你都準備好了嗎？

台麗：帶了件雪衣，別的我想到時候再買。不知道下**起**雪**來**是什麼樣子？

・臺灣的水果
（臺灣省青果運銷合作社提供）

・臺灣的水果
（臺灣省青果運銷合作社提供）

・臺灣的水果
（臺灣省青果運銷合作社提供）

・做糖用的甘蔗（范慧貞提供）

偉立：下雪的時候到處都是白的，很漂亮。不過雪融化了以後，路上又髒又滑，這時候你就會覺得還是夏天好了。夏天只有中午比較熱，晚上就涼快了。

（台麗又咳嗽）

偉立（拿出一個蘋果）：啊，我有一個蘋果，給你吧，病人。我們有句話說：「一天吃一個蘋果，就不必看醫生了。[4]」

台麗：謝謝。美國的蘋果**是**很好吃，可是我現在最想的就是鳳梨。臺灣的鳳梨又香又甜，顏色也很漂亮。

偉立：李平也這麼說。他還說他家那兒有一條河，附近出產的米和西瓜是全臺灣最好吃的[5]。

台麗：對，對，對，真的很不錯。除了鳳梨、西瓜以外，還有香蕉、葡萄……好多好多水果。

偉立：佛羅里達州、加州[6]也出產很多水果，**像**葡萄柚、柳橙、葡萄、李子**什麼的**。

台麗：你們中西部大平原出產的小麥、玉米是有名的，我們每年都進口不少。

偉立：中國人喜歡喝茶，臺灣也產茶嗎？

台麗：北部山區出產的茶很多、也很好。算起來我們的天然資源**並不**多，尤其是礦產，像煤、石油差不多都沒有，所以政府跟農民都在研究怎麼樣可以有更多更好的農產品，現在不但夠自己吃，還可以出口了。

偉立：我知道，在你心裡，臺灣什麼都好。

台麗：那當然。你知道我還想什麼嗎？海鮮。臺灣的魚蝦又便宜又新鮮，種類又多。看！你害我更想家了。

（公共汽車來了）

偉立：真對不起。我的車來了，我得走了。再見。

台麗：再見。

生詞及例句

1. 氣候 (qìhòu)　*N*: **climate**

　這裡的氣候不錯，冬天不冷，夏天也不熱。

2. 出產 (chūchǎn)

N/V: **natural product, product / to produce**

　(1) 我們的出產不夠，所以得跟外國買。

　(2) 你們那一州出產什麼水果？

產 (chǎn)　*V*: **to produce, yield**

　臺灣山區產茶嗎？

3. 準時 (zhǔnshí)　*A/SV*: **to be punctual, on time**

　(1) 今天你來晚了，請你明天準時來。

　(2) 他跟人約會總是很準時。

4. 感冒 (gǎnmào)　*N/V*: **flu, cold / to have a flu or cold**

　我早上起來就頭疼，大概是感冒了。

5. 咳嗽 (késòu)　*V/N*: **to cough / a cough**

　(1) 他上個星期開始咳嗽，咳了好幾天了。

　(2) 他的咳嗽還沒好。

6. 適應 (shìyìng)　*V*: **to adapt to**

　我剛搬家，對新環境還不太能適應。

7. 暖和 (nuǎn·huo) *SV*: **to be warm**

外面好冷，一進屋子就覺得暖和多了。

8. 度 (dù)

M: **degrees [unit of measure for angles, temperature]**

臺北最熱的時候，有九十多度。

9. 零下 (língxià) *N*: **below zero**

這幾天冷得不得了，夜裡都是零下兩三度。

10. 裝暖氣 (zhuāng//nuǎnqì) *VO*: **to equip with heating**

他房間裡沒裝暖氣，所以比較冷。

裝 (zhuāng) *V*: **to install; to load, pack, fill**

你為什麼不把電話裝在客廳裡？

暖氣 (nuǎnqì) *N*: **heating; warm air**

冷氣 (lěngqì) *N*: **air conditioning; cold air**

11. 一般來說（一般說來、一般而論）(yìbānláishuō)

IE: **generally speaking**

一般來說，中國人喝茶的比喝咖啡的多。

一般 (yìbān) *AT*: **common, general**

在臺灣，一般六樓的公寓都有電梯。

12. 晴天 (qíngtiān) *N*: **clear day, sunny day**

13. 季 (jì) *M*: **season**

臺灣一年四季都出產很多水果。

季節 (jìjié) *N*: **season**

雨季 (yǔjì) *N*: **rainy season**

乾季 (gānjì) *N*: **dry season**

有些地方一年只有兩個季節，就是雨季跟乾季。

季風 (jìfēng) *N*: **monsoon**

14. 濕／溼 (shī) *SV*: **to be damp, moist, humid, wet**

冬天下雨，又冷又濕，很不舒服。

濕度 (shīdù) *N*: **humidity**

濕熱 (shīrè) *SV*: **to be hot and humid**

15. 並 (bìng)

A: **used before a negative for emphasis**（**see 文法練習第五**）

(1) 學中文並沒有你想的那麼難。

(2) 張：你為什麼到你爸爸公司去上班？

李：我並不願意去，可是我爸爸一定要我去。

並且／而且 (bìngqiě/érqiě)

CONJ: **and, besides, moreover, furthermore**

16. 氣溫 (qìwēn) *N*: **air temperature**

這幾天的氣溫很高，熱得不得了。

體溫 (tǐwēn) *N*: **body temperature**

溫度 (wēndù) *N*: **temperature**

17. 變化 (biànhuà) *N*: **change, transformation**

臺北市這幾年的變化很大，很多地方我都不認得了。

變 (biàn)

V: **to change, become different, to transform**

她小時候很難看，現在大了，變漂亮了。

18. 尤其是 (yóuqíshì) *A*: **especially, above all**

我什麼水果都喜歡吃，尤其是西瓜。

19. 颳風 (guā//fēng) *VO*: **for wind to blow**

現在外面颳著風、下著雨，你還要出去嗎？

20. 雪衣 (xuěyī) *N*: **snow suit**

21. 到處 (dàochù) *N*: **everywhere**

今天街上到處都是人，你開車要慢一點。

22. 融化 (rónghuà) *V*: **to melt, to thaw**

是下雪的時候冷，還是雪融化的時候冷？

23. 滑 (huá)

SV/V: **to be slippery, smooth / to slip, skate, slide, glide**

剛下過雨，路上很滑，你走慢一點吧！

滑雪 (huá//xuě) *VO*: **to ski**

24. 涼ㄌㄧㄤˊ快ㄎㄨㄞˋ (liángkuài)

SV: **to be nice and cool, comfortably cool**

房間裡有冷氣，比外面涼快不少。

涼ㄌㄧㄤˊ (liáng) *SV*: **to be cool; to be cold**

快吃吧！菜涼了就不好吃了。

25. 鳳ㄈㄥˋ梨ㄌㄧˊ (fènglí) *N*:**pineapple**

26. 香ㄒㄧㄤ蕉ㄐㄧㄠ (xiāngjiāo) *N*: **banana**

27. 葡ㄆㄨˊ萄ㄊㄠˊ柚ㄧㄡˋ (pútáoyòu) *N*: **grapefruit**

28. 柳ㄌㄧㄡˇ橙ㄔㄥˊ (liǔchéng) *N*: **orange**

29. 小ㄒㄧㄠˇ麥ㄇㄞˋ (xiǎomài) *N*: **wheat**

30. 玉ㄩˋ米ㄇㄧˇ (yùmǐ) *N*: **corn, maize**

玉ㄩˋ (yù) *N*: **jade**

米ㄇㄧˇ (mǐ) *N*: **uncooked rice**

31. 進ㄐㄧㄣˋ口ㄎㄡˇ (jìnkǒu) *V/AT*: **to import/imported**

(1)這幾年臺灣從美國進口了很多蘋果、玉米。

(2)從前在臺灣，進口車的價錢非常高，一般人都買不起。

出ㄔㄨ口ㄎㄡˇ (chūkǒu) *V*: **to export**

32. 天ㄊㄧㄢ然ㄖㄢˊ資ㄗ源ㄩㄢˊ (tiānrán zīyuán) *N*: **natural resource**

天ㄊㄧㄢ然ㄖㄢˊ (tiānrán) *AT*: **natural**

資ㄗ源ㄩㄢˊ (zīyuán) *N*: **resource**

33. 礦ㄎㄨㄤˋ產ㄔㄢˇ (kuàngchǎn) *N*: **minerals, mineral products**

我國的礦產除了金、銀以外，還有鐵。

34. 煤ㄇㄟˊ (méi) *N*: **coal**

煤ㄇㄟˊ礦ㄎㄨㄤˋ (méikuàng) *N*: **coal mine**

35. 石ㄕˊ油ㄧㄡˊ (shíyóu) *N*: **petroleum, oil**

石ㄕˊ頭ㄊㄡˊ (shí·tóu) *N*: **stone**

油ㄧㄡˊ (yóu) *N/SV*: **oil / to be oily**

油ㄧㄡˊ膩ㄋㄧˋ (yóunì)

SV: **(said of food) to be greasy or oily**

油炸的東西太油膩，吃太多，對身體不好。

汽ㄑㄧˋ油ㄧㄡˊ (qìyóu) *N*: **gasoline, petrol**

36. 農ㄋㄨㄥˊ產ㄔㄢˇ品ㄆㄧㄣˇ (nóngchǎnpǐn) *N*: **agricultural product**

米、麥、青菜、水果什麼的，都是農產品。

37. 新ㄒㄧㄣ鮮ㄒㄧㄢ (xīnxiān) *SV*: **to be fresh**

鄉下車少，空氣當然新鮮。

鮮ㄒㄧㄢ (xiān) *SV*: **to be delicious, tasty ; to be fresh**

(1) 這個雞湯的味道很鮮，好喝極了。

(2) 她買了些鮮花放在辦公室裡。

海ㄏㄞˇ鮮ㄒㄧㄢ (hǎixiān) *N*: **sea food**

38. 種ㄓㄨㄥˇ類ㄌㄟˋ (zhǒnglèi) *N*: **type, variety, kind**

這個市場，青菜的種類最多，青花菜、芥蘭菜都有。

類ㄌㄟˋ (lèi) *M*: **kind, type, class, category**

這一類的書都有很多畫，適合五、六歲的小孩看。

39. 害ㄏㄞˋ (hài) *V*: **to cause trouble to, to impair**

我男朋友急著要我跟他一起出門，害我飯都來不及吃。

40. 想ㄒㄧㄤˇ家ㄐㄧㄚ (xiǎng//jiā)

VO/SV: **to miss home / to be homesick**

你離開家快一年了，一定常想家吧？

專有名詞 Proper Names

1. 華ㄏㄨㄚˊ氏ㄕˋ (Huá Shì) Fahrenheit
2. 佛ㄈㄛˊ羅ㄌㄨㄛˊ里ㄌㄧˇ達ㄉㄚˊ州ㄓㄡ (Fuóluólǐdá Zhōu) the state of Florida
3. 加ㄐㄧㄚ州ㄓㄡ (Jiā Zhōu) the state of California

注釋

1. "冬天差不多是十三、四度。再冷也不會到零下。"This is the weather of the valleys and the plains in Taiwan. In high mountains, the temperature may drop to below zero Celsius in winters. The people in Taiwan talk about temperature in Celsius, and that is why 台麗 still tells the temperature in Celsius.
2. "南部晴天的時候多，比北部暖和" The Tropic of Cancer goes through 嘉義縣 (Jiāyì Xiàn, Chia-yih County). Most of Taiwan is north of the Tropic of Cancer, in the subtropics. There is more sunshine in the south, and the temperature there is a little higher on average than in the north. The average temperature is above 20˚C (68˚F) for 8 to 9 months in the north, whereas it is above 20˚C for 10 months in the south.
3. "春天秋天的氣溫變化很大" The spring and autumn in Taiwan are both short, with frequent and wide changes in temperature. Sometimes the morning and evening temperatures differ by more than 10˚C (50˚F). Temperatures may also vary up to 10˚C from one day to the next.
4. "一天吃一個蘋果，就不必看醫生了。" is the familiar saying: "An apple a day keeps the doctor away."
5. "........有一條河，附近出產的米和西瓜是臺灣最好吃的。" This is a reference to 濁水溪 (Zhuóshuǐ Xī), the longest river (186 KM) in Taiwan, located on the western part of the island. The longest river on the east has a length of 84 KM. The main agricultural products in the 濁水溪 area are watermelon and rice.
6. 加州 is the short name for 加利福尼亞州 (Jiālìfúníyǎ Zhōu), the State of California.

文法練習

☞ 一 怎麼(一)回事　What is going on? What happened?

⊙今天怎麼回事？　What is going on today?

用法說明：覺得情況不平常或奇特時，都可用這句話詢問事情發生的原因或經過。

Explanation : This is used to inquire further about a situation one feels is unusual or peculiar.

練習：根據所給情況用「怎麼回事」發問。

Exercise : Please inquire about the given situations using "怎麼回事".

1. 下班時間還沒到，去找朋友，看見公司裡只有朋友一個 人，別人都走了。

   You go to visit a friend during office hours, and you see that your friend is alone. Everyone else has left the office.

   →怎麼回事？別人都到哪裡去了？

   What happened? Where did everybody else go?

2. 看到同學的臉白得像紙一樣。

   ....

3. 看見妹妹的房間地上有很多髒東西。

   ....

4. 昨天才買的錶，今天就停了。

   ....

5. 室友這個星期都很晚回來，今天碰見他。

   ....

☞ 二 以為……，沒想到……

......thought that......, ...didn't think that......

⊙我以為只是小感冒，沒想到咳了這麼久。

I thought that this was only a small cold, I had no idea that I would have a cough for this long.

用法說明：「以為」後面是不正確的想法，「沒想到」後面是「意料之外」的事實。

Explanation : Following 以為 is a mistaken thought idea (which one previously believed to be true), after 沒想到 is the unexpected or unpredictable truth.

練習：請用「以為……，沒想到……」改寫下面各句。

Exercise : Please rewrite the sentences below using "以為……，沒想到……".

1. 我想他是學生，可是我弄錯了，他是老師。
   I thought he was a student, but I was mistaken: He's a teacher.
   →我以為他是學生，沒想到他是老師。
   I thought that he was a student. I had no idea that he was a teacher.
2. 他想做中國菜很容易，可是他錯了，麻煩得不得了。
   ……………………………………………………………………
3. 張小姐想這裡的冬天非常冷，可是她錯了，一點也不冷。
   ……………………………………………………………………
4. 大家都想他的病沒希望了，可是大家都錯了，他好了。
   ……………………………………………………………………
5. 我看她只有三十多歲，可是她告訴我她已經五十多歲了。
   ……………………………………………………………………

☞ 三 再……也……　No matter how.......

⊙再冷也不會到零下。

No matter how cold it gets it won't go below zero.

用法說明：用於假設的情況，有「即使」或「無論怎麼」的意思。用「再」將情況推到最高程度，但即使在最高程度的情況下，「也」後面的結論仍然不變。「再」為副詞，用來修飾跟在後面的 SV、V, 或 AV。

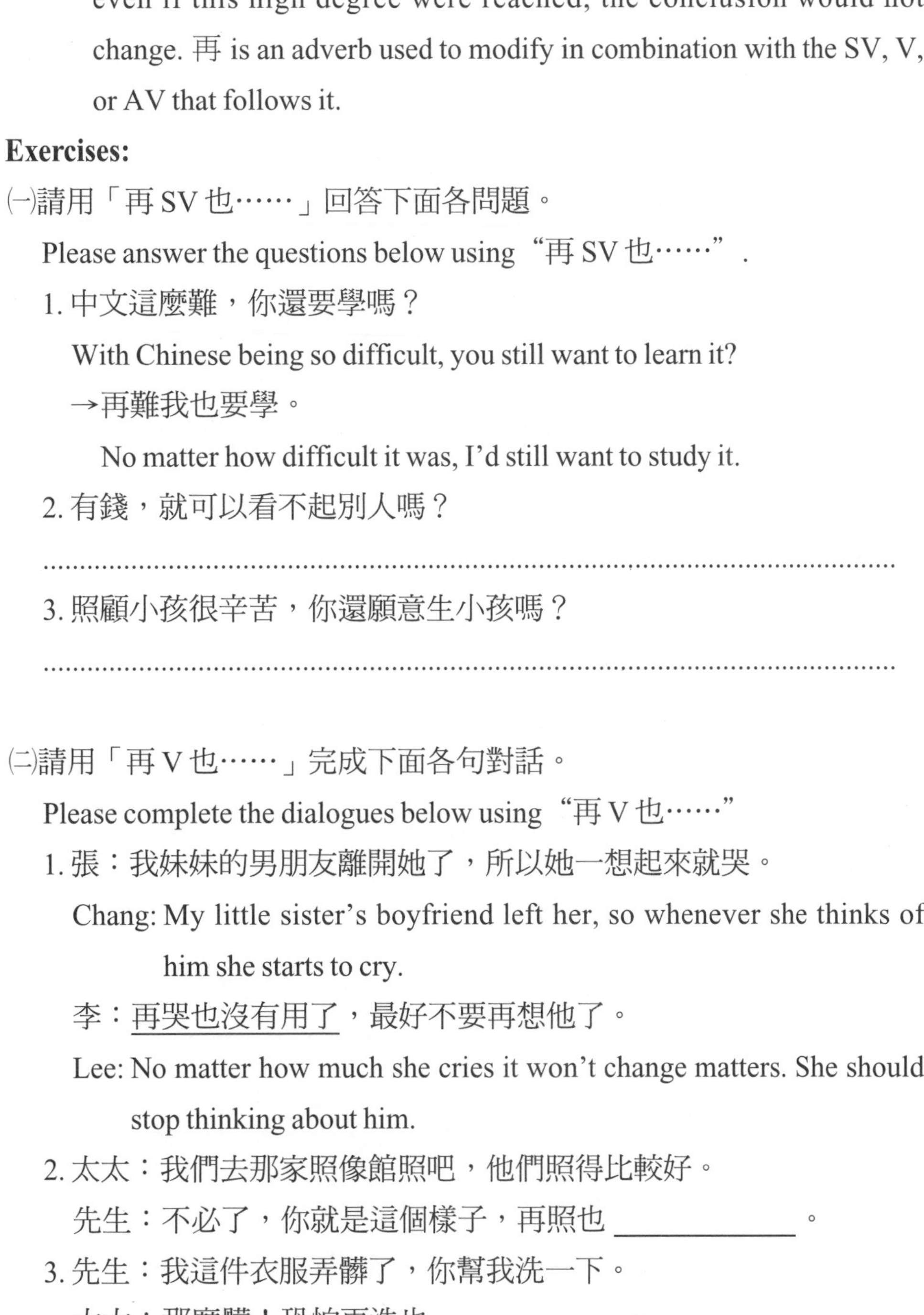

Explanation : This pattern is used in a hypothetical situation, and means "even if" or "no matter how......" The clause following 再 is an exaggerated and hypothetical expression of degree; the clause following 也 affirms that, even if this high degree were reached, the conclusion would not change. 再 is an adverb used to modify in combination with the SV, V, or AV that follows it.

練習：Exercises:

(一)請用「再SV也……」回答下面各問題。

Please answer the questions below using "再SV也……".

1. 中文這麼難，你還要學嗎？

   With Chinese being so difficult, you still want to learn it?

   →再難我也要學。

   No matter how difficult it was, I'd still want to study it.

2. 有錢，就可以看不起別人嗎？

   ....

3. 照顧小孩很辛苦，你還願意生小孩嗎？

   ....

(二)請用「再V也……」完成下面各句對話。

Please complete the dialogues below using "再V也……"

1. 張：我妹妹的男朋友離開她了，所以她一想起來就哭。

   Chang: My little sister's boyfriend left her, so whenever she thinks of him she starts to cry.

   李：再哭也沒有用了，最好不要再想他了。

   Lee: No matter how much she cries it won't change matters. She should stop thinking about him.

2. 太太：我們去那家照像館照吧，他們照得比較好。

   先生：不必了，你就是這個樣子，再照也 ____________ 。

3. 先生：我這件衣服弄髒了，你幫我洗一下。

   太太：那麼髒！恐怕再洗也 ____________ 。

㈢請用「再SV＋的＋N也……」完成下面各句對話。

Please complete the following dialogues using "再SV＋的 ＋N也……"

1. 張：這次考試考了很多書裡沒有的東西。

Chang: The test this time covered a lot of material which wasn't in the book.

李：是啊！這麼難，再用功的學生也考不好。

Lee : True! With a test this hard, no matter how hard-working a student was, he/she would still do poorly.

2. 張：沒想到這麼好的學校會有他這麼壞的學生！

李：不必奇怪，再好的學校也________。

3. 張：這麼貴的衣服，誰買得起呢？

李：你放心！再貴的衣服也________。

㈣請用「再AV＋V也……」完成下面各句對話。

Please complete the following dialogues using "再AV＋V也……".

1. 張：這裡的風景真好，你畫一張吧！

Chang: The scenery here is really great. Why don't you do a painting?

李：不行！這麼美的風景，我再會畫也畫不好。

Lee: Impossible! With such a beautiful scene, no matter how talented I was , I still wouldn't be able to do it justice.

2. 張：老師要走了，有什麼話快說吧！

李：是啊！老師走了的話，再想說也________。

3. 張：我聽說你很能吃，所以我做了這麼多菜。

李：太多了吧？我再能吃也________。

☞ 四 一般來說（一般而論） Generally speaking,......

⊙一般來說，南部晴天的時候多，比北部暖和。

Generally speaking, there are more clear days in the South, and the temperature is warmer than the North.

用法說明：一般來說強調「大部分的狀況都是這樣」。

Explanation : 一般來說 emphasizes that something is true in most instances and means "generally speaking."

練習：請用一般來說回答下面各問題。

Exercise : Please use 一般來說 to answer the following questions.

1. 西方小孩比東方小孩獨立嗎？

   Are Western children more independent than Eastern children?

   →一般來說，西方小孩比較獨立。

   Generally speaking, Western children are more independent than Eastern children.

2. 廣東菜辣不辣？

   ……………………………………………………………………………………

3. 這裡的秋天，氣溫變化很大嗎？

   ……………………………………………………………………………………

4. 補習班的學習環境怎麼樣？

   ……………………………………………………………………………………

5. 學校附近的房子房租都很便宜吧？

   ……………………………………………………………………………………

☞ 五 並不／沒

not at all (indicates contradiction of the previous speaker's statement)

⊙夏天又濕又熱，並不舒服。

It is both hot and humid in the summer, so (contrary to what you might think) it is really uncomfortable.

用法說明：「並」放在「不」或「沒」之前，加強否定的語氣，說明真實情況跟某種看法或一般看法不一樣。

Explanation : When 並 is placed in front of 不 or 沒, it strengthens the negative tone and indicates that the true situation differs from certain opinion or the general view.

練習：Exercises:

㈠請用「並不／沒」改寫下面各句。

Please rewrite the sentences below using“並不／沒”

1. 大家都說這部電影很好看，可是我覺得不怎麼好看。

Everybody says that this movie is very good, but I don’t think it’s particularly good.

→大家都說這部電影很好看，可是我覺得並不好看。

Everybody says that this movie is very good, but I think it’s actually bad.

or→大家都說這部電影很好看，可是我並不覺得好看。

Everybody says that this movie is very good, but I, in fact, think it’s bad.

2. 我以為他去過臺灣，可是他說他沒去過。

……………………………………………………………………………………

3. 我室友學過三年中文，可是說得不太好。

……………………………………………………………………………………

4. 沙漠裡不是一點水也沒有。

……………………………………………………………………………………

5. 成績好的學生不一定都很用功。

……………………………………………………………………………………

㈡請用「並不／沒」完成下面對話。

Please complete the following dialogues using“並不／沒”

1. 張：你每天都來得這麼早，你住的地方很近吧？

Chang: You come so early every morning. Your home must be really close to here.

李：<u>我住得並不近，不過我都很早出門。</u>

Lee: No, in fact I don’t live very close at all, but I leave very early.

2. 張：這件事情，我以為他已經告訴你了。

李：________________________________。

3. 張：他這麼聰明，成績一定很好。

李：______________________________。

4. 張：他真幫了你一個大忙。

李：______________________________。

5. 張：我這麼做是不是錯了？

李：______________________________。

☞ 六 V 起 O 來...... When......starts V

⊙尤其是颳起風來，真是冷得不得了。

Especially when the wind starts blowing, it is unbearably cold.

⊙不知道下起雪來是什麼樣子。

I wonder what it's like when it snows?

用法說明：「V 起 O 來」放在句子前面的時候，用法跟第一課的一、(I) 一樣，只是多一個受詞，而這個受詞一定要放在「起來」的中間，不可以放在「起來」的後面。說話者說明情況與剛剛提到的或預想的情況有甚麼不同。

Explanation : When "V 起 O 來" is founded at the beginning of the sentence, its usage is the same as in chapter 1, No. 1, Part 1. However when an object is given, the object must be placed between the「起」and the「來」of the「起來」.

練習：請完成下面各對話。

Exercise: Please complete the dialogues below.

1. 張：他平常很多話都不敢說，為什麼喝了酒就不一樣了？

Chang : Usually he's afraid to speak out. Why is he different after he drinks?

李：<u>他一喝起酒來就什麼都不怕了。</u>

Lee : As soon as he starts drinking, he's not afraid of anything.

2. 張：小王已經做了好幾個小時的事了，怎麼還不來吃飯？

李：他做起事來 ______________________。

3. 張：你妹妹說話聲音很低，沒想到唱歌聲音那麼高。

李：是啊！她唱起歌來 ______________________。

4. 張：我哥哥對什麼都不喜歡，只有說到籃球的時候才有興趣。
   李：就是嘛！一說起籃球來，他 ________________________ 。
5. 張：你第一次離開家，一定很想爸爸媽媽吧？
   李：是啊！每次想起他們來 ________________________ 。

☞ 七 是 (A)SV

⊙美國的蘋果是很好吃。

American apples are quite delicious (indeed).

用法說明：中文裡，「SV」的前面本來不需用「是」，但如果要表示強調或肯定對方的看法，就可加「是」。

Explanation : In Chinese, it is not necessary to place 是 in front of a SV, but 是 can be added for emphasis or for affirmation of the other party's statement or opinion.

練習：請用「是 (A) SV」完成下面各對話。

Exercise : Please complete the dialogues below using "是 (A) SV"

1. 張：我覺得這裡的氣溫變化非常大。
   Chang: I think that the temperature changes here are quite drastic.
   李：嗯，這裡的氣溫變化是非常大。
   Lee: Uh huh, the temperature changes here are indeed quite drastic.
2. 張：美國的天然資源很多。
   李：________________________ 。
3. 張：這塊牛肉的味道好像不太新鮮了。
   李：________________________ 。
4. 張：天天吃學校的大鍋菜，你不會膩嗎？
   李：________________________ 。
5. 張：聽說臺灣的夏天濕熱得不得了，是真的嗎？
   李：________________________ 。

☞ 八 像……什麼的 such as...... and so on.

⊙……，像葡萄柚、柳橙、香蕉、葡萄、李子什麼的。

......, such as grapefruit, oranges, bananas, grapes, pears, and so on.

用法說明：「像」是例如的意思，舉例說明時，因要舉出的東西太多，沒辦法一一列出，只要說出幾個，放在「像」的後面即可。

Explanation :像 means " for example, such as. " It is used to introduce a list when there are too many items for the speaker to list one by one and he/she just wants to mention a few sample items.

練習：請用「像……什麼的」完成下面各句。

Exercise : Please complete the following sentences using "像…… 什麼的" .

1. 我吃過很多中國菜，<u>像宮保雞丁、青豆蝦仁、芥蘭牛肉什麼的。</u>
   I've eaten lots of Chinese food: for example, Gongbao chicken, shrimp with peas, beef and broccoli, etc.
2. 我剛搬家，廚房裡的東西像＿＿＿＿＿＿＿＿都還沒買。
3. 他去過不少國家，像＿＿＿＿＿＿＿＿都去玩過。
4. 他學過幾種語言，像＿＿＿＿＿＿＿＿，都說得不錯。
5. 你應該常做運動，像＿＿＿＿＿＿＿＿，對身體都很好。

九 害 cause (in a harmful way)

⊙你害我更想家了。

You're causing me to miss home even more.

用法說明：這個「害」是「讓」或「使」的意思，語氣強烈一點，而且都是負面的。

Explanation : This 害 means " to make, to cause ". The tone is fairly strong and is always negative.

練習：請用「害」改寫下面各句。

Exercise : Please rewrite the following sentences using 害.

1. 你說這些話，會讓他睡不著覺的。
   If you tell him all this it's going to make him unable to fall asleep at night.
   →你說這些話，會害他睡不著覺的。
   If you tell him all this it's going to make him unable to fall asleep at night. (implication is more negative: you will cause him to suffer).

2. 我給這個孩子穿得太少，所以孩子感冒了。

....

3. 天氣這麼壞，我們不能出去野餐了。

....

4. 物價太高，大家沒辦法生活了。

....

5. 他常常請我吃飯，所以我胖了不少。

....

課室活動

遊戲 (yóuxì, game)

1. This game is called 碰球. The teacher writes down on individual cards different types of agricultural produce, industrial produce and minerals the class has learned. Each student is given one card and asked to remember the item written on it. The students then form a circle, each holding their card in front of him/her so that it is visible to the other students. One student starts the game by saying : 我的 X 碰 Y。e.g., 我的香蕉碰西瓜。The student representing 西瓜 must immediately respond by saying something such as : 我的西瓜碰鳳梨。

2. As a penalty, any student who fails to respond or who responds incorrectly must tell the class some of the produce/minerals of a chosen state, e.g., 加州出產葡萄、李子⋯⋯。Each state can be mentioned only once.

短文

簡介臺灣(二)

台灣是個海島，一般來說，下雨的機會很大，可是因為夏天颱西南季風，這時就是西南部的雨季。到了冬天，沒颱東北季風，就是北部的雨季。這種冬雨，不但溼又冷，而且下的時間又長，所以台灣北部的氣候跟南部比起來，就差多了。另外每年四、五月是梅雨季節，差不多要下一個月的雨。梅雨下完了，天氣就熱起來了。

台灣溼熱的氣候，很適合農業的發展，所以農產品的種類非常多，除了米、茶以外，像甘蔗[2]、甘藷[3]、橘子、鳳梨、香蕉、花生[4]什麼的，也都又多又好。

台灣的天然資源，除了北部以前出產過煤跟金子以外，現在已經沒什麼礦產了。又因為山多，森林[5]也多，而且四邊都是海，所以漁業[6]也非常重要。

Vocabulary:

1. 梅雨 (méiyǔ) : (literally: plum rains) heavy spring rains

2. 甘蔗 (gānzhè): sugar cane

3. 甘薯 (gānshǔ): sweet potato, yam
4. 花生 (huāshēng): peanuts
5. 森林 (sēnlín): forest
6. 漁業 (yúyè): fishing industry

毛衣 (máoyi, sweater)

毛 (máo, hair)

第六課

考不完的試

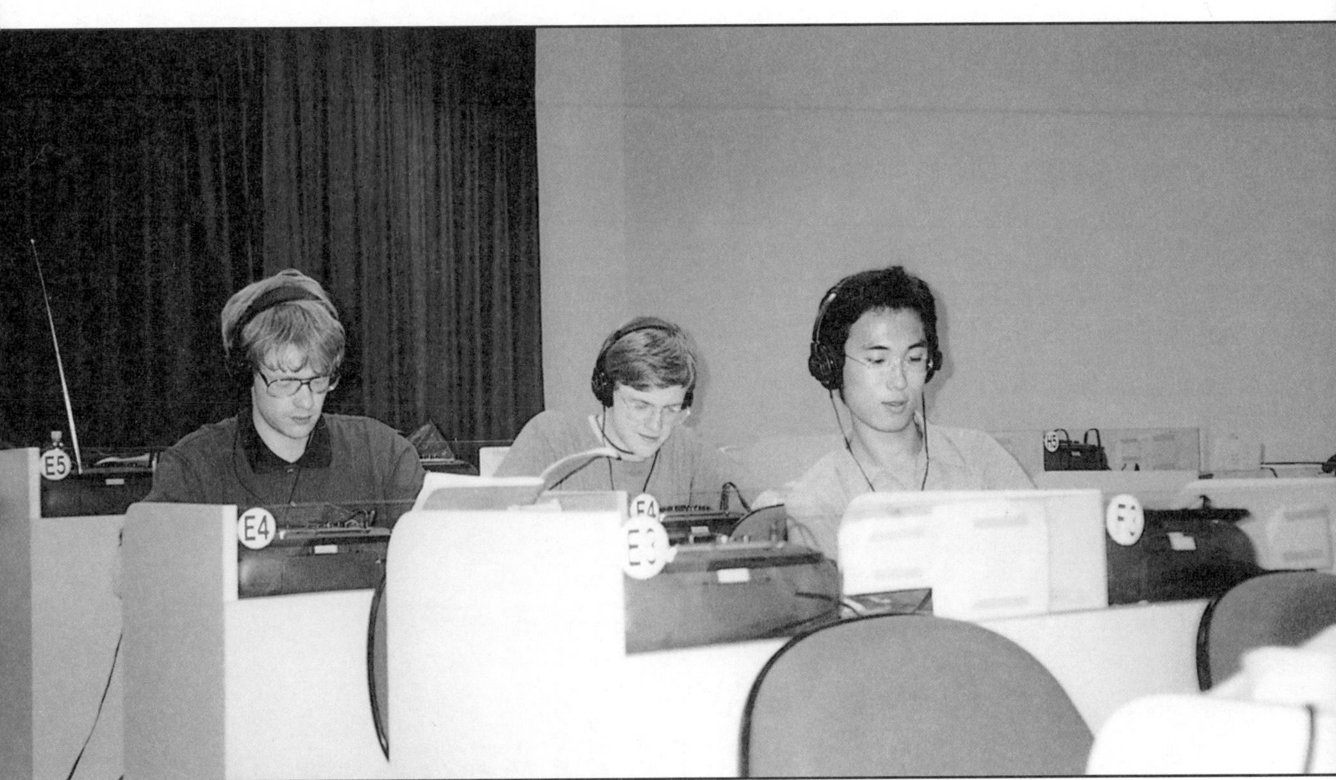

・學生在語言實驗室聽錄音帶（范慧貞提供）

（下課以後，高偉立走到前面找教授談話）

偉立：張老師，我剛剛看了考卷，有幾個地方不太明白。

教授：**哦**？什麼地方有問題？

偉立：我這題翻譯跟老師的差不多，為什麼要扣兩分呢？

教授：我看看。噢！「就」應該在主詞後面。文法錯了，當然要扣分。

偉立：還有這個呢？

教授：你把「再見」的「再」寫**成**「現在」的「在」了。下次小心一點兒。你考得不錯嘛！

偉立：我這次分數比上次低。題目不難，我都會，可是還寫錯，我太不小心了！所以我很生自己的氣。

教授：別生氣了！考試也是一種練習，可以讓老師跟你自己了解你複習得夠不夠，學過的東西都記**住**了沒有。

偉立：還可以看出學生小心不小心。

教授：對了！還有問題嗎？

偉立：沒有了。謝謝，再見。

※ ※ ※ ※ ※ ※

（林建國踢開房門，把書往桌上一扔）

偉立：你怎麼啦？生什麼氣？

建國：今天心理學考得好爛[1]！昨天看的都沒考，真倒楣！

偉立：別的同學考得怎麼樣？

建國：不知道。不過，他們好像考得不錯。

偉立：先別難過，我們想想問題在哪裡。是不是你念書的方法不對？

建國：我高中也是這樣念的啊！

偉立：噢，我明白了。念大學跟念高中不一樣，一定得自動自發，才會有好成績。

國立台灣師範大學
國語教學中心

MANDARIN TRAINING CENTER
NATIONAL TAIWAN NORMAL UNIVERSITY

學 業 證 明 書
RECORD OF STUDY

姓 名 NAME: DAVID BAXTER (IN ENGLISH) 白大為 (IN CHINESE)

註册起訖日期 PERIOD(S) OF ENROLLMENT	個別班 INDIVIDUAL TUTORIAL	合 班 SMALL GROUP CLASS	正式生 FULL TIME	選讀生 PART TIME
Sep. 1, 1991 -- Aug. 31, 1993		X	X	

應上課時數 TOTAL NO. OF CLASS HOURS THE STUDENT ENROLLED FOR	878
實際上課時數 TOTAL NO. OF CLASS HOURS THE STUDENT ACTUALLY STUDIED	802

所 用 材 料 STUDY MATERIALS		成績 GRADE%
國語會話(一)	SPEAK CHINESE (THE REVISED EDITION)	93
實用國語會話(二)	PRACTICAL CHINESE DIALOGUES II	88
今日台灣	TAIWAN TODAY	90
中國的風俗習慣	CHINESE CUSTOMS AND TRADITIONS	88
中國歷史故事(一)	STORIES FROM CHINESE HISTORY I	86
新選廣播劇	NEW RADIO PLAYS	89
國語日報	MANDARIN DAILY NEWS	87

備 註 REMRKS

EXPLANATION

The Mandarin Training Center is a non-credit-granting language training institute and students may study here for as long or as short a time as they please. Thus students neither have a cumulative grade point average nor class rank.

"Full time" means ten or more hours of study per week; "part time" means nine or less hours of study per week.

The grading system used at this Center — the same as the system used at all public schools and universities in Taiwan — is as follows:

80—100 = A; 70—79 = B; 60—69 = C; 50—59 = Pass Conditional (upon make-up exam); 49 & Below = F.

文 號 FILE NO: 學 RS 08345

March 20, 1994
發出日期 Date of Issue

Teh-ming Yeh
主任 葉德明 Teh-ming Yeh, Director

81.5. 3,000

· 學生學業證明書
（范慧貞提供）

建國：你的意思是——

偉立：平常要**多**看書，發現問題就去請教老師，也可以跟同學討論。

建國：對！一次小考考壞了沒關係，我現在就開始用功，期中考、期末考就不會有問題了。你得給我加油啊！

※ ※ ※ ※ ※ ※

（系辦公室）

偉立：胡老師，你好。**咦**，張老師不在？我的作業交給你，好不好？

助教：好啊，我正在改你們的作業呢[2]。

偉立：你今天臉色不太好，不舒服嗎[3]？

助教：大概是睡得不夠吧。明天要考法文，下星期一要交報告，這幾天**不但**要看書，查資料，**還**要上課，改作業，差不多天天開夜車[4]，累得不得了。

偉立：當助教真辛苦，還是只做學生比較好。

助教：是啊。我在臺灣念大學的時候，報告沒這麼多，也不必工作，輕鬆多了。

偉立：那你們的考試很多**嘍**？

助教：也**不算**多，你只要把書上或是老師說的背下來，考試及格[5]一定沒問題。

偉立：什麼都要背嗎？那我死定了[6]。

助教：當然不是什麼都要背，其實背書也沒有你想的那麼難。

你們老師不叫你們背書嗎？

偉立：很少。

助教：所以啦，要是你常常背，大概就不會覺得那麼難了。

偉立：我**寧可**寫報告，**也**不要背書。

助教：背書是很無聊，可是有些東西**非**背**不可**。學語言更需要背。

偉立：我們老師總是鼓勵我們要有自己的想法，寫報告比背書有意思多了。

助教（看看錶）：我得去上課了，再見。

偉立：再見。

生詞及例句

1. 考卷 (kǎojuàn) *N*: **exam paper, test booklet（M：份）**

今天有二十個人來考試，請準備二十份考卷。

2. 翻譯 (fānyì)

V/N: **to translate, interpret / translator, interpreter, translation**

(1)這句中國話用英文應該怎麼說？你會不會翻譯？

(2)他跟外國人談生意的時候，常常帶著一個翻譯。

(3)這本書的日文翻譯不太好，很多意思都弄錯了。

翻 (fān)

V: **to translate; to turn (over, upside down, up, etc.); to rummage, to search**

(1)我們兩國生活習慣不一樣，有些句子翻譯的時候很難翻。

(2)各位同學，今天我們念第六課，請翻到第八十五頁。

(3)中國人在船上吃魚，吃完了一面，不可以把魚翻過來再吃，因為他們怕船也會翻過來。

(4)小偷沒偷走什麼東西，可是把我的衣服翻亂了。

(5)這本雜誌，我沒有時間慢慢地看，只隨便翻了一下。

3. 扣分 (kòu//fēn) *VO*: **to deduct points, take off credit**

扣 (kòu) *V*: **to deduct**

老師說寫錯一個字要扣一分。

4. 主詞 (zhǔcí) *N*: **subject (of a sentence)**

詞 (cí) *N*: **word**

名詞 (míngcí) *N*: **noun**

動詞 (dòngcí) *N*: **verb**

5. 文法 (wénfǎ) *N*: **grammar**

6. 成 (chéng)

V/PV/RE: **to become, to turn into, to complete/ to V as / [RE indicates success, completion, or accomplishment of an action]**

(1)他們才認識三個月就成了好朋友了。

(2)對不起，李先生，我把你看成張先生了。

(3)我的錢不夠，我想我去不成了。

7. 分數 (fēnshù) *N*: **score, grade (in an exam, course)**

分 (fēn) *M*: **point (s)(in an exam)**

他這次考試的分數是全班最高的，九十六分。

8. 低 (dī) *SV*: **to be low**

一般來說，男人的聲音比較低。

9. 題目 (tímù) *N*: **title, subject , topic**

這篇文章的題目是「中國的出產」，也介紹了很多農產品。

題 (tí)

M: **for question or problem (in a test or an exercise)**

考卷上一共有十個題目，第一題最容易。

10. 了解 / 瞭解 (liǎojiě)

V/N: **to know, to understand / knowledge, understanding**

你們剛認識，所以你不了解他。

11.複ㄈㄨˋ習ㄒㄧˊ／溫ㄨㄣ習ㄒㄧˊ(fùxí/wēnxí) *V*: **to review ; to revise**

下了課以後，得常複習，要不然很快就忘了。

12.記ㄐㄧˋ住ㄓㄨˋ(jì//zhù)

RC: **to remember, to fix in the mind, to commit to memory**

他的電話號碼很難記，我總是記不住。

13.踢ㄊㄧ開ㄎㄞ(tī//kāi)

RC: **to kick away (literally or figuratively)**

(1)你為什麼把狗踢開？你不喜歡狗嗎？

(2)他覺得我對他沒有幫助了，就想把我踢開了。

踢ㄊㄧ (tī) *V*: **to kick**

馬生氣的時候才會踢人。

踢ㄊㄧ到ㄉㄠˋ(tī//dào) *RC*: **to kick**

他沒踢到我，因為我跑得快。

14.心ㄒㄧㄣ理ㄌㄧˇ學ㄒㄩㄝˊ(xīnlǐxué) *N*: **psychology**

心ㄒㄧㄣ理ㄌㄧˇ(xīnlǐ) *N*: **thought and ideas; mentality**

你做生意，要懂客人心理，兩塊九毛雖然只比三塊便宜一毛，但是願意買的人就多了。

15.爛ㄌㄢˋ(làn)

SV: **to be worn out ; to be rotten, decayed; (slang) rotten, terrible**

(1)這本書真爛， 連書名都翻譯錯了。

(2)這個蘋果放了一個星期，快爛了，不能吃了。

16.倒ㄉㄠˇ楣ㄇㄟˊ(dǎoméi)

SV: **to have bad luck or an unlucky break; to get into trouble**

他不但丟了書，還丟了錢，真倒楣！

倒ㄉㄠˇ(dǎo)

V/RE: **to fall over, [RE indicates toppling or falling over of the subject]**

(1)上次大地震，房子倒了二十幾間。

(2)他不小心碰倒了桌上的茶杯。

17. 高ㄍㄠ 中ㄓㄨㄥ (gāozhōng)

N: **senior high school (10th, 11th and 12th grades)**

18. 自ㄗˋ 動ㄉㄨㄥˋ 自ㄗˋ 發ㄈㄚ (zìdòng zìfā)

IE: **self–motivated and spontaneous**

這個孩子做什麼事都自動自發，從來不要我叫他。

自ㄗˋ 動ㄉㄨㄥˋ (zìdòng)

AT/SV/A: **to be automatic, voluntary/automatically, voluntarily**

他的照像機是全自動的，誰都會用。

被ㄅㄟˋ 動ㄉㄨㄥˋ (bèidòng) *SV*: **to be passive**

他很被動，什麼事都要別人說了，才去做。

19. 如ㄖㄨˊ 果ㄍㄨㄛˇ (rúguǒ) *A*: **if, in case, in the event of**

如果你不願意幫忙，應該早一點告訴他。

20. 討ㄊㄠˇ 論ㄌㄨㄣˋ (tǎolùn) *V*: **to discuss (formally)**

這個問題我們已經跟張教授討論過了。

21. 難ㄋㄢˊ 過ㄍㄨㄛˋ (nán'guò) *SV*: **to be sad, to be distressed**

他的女朋友離開他了，所以他很難過。

22. 期ㄑㄧˊ 末ㄇㄛˋ 考ㄎㄠˇ (qímòkǎo)

N: **final exam (at the end of the term)**

期ㄑㄧˊ 中ㄓㄨㄥ 考ㄎㄠˇ (qízhōngkǎo) *N*: **mid-term exam**

補ㄅㄨˇ 考ㄎㄠˇ (bǔkǎo)

N/V: **make-up exam / to take a make-up exam**

(1)他的分數太低，一定得補考。

(2)補考的成績要是不好的話，他就得再念一年了。

23. 加ㄐㄧㄚ 油ㄧㄡˊ (jiā//yóu)

VO: **to make an extra effort, "Step on it !" ; to oil, lubricate, refuel; to cheer (an athlete)**

加ㄐㄧㄚ 油ㄧㄡˊ 站ㄓㄢˋ (jiāyóuzhàn)

N: **gasoline (petrol) filling station**

(1)沒油了，我們先去加油站加油吧！

(2)加油吧！只要你用功，一定可以考好的。

24. 作ㄗㄨㄛˋ業ㄧㄝˋ (zuòyè) *N*: **homework**

老師留的作業太多，我還沒寫完。

25. 臉ㄌㄧㄢˇ色ㄙㄜˋ (liǎnsè) *N*: **complexion; facial expression**

(1) 他的臉色很黃，是不是病了？

(2) 他的臉色很難看，真的生氣了。

26. 報ㄅㄠˋ告ㄍㄠˋ (bàogào)

V/N: **to report, to make known / a report (written or spoken)**

(1) 每天晚上電視幾點報告新聞？

(2) 我今天晚上要寫報告，不能出去玩。

27. 查ㄔㄚˊ (chá)

V: **to check, examine, inspect; to look into, investigate; to look up, consult**

我不知道火車站的電話號碼是多少，請你幫我查查。

28. 當ㄉㄤ (dāng) *V*: **to work as, to serve as**

他從小就想當醫生。

29. 助ㄓㄨˋ教ㄐㄧㄠˋ (zhùjiào) *N*: **teaching assistant**

張教授要我們把作業交給王助教改。

30. 輕ㄑㄧㄥ鬆ㄙㄨㄥ (qīngsōng)

SV/V: **to be relaxed, easy, comfortable; to relax, wind down**

(1) 作業都做完了，考試也考完了，我覺得真輕鬆。

(2) 考試考完了，我想去看電影，輕鬆輕鬆。

鬆ㄙㄨㄥ (sōng) *SV*: **to be relaxed, lenient, slack, loose**

那個老師對學生太鬆了，所以學生都不用功。

31. 背ㄅㄟˋ書ㄕㄨ (bèi//shū)

VO: **to recite a passage from memory; act of memorizing a passage**

老師叫我們背書，我念了二十次才記住。

背ㄅㄟˋ (bèi)

V/N: **to memorize, to learn by heart, to recite from memory / the back of the body, the back of an object**

(1) 這幾個句子太難，我背了半天還記不住。

(2)他的背疼得不得了，躺在床上休息呢。

背ㄅㄟˋ下ㄒㄧㄚˋ來ㄌㄞˊ (bèi//xiàlái)

RC: **to memorize, to commit to memory**

請你們回去把這一課都背下來。

32. 及ㄐㄧˊ格ㄍㄜˊ (jígé)

V: **to pass a test, pass an examination / to be qualified**

這次考試比較難，所以五十分就算及格了。

33. 死ㄙˇ定ㄉㄧㄥˋ了˙ㄌㄜ (sǐdìng·le)　　*IE*: **(slang) will surely die**

我媽叫我十點回家，現在十二點了，我死定了！

死ㄙˇ (sǐ)　　*V/SV*: **to die/to be dead**

他很小的時候，父母就死了。

34. 其ㄑㄧˊ實ㄕˊ (qíshí)　　*A*: **actually, in fact, as a matter of fact**

他說他會做飯，其實他只會烤麵包。

35. 寧ㄋㄧㄥˊ可ㄎㄜˇ／寧ㄋㄧㄥˊ願ㄩㄢˋ (níngkě/níngyuàn)

AV: **would rather, had better, would sooner**

我寧可吃烤麵包，也不要吃麥當勞的炸雞。

36. 無ㄨˊ聊ㄌㄧㄠˊ (wúliáo)

SV: **to be bored ; to be boring and uninteresting; to be a nuisance; to be nonsensical**

(1)我一個人在家很無聊，所以想約朋友去跳舞。

(2)我昨天在車上碰到一個很無聊的人，他總是想找我說話。

37. 非ㄈㄟ……不ㄅㄨˋ可ㄎㄜˇ (fēi......bùkě)

PT: **must, have to, is indispensable, will inevitably**

不考試就不能畢業，所以你非考不可。

38. 想ㄒㄧㄤˇ法ㄈㄚˇ (xiǎngfǎ)　　*N*：**way of thinking, point of view**

他的想法很奇怪，一般人很難了解他。

看ㄎㄢˋ法ㄈㄚˇ (kànfǎ)

N: **point of view, opinion, way of looking at things**

做ㄗㄨㄛˋ法ㄈㄚˇ (zuòfǎ)　　*N*: **way of doing things**

說ㄕㄨㄛ法ㄈㄚˇ (shuōfǎ)

N: **way of speaking, an orally expressed view**

教ㄐㄧㄠ 法ㄈㄚˇ (jiāofǎ) *N*: **teaching method, way of teaching**

歎詞跟語助詞 Interjections and Particles

1. 哦ㄛˊ (ó) *I:* **[indicates doubt ; "really?!"]**

   張：我昨天給你打過電話。

   李：哦？沒有人告訴我啊！

2. 咦ㄧˊ (yí) *I:* **[indicates surprise]**

   咦？你怎麼有我的電話號碼？

3. 嘍˙ㄌㄡ (·lou) *P:* **[indicates exclamation or interrogation]**

   我們就這麼辦嘍？

注釋

1. 爛 is a slang term used in Taiwan, popularized by some television programs in the early '80s. 爛 literally means "decayed or rotten", but in this case it is used to describe something which is lousy or extremely bad. Originally it was used in this manner mostly by young people, but it has since become widely used and does not sound as extreme as it did several years ago.
2. "我正在改你們的作業呢！" means: "I'm right in the middle of correcting your assignments."
3. "你今天臉色不好，不舒服嗎？" means: "You don't look well today. Are you not feeling well?" This is an expression of concern. Some other ways to say this are: "你還好吧？(Are you all right?)" and "你怎麼了？ (What's the matter with you ? or What's wrong with you?)" However, the latter is considered somewhat straightforward and impolite and should not be used when speaking with an elder .

4. 開夜車 is a slang term used by students meaning: “to stay up late at night in order to complete an assignment or study for an exam”, “to burn the midnight oil”.

5. 考試及格 means “to pass an exam”. One usually has to get a grade of at least 60 points in order to pass an exam in Taiwan.

6. 死定了 is a slang term used by young people. It literally means “one will certainly die.” It is used to describe the dire importance of a particular situation. It is similar to saying: “That will be the death of me (if something happens).” Another Chinese pattern to convey the same meaning is “……完了”.

文法練習

☞ 一 N_1 V 成 N_2 N_1 turned into N_2 (via V)

⊙你把「再見」的「再」寫成「現在」的「在」了。

You wrote the 再 from 再見 like the 在 from 現在.

用法說明： 這個「成」是 PV，是「成為」的意思，N_1 經由 V 這個動作成為 N_2。因為也有「處置」的作用，所以常跟「把」一起用。動詞如果是看、聽、說、寫、念，就有「弄錯了」的意思。

Explanation: 成 is used here as a post verb. It means the same thing as 成為 (to turn into, become). Thus, this pattern can be translated as “N_1 becomes N_2 via the action of V”. 把 is often used together with this pattern because the sentence shows manipulation of an object. If the main verb is 看, 聽, 說, 寫, and 念 then this pattern usually indicates that the change or manipulation was faulty or resulted in a mistake.

練習： Exercise:

㈠請根據提示，用「V 成」完成下面各句。

Please use the "V 成" pattern to complete the following sentences using the information provided in the parentheses.

1. 這間書房，他打算<u>改成客房</u>，因為常有客人來住。（客房、改）
   He plans to convert this study into a guest room because guests often stay over.
2. 這篇文章是用法文寫的，我看不懂，你幫我 ＿＿＿＿＿＿＿＿，好不好？（英文、翻）
3. 我覺得她頭髮的樣子很好看，我也想 ＿＿＿＿＿＿＿＿。（她那個樣子、剪）
4. 我們有六個人，這個蛋糕當然得 ＿＿＿＿＿＿＿＿。（六塊、分）
5. 這個地方原來只有兩萬人，現在已經 ＿＿＿＿＿＿＿＿。（一個大城市、發展）

㈡請根據提示，用「V 成」跟「把」完成下面各句。

Please use the "V 成" and 把 pattern to complete the following sentences using the information provided in parentheses.

1. 你聽錯了，你<u>把十四聽成四十了</u>。（十四、四十、聽）
2. 他的中國話真不好，又 ＿＿＿＿＿＿＿＿。（綠、路、念）
3. 李小姐站得太遠，所以我 ＿＿＿＿＿＿＿＿。（她、張小姐、看）
4. 我同學 ＿＿＿＿＿＿＿＿，真好笑！
   （我哥哥是做麵包的、我哥哥是麵包做的、說）
5. 我弄不清楚這兩個字怎麼用，常常 ＿＿＿＿＿＿＿＿。（得、的、寫）

二 V 住

(indicates the resulting stabilization, or fixation of an action)

⊙學過的東西都記住了沒有?

Do you (solidly) remember everything that you have studied?

用法說明： 這個「住」是 RE，表示「穩固」。RC 的 Actual Type 跟 Potential Type 都可用。

Explanation: This 住 is a RE (resultative verb ending), and it indicates the stabilization or fixation of a verb's action. The RC can be used in either Actual Type form or Potential Type form.

練習： 請根據所給「V住」填入合適的RC。

Exercise: Please fill in the appropriate RC in accordance with the provided「V住」.

1. 記住：
   (1) 他的電話號碼很好記，你一定記得住。
   His phone number is easy to memorize: You'll definitely remember it.
   (2) 這本書，我才念了一次，當然 ________________ 。
   (3) 這些句子，我背了半天，可是一個字都 ________________ 。
2. 坐住：
   (1) 三個月大的孩子，怎麼 ________________ ？
   (2) 他很愛玩，在家裡一分鐘也 ________________ 。
3. 站住：
   (1) 沒關係，我不累，不必坐，我還 ________________ 。
   (2) 他 ________________ ，得找個椅子坐下來了。
   (3) 我一叫他，他就 ________________ 。
4. 拿住：
   (1) 這麼大的杯子，小孩一定 ________________ 。
   (2) 那個瓶子，他 ________________ ，就打破了。
5. 停住：
   (1) 他的車開得太快， ________________ ，所以出事了。
   (2) 飛機剛起飛，怎麼 ________________ ?!

☞ 三 多 V(O)　V more

⊙平常要多看書。

(You) need to read more in general.

用法說明：「多」在此做副詞用，修飾後面的動詞，強調程度應該加強。客套話可重疊「多」。如欲說明程度，可在V之後加上「一點」、「一些」或「Nu–M」。此時「多」就不可重疊。

Explanation: 多 is used here as an adverb which describes the verb that follows, indicating increased frequency or degree. To soften the tone of 多 and make it more polite, it can be repeated. To indicate only a small or specific increase in frequency, place 一點, 一些, or "Nu M" after the verb without repeating 多.

練習：請把「多」插入下面各句適當位置。

Exercise: Please place 多 in the appropriate place in the following sentences.

1. 這件事很清楚，不必我說。

   This matter is very clear; I don't need to explain it.

   →這件事很清楚，不必我多說。

   This matter is very clear; I don't need to explain further.

2. 運動對身體健康有很大的幫助。

   ....

3. 再吃一點嘛！我做的菜不好吃嗎？

   ....

4. 一袋蘋果不夠，你應該再買一些。

   ....

5. 你不必今天就回去，在這裡住幾天吧！

   ....

6. 以後要麻煩你照顧我的孩子了。（「多」可重疊）

   ....

7. 我什麼都不懂，要跟你學習。（「多」可重疊）

   ....

☞ 四 不但……，還……　Not only......, but also......

⊙這幾天不但要看書、查資料，還要上課、改作業……

Lately, I not only have had to study and do research, but I also have had to go to class, correct homework...

用法說明：這個句型跟第四課的「不但……，也……」差不多，但是用「還」時，程度比用「也」更進一步。

Explanation: This sentence pattern is very similar to the "不但…，也…" pattern found in Chapter 4; however, the use of 還 instead of 也 implies a slightly stronger tone.

練習：請用「不但……，還……」完成下面句子。

Exercise: Please use the "不但……，還……" pattern to complete the following sentences.

1. 他不但有三輛汽車，還有一架小飛機。

   Not only does he have three cars, but he also has a small airplane.

2. 張先生不但念過大學，還 ______________________。
3. 王小姐不但去過歐洲，還 ______________________。
4. 這個地方不但有公路，還 ______________________。
5. 老李真倒楣，不但被偷過，還 ______________________。

☞ 五 不算
(is not, does not count as, should not be considered as)

⊙也不算多。

(Here,也 indicates a contradiction of the previous speaker's statement)
But that isn't much.

用法說明：「不算」就是「算是」的否定。（請參考第二課文法練習二）

Explanation: 不算 is the opposite of 算是.

練習：請把下面各句改成「不算」的句子。

Exercise: Please change the following sentences into the 不算 form.

1. 在這個學校申請獎學金算是容易的。

   It's quite easy to apply for a scholarship at this school.

   →在這個學校申請獎學金不算難。

   It's not difficult to apply for a scholarship at this school.

2. 那個學生的成績在班上算是高的。

....

3. 教書的工作算是辛苦的。

....

4. 這個冰箱的價錢跟你的比起來算是便宜的。

....

5. 你們這兒的火車一小時跑一百五十公里算是快的。

....

☞ 六 寧可 VP_1，也 VP_2（寧願……，也……）would rather VP_1 than VP_2

⊙我寧可寫報告，也不要背書。

I would rather write a report than memorize a passage.

用法説明： VP_1 本來是不喜歡做的事，但因不願改變 VP_2的情況，VP_1 變得可以接受了。

Explanation: In this pattern VP_1 is something the subject doesn't really want to do, but rather something he is willing to accept, in order to avoid a change in the situation given by VP_2. This pattern implies that although VP_1 is not completely ideal, in comparison with VP_2 it is the more acceptable alternative. If VP_1 is positive, then VP_2 needs to be negative. But when VP_1 is negative, VP_2 can be either positive or negative.

練習： 請用「寧可……，也……」完成下面對話。

Exercise: Please use the "寧可……，也……" pattern to complete the following dialogues.

1. 張：你怎麼在家裡洗衣服，沒跟他去看電影？

   Chang: Why did you stay home washing clothes instead of going to the movies with him?

   李：那個人很沒趣，我寧可在家洗衣服，也不要跟他去看電影。

   Li: That guy is very uninteresting ; I'd rather stay at home and wash clothes than go to the movies with him.

2. 張：錢那麼少，你為什麼不換工作？

李：這個工作可以學到很多東西，所以我 ________________ 。

3. 張：學校的大鍋菜吃膩了，我們到郵局旁邊那家飯館去吃吧！

李：那家飯館的菜太難吃，我 ________________ 。

4. 張：快睡吧，天快亮了。

李：這本書太好看了，我寧可不 ________________ 。

5. 張：你跟王小姐借一件衣服去參加舞會吧！

李：我不喜歡她，我寧可沒有 ________________ 。

七 非……不可

have to, definitely must, is indispensable (for a particular action)

⊙……可是有些東西非背不可。

......but there are some things you must memorize .

用法說明：「非……不可」的意思是「不……不行」。

Explanation: This pattern indicates that you must definitely carry out a specific action due to either necessity or strong desire.

練習：請用「非……不可」完成下面對話。

Exercise: Please use "非……不可" to complete the dialogues below.

1. 張：怎麼樣才會有好成績？

Chang: What must one do to get good grades?

李：要有好成績，非用功不可。

Li: If you want to have good grades, you must work very diligently.

2. 張：這裡的冬天需不需要裝暖氣？

李：冬天的溫度都在零下， ________________ 。

3. 張：哎喲！怎麼辦？我把哥哥的照像機弄壞了。

李：如果他知道了， ________________ 。

4. 張：急什麼？再坐一會兒嘛！

李：不行，還有半個小時火車就要開了，我 ________________ 。

5. 張：你怎麼又要找房子？

李：我的房東要賣房子，所以我 ________________ 。

☞ 八 歎詞跟語助詞用法
The use of Interjections & Modal Parttcles

㈠哦 Oh, (really)?

⊙哦，什麼地方有問題？

Oh (really)? Where is the problem?

用法說明：放在句首，語調高揚，對聽到的情況表示疑惑、驚訝。

Explanation: When 哦 is placed at the beginning of a sentence and spoken with a questioning tone, it indicates doubt or surprise about what one has just heard.

練習：請用「哦」完成下面對話。

Exercise: Please use 哦 to complete the following dialogues.

1. 張：王教授這個週末要請我們吃飯。

   Chang: Professor Wang wants to treat us to a meal this weekend.

   李：哦，真的嗎？

   Li: Oh, really?

2. 張：我室友下個月就要去臺灣學中文了。

   李：哦，________________ 。

3. 張：林小姐病了好幾個星期了。

   李：哦，________________ 。

4. 張：上次考試，我的學生有一半不及格。

   李：哦，________________ 。

5. 張：我哥哥大學畢業了，可是還不想找工作。

   李：哦，________________ 。

㈡咦 Yi? (What?) (indicates surprise)

⊙咦，張老師不在？

Huh? Teacher Zhang isn't here?

用法說明： 放在句首，語調高揚，對眼前的狀況表示驚訝或疑問。近似自言自語。

Explanation: 咦 is placed at the beginning of a sentence and is spoken with a questioning tone, indicating doubt or surprise about what one has just seen, as if the speaker is talking to himself.

練習： Exercise

㈠根據所給情況，用「咦」表示驚訝或疑問。

Please use 咦 to indicate surprise or doubt about the provided situations.

1. 開燈，可是燈不亮。

You turned on the switch, but the light doesn't shine.

→咦，燈壞了？

Huh? Is the light broken?

2. 早上起來，看見廚房地上都是水。

→咦，____________？

3. 吃晚飯的時候回家，發現沒有人在家。

→咦，____________？

4. 室友出門，可是你看見他的鑰匙還放在桌上，沒帶走。

→咦，____________？

5. 聽說陳助教去了日本，可是今天在路上遠遠地看見他。

→咦，____________？

㈡請在「欸」、「哦」、「咦」三詞當中選擇合適的填進空格裡。

Please choose the most appropriate of the three exclamations 欸, 哦, and 咦 to fill in the blanks.

1. ____________，電視怎麼沒聲音了？
2. （看錶）____________，他不是說好了三點一定到嗎？
3. ____________，聽你的意思，好像不願意幫忙。
4. ____________，我記得你不吃辣的，怎麼點了宮保雞丁？
5. ____________，誰把我的桌子搬走了？
6. ____________，你已經知道他出國的事了？

㈢嘍 (indicates exclamation or interrogation)

⊙那你們的考試很多嘍？

So you have a lot of tests?

用法說明：「嘍」是「了」跟「o」或「ou」的合音。「了」在此強調達到某一程度。放在句尾，語調高平，徵詢對方以求確定。

Explanation: 嘍 is the combined sound of 了 and "o". The 了 here emphasizes that a certain level is reached. 嘍 is placed at the end of a statement and pronounced with a high flat tone to ask the other party to confirm the statement.

練習：請用「嘍」完成下面對話。

Exercise: Please complete the following dialogues using 嘍.

1. 張：我們要去歐洲旅行三個月。

   Chang: We want to travel in Europe for three months.

   李：那你們帶的行李一定不少嘍？

   Li: Then I guess you'll have to bring a lot of luggage, huh?

2. 張：這學期，我只選了兩門課。

   李：那 ________________ ？

3. 張：我一天見不到我女朋友就沒辦法念書。

   李：那 ________________ ？

4. 張：這次考試，全班都考得很好。

   李： ________________ ？

5. 張：上週末我一個人在家，電視也壞了，真不知道做什麼才好。

   李： ________________ ？

課室活動

Role playing:

1. Two students : One acts as a strict teacher, the other as a student who has not finished his/her homework. The student offers excuses to avoid being punished.

Some useful supplementary words include: 嚴 (yán; to be strict),罰 (fá; to punish), 原諒 (yuánliàng; to forgive), 原因 (yuányīn; reason), 懶 (lǎn; to be lazy), 藉口 (jièkǒu; excuse).

2. Two students: One acts as a parent, the other as a young teenage daughter who has been sitting in front of the TV set for two hours. The parent knows that the daughter has not prepared for her exam tomorrow. The two should improvise a conversation suitable for this situation. Some useful supplementary words include: 數學 (shùxué; mathematics), 歷史 (lìshǐ; history), 化學 (huàxué; chemistry), 公式 (gōngshì; formula), 節目(jiémù; program), 催 (cuī; to urge; hurry along), 管 (guǎn; to discipline; to be concerned about; to be in charge of; to manage).

下星期一考心理學。

下星期二考法文。

下星期三考地理。

我快變成「烤鴨」了！

短文

老師的話

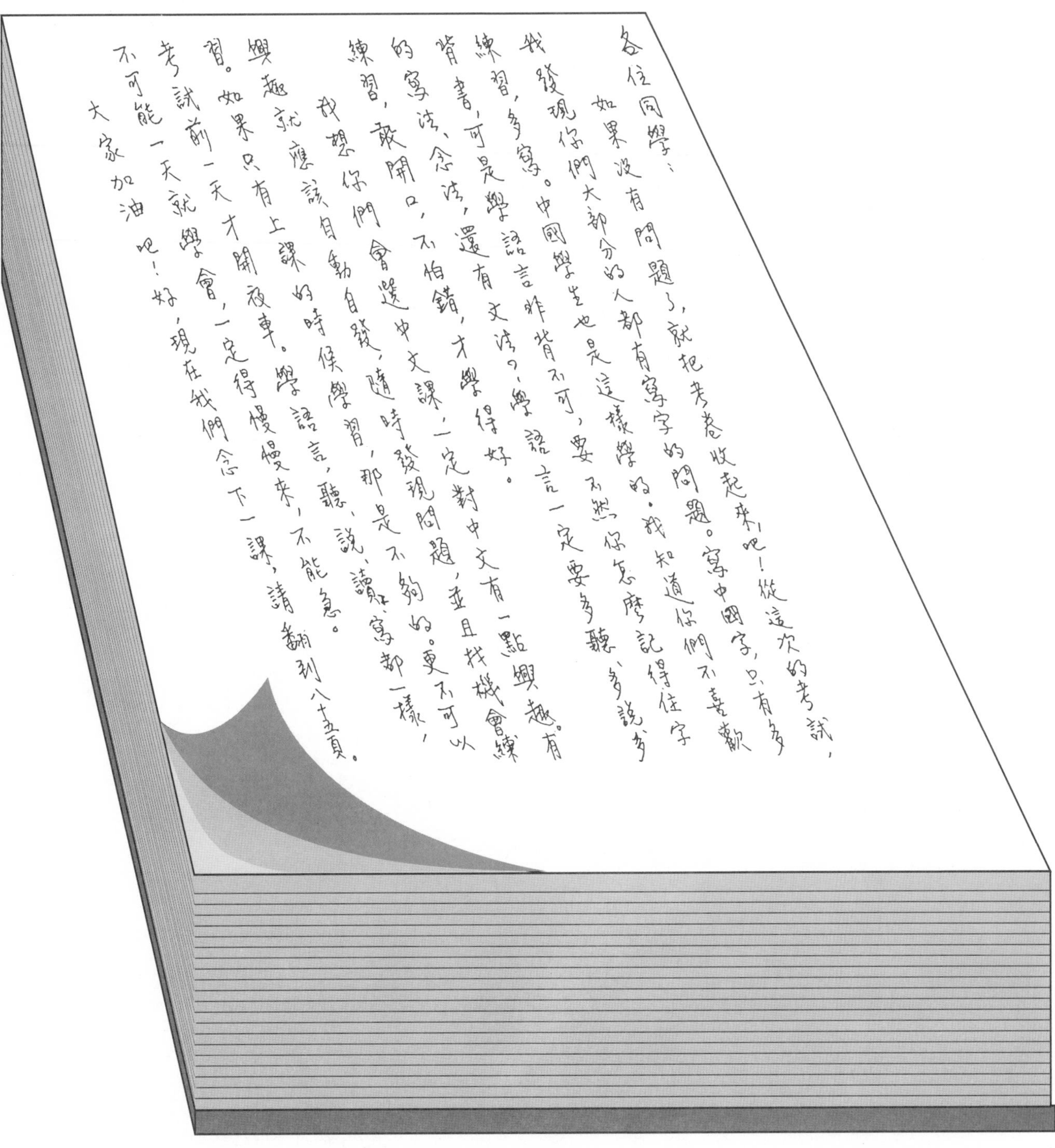

各位同學：

如果沒有問題了，就把考卷收起來吧！從這次的考試，我發現你們大部分的人都有寫字的問題。寫中國字，只有多練習，多寫。中國學生也是這樣學的。我知道你們不喜歡背書，可是學語言非背不可，要不然你怎麼記得住字的寫法、念法，還有文法呢？學語言一定要多聽、多說、多練習，敢開口，不怕錯，才學得好。

我想你們會選中文課，一定對中文有一點興趣。有興趣就應該自動自發，隨時發現問題，並且找機會練習。如果只有上課的時候學習，那是不夠的。更不可以考試前一天才開夜車。學語言，聽、說、讀、寫都一樣，不可能一天就學會，一定得慢慢來，不能急。

大家加油吧！好，現在我們念下一課，請翻到八十五頁。

Vocabulary:

1.收起來 (shōuqǐ·lái): to put away

2.讀 (dú): to read

第七課

念大學真不容易

・軍事訓練（新聞局提供）

（活動中心，李平端著咖啡找位子）

李平：嗨，你也在這裡啊？看什麼書？

建國：心理學。我上次考得好爛，下星期再考不好，就慘了。

李平：難怪你這麼用功。下星期還早嘛！

建國：可是我心裡壓力好大啊！

李平：**才**一個小考**就**讓你有這麼大的壓力，要是你還在臺灣，恐怕早就變成神經病了。

建國：太誇張了吧？我記得我小時候，考試也不怎麼多啊！

李平：那是因為你只念到小學三年級，沒考過高中、大學[1]。

（偉立走過來）

偉立：嗨！你們好，在談什麼？

李平：剛剛他說考試有壓力，我告訴他臺灣的學生要念高中、大學都得通過考試。因為人人都想念大學[2]，有的人要上有名的大學，有的人要念熱門的科系，所以很早就開始準備，差不多每天都有複習考。下了課還要去補習。這**才**是壓力。

偉立：天哪！那他們一定不敢出去玩了，恐怕連睡覺的時間都不夠。

李平：這樣已經不錯了。從前我爸媽他們還要考初中呢！那時候義務教育只有六年[3]。

偉立：你們也有SAT[4]嗎？

李平：沒有，可是我們有大學聯考。就是每年七月所有的大學聯合起來，在同一天舉行考試。每年有十萬多人參加，只錄取三萬多人[5]，競爭非常激烈。

建國：**幸虧**我們家移民了，**要不然**我一定念不了大學。

李平：有的父母怕孩子受不了這種壓力，就想辦法把他們送到外國去念書。像我舅舅，就把我表弟送來了。

・大專聯考父母陪考情形(《中國時報》黃錦彥攝影)

建國：他現在在哪裡？他多大了？

李平：洛杉磯，住在他姑姑家。念八年級了。他在臺灣的時候，不喜歡背書，有好幾科不及格。我舅舅擔心他考不上大學，他自己也願意到外國看看，所以就來了。

偉立：現在情形怎麼樣？

李平：他來了半年了。雖然他喜歡老師的教法，但是上課的時候不敢問問題，下了課功課常做得不對，也不知道怎麼寫報告，所以成績並不理想。

建國：我剛來的時候也一樣。他**會**慢慢適應**的**。

李平：我也這麼希望。我覺得他的問題是父母不在這兒，心裡很孤單。雖然有姑姑照顧，但總還是不夠。你知道，有的事情你只會跟父母說，不好意思告訴別人。

偉立：嗯，這真是麻煩。

李平：是啊。我們政府已經注意到這些小留學生的問題[6]，大家也發現把孩子送出來念書，並不是最好的辦法。

建國：你剛剛說十萬人才錄取三萬人，沒考上的人，工作好找嗎？

李平：高中畢業找工作並不容易。所以有的就進專科學校[7]學習一種技術，有的補習一年再考，可是男孩子**滿**了十八歲就得先去當兵[8]了。

建國：這些人**只好**當完兵再考大學嘍？

李平：是啊！

偉立：那麼多人都要念大學，人人都念得起嗎？

李平：臺灣的大學，**不管**公立私立的，學費**都**沒有美國那麼高[9]，我們政府的想法是如果學費太高，有錢人才念得起大學，那很不公平。

偉立：**像**你**這樣**出國留學的人多不多？

李平：不少。有的人覺得大學學得還不夠，**不是**在國內念研究所，**就是**出國留學。

建國：噢，對了！你的論文寫完了嗎？以後有什麼打算？

李平：寫**得差不多了**。拿到學位以後，我想回臺灣工作。

建國：他們一定很歡迎你這位李博士回國服務。

生詞及例句

1. 活ㄏㄨㄛˊ動ㄉㄨㄥˋ中ㄓㄨㄥ心ㄒㄧㄣ (huódòng zhōngxīn)　*N*: **activity center**

   活ㄏㄨㄛˊ動ㄉㄨㄥˋ (huódòng)

   V/N: **to move about, to exercise / activity**

   (1) 人老了，應該常活動，總是坐著並不好。

   (2) 我常常參加別系的活動，所以認識的人比較多。

   中ㄓㄨㄥ心ㄒㄧㄣ (zhōngxīn)　*N*: **center, heart, central point**

   這個語言中心只教學生德文跟法文。

2. 端ㄉㄨㄢ (duān)

   V: **to hold something level with both hands; to carry**

   端著盤子的那位小姐是不是你們的助教？

3. 位ㄨㄟˋ子˙ㄗ (wèi·zi)　*N*: **seat, place, position**

   車上還有幾個位子，你們要不要坐？

4. 慘ㄘㄢˇ (cǎn) *SV*: **to be tragic, pitiful, miserable**

(1)你姐姐發現你把她的照像機弄壞了，你就慘了。

(2)這個地方因為地震死了很多人，真慘！

5. 壓ㄧㄚ 力ㄌㄧˋ (yālì) *N*: **pressure, stress**

他的工作太多，壓力很大。

壓ㄧㄚ (yā) *V*: **to press, to push down, to weigh down**

風太大，請你拿本書把這些紙壓著。

6. 變ㄅㄧㄢˋ 成ㄔㄥˊ (biànchéng)

V: **to become, to change into, transform into**

病好了以後，他變成一個不愛說話的人了。

7. 神ㄕㄣˊ 經ㄐㄧㄥ 病ㄅㄧㄥˋ (shénjīngbìng)

N: **insanity, mental illness (usually used in anger or jest as an exaggeration, rather than to describe actual insanity)**

今天這麼熱，你還穿這麼多衣服，真是神經病。

神ㄕㄣˊ 經ㄐㄧㄥ (shénjīng) *N*: **nerve**

神ㄕㄣˊ (shén) *N*: **god**

8. 誇ㄎㄨㄚ 張ㄓㄤ (kuāzhāng)

SV: **to be exaggerated, to be overstated**

他說他家的房子住得下一百個人，真是太誇張了。

9. 通ㄊㄨㄥ 過ㄍㄨㄛˋ (tōngguò) *V*: **to pass , pass through**

聽說這次心理學期末考很容易，大家都通過了。

10. 熱ㄖㄜˋ 門ㄇㄣˊ (rèmén)

SV: **to be in great demand, to be very popular (area of study, learning, subject, field)**

這幾年學電腦很熱門，連很小的孩子都去學了。

冷ㄌㄥˇ 門ㄇㄣˊ (lěngmén) *SV*: **opposite of 熱門**

11. 天ㄊㄧㄢ 哪˙ㄋㄚ (tiān·na)

IE: **Goodness!, Good heavens!, Gracious!**

天哪！他怎麼這麼胡塗？忘了今天是期末考了。

哪˙ㄋㄚ (·na)

P: **(following words that end in "an", "en", serves the same function as "啊")**

12. 初中(chūzhōng)

N: **junior high school (7th,8th and 9th grades)**

我比別人早念一年書，十一歲就念初中了。

13. 義務教育(yìwù jiàoyù) *N*: **compulsory education**

我們小學、初中都是義務教育，非念不可。

義務(yìwù) *N*: **duty, obligation, responsibility**

雖然我是你妹妹，可是我沒有義務給你介紹女朋友吧?!你自己去找啊！

教育(jiàoyù) *N*: **education**

這個州的教育辦得很好，到處都有學校。

教育部(jiàoyùbù) *N*: **the Ministry of Education**

14. 聯合(liánhé) *V*: **to combine, to unite, to ally**

他們打算聯合另外兩所學校一起考試。

聯合國(Liánhé Guó) *N*: **United Nations**

聯考(liánkǎo)

N: **a standardized entrance exam for school (high school, college, etc.)**

今年參加高中聯考的學生比去年多了三千人。

15. 同一天(tóngyìtiān) *Dem-Nu-M*: **the same day**

沒想到我的生日跟他的同一天，都是三月十一號。

同(tóng) *CV/DEM*: **together, with; same**

(1)我每天同他一起去上學。

(2)我們在同一棟大樓上課，所以我常常碰到他。

不同（不一樣）(bùtóng)

SV: **to be different from, distinct from**

(1)我跟他的習慣不同，他早睡早起，我晚睡晚起。

(2)「大」跟「太」這兩個字有什麼不同？。

同樣(tóngyàng) *AT*: **the same, similar**

我們對教育有同樣的看法，都覺得學習環境對學生很重要。

16. 舉ㄐㄩˇ行ㄒㄧㄥˊ(jǔxíng)

V: **to hold (a meeting, ceremony, etc.), to convene, take place**

我們要給她舉行一個生日舞會。

舉ㄐㄩˇ(jǔ) *V*: **to hold up, raise, lift**

警察叫小偷把手舉起來。

舉ㄐㄩˇ手ㄕㄡˇ(jǔ//shǒu)

VO: **to raise one's hand (to vote or to speak-up)**

有問題的人請舉手。

舉ㄐㄩˇ重ㄓㄨㄥˋ(jǔ//zhòng) *VO/N*: **weight lifting**

17. 錄ㄌㄨˋ取ㄑㄩˇ(lùqǔ)

V: **to admit, to accept (applicants after an examination or application process)**

想進我們公司做事的人很多，可是我們只錄取了三個人。

18. 競ㄐㄧㄥˋ爭ㄓㄥ (jìngzhēng) *V/N*: **to compete / competition**

只有一個工作機會，可是競爭的人有幾百個。

19. 激ㄐㄧ烈ㄌㄧㄝˋ(jīliè)

SV: **(of action and argument) to be intense, sharp, fierce, acute, violent**

他們打得太激烈了，有人被打死了。

20. 幸ㄒㄧㄥˋ虧ㄎㄨㄟ (xìngkuī) *A*: **fortunately, luckily**

幸虧沒下雨，要不然就不能去野餐了。

21. 舅ㄐㄧㄡˋ舅˙ㄐㄧㄡ (jiù·jiu) *N*: **uncle (mother's brother)**

舅ㄐㄧㄡˋ媽ㄇㄚ (jiùmā) *N*: **aunt (wife of mother's brother)**

22. 表ㄅㄧㄠˇ弟ㄉㄧˋ(biǎodì)

N: **younger male cousin (on mother's side or paternal aunt's side)**

表ㄅㄧㄠˇ哥ㄍㄜ (biǎogē)

N: **older male cousin (on mother's side or paternal aunt's side)**

表ㄅㄧㄠˇ姐ㄐㄧㄝˇ(biǎojiě)

N: **older female cousin (on mother's side or paternal aunt's side)**

表ㄅㄧㄠˇ妹ㄇㄟˋ(biǎomèi)

N: **younger female cousin (on mother's side or paternal aunt's side)**

23. 擔ㄉㄢ心ㄒㄧㄣ (dān//xīn)

VO/SV: **to worry / to be worried, concerned**

(1) 她好晚才回來，害我擔了半天的心。

(2) 她好晚才回來，我擔心得不得了。

24. 考ㄎㄠˇ上ㄕㄤˋ (考ㄎㄠˇ取ㄑㄩˇ) (kǎo//shàng) (kǎo//qǔ)

RC: **to pass an entrance examination (for school, a job, a license, etc.)**

恭喜你考上了最好的大學。

25. 情ㄑㄧㄥˊ形ㄒㄧㄥˊ (qíng·xíng)

N: **situation, condition, circumstances**

小張的爸爸還沒有找到工作，媽媽又病了，所以最近他家的情形不好。

26. 理ㄌㄧˇ想ㄒㄧㄤˇ (lǐxiǎng) *SV/N*: **to be ideal / ideal**

(1) 我很久沒練習寫字了，成績一定不理想。

(2) 我的理想是進大公司做事。

27. 孤ㄍㄨ單ㄉㄢ (gūdān) *SV*: **to be alone, to be lonely**

你一個人住那麼大的房子，不覺得孤單嗎？

28. 不ㄅㄨˋ好ㄏㄠˇ意ㄧˋ思˙ㄙ (bùhǎoyì·si)

IE: **to find it embarrassing, to be ill at ease; to feel shy or bashful, ashamed**

我已經二十歲了，不好意思再跟父母要錢。

29. 注ㄓㄨˋ意ㄧˋ (zhùyì) *V*: **to pay attention to, to take notice of**

各位請注意，飛機要起飛了。

30. 專ㄓㄨㄢ科ㄎㄜ學ㄒㄩㄝˊ校ㄒㄧㄠˋ (zhuānkē xuéxiào)

N: **a technical college, vocational school**

臺灣的專科學校有兩年的、三年的，也有五年的。

科ㄎㄜ系ㄒㄧˋ (kēxì)

N: **department (in a college or university)**

這個大學有很多科系。

科ㄎㄜ (kē)

M: **a branch of academic or vocational study; a division or subdivision of an administrative unit or section**

感冒應該看哪一科的醫生？

31. 技ㄐㄧˋ術ㄕㄨˋ (jìshù) *N*: **skill, technique; technology**

他開車的技術不錯，你放心。

32. 當ㄉㄤ 兵ㄅㄧㄥ (dāng//bīng)

VO: **to join the army, to serve in the military**

在臺灣，當兵是義務。

33. 只ㄓˇ好ㄏㄠˇ (zhǐhǎo)

A: **can only, cannot but, have no alternative but**

太晚了，沒有公車了，我只好走路回宿舍。

34. 不ㄅㄨˋ管ㄍㄨㄢˇ/不ㄅㄨˋ論ㄌㄨㄣˋ/無ㄨˊ論ㄌㄨㄣˋ……都ㄉㄡ……
(bùguǎn/búlùn/wúlùn......dōu......)

PT: **no matter (what, how, whether, etc.), regardless of**

不管大人、小孩，坐公車都得買票。

管ㄍㄨㄢˇ (guǎn)

V: **to be in charge of, to run, be responsible for; to mind, attend to, bother about, to be concerned about**

你別管他，讓他自己決定吧。

他已經坐下了，地上好髒，他也不管。

管ㄍㄨㄢˇ不ㄅㄨˋ了ㄌㄧㄠˇ (guǎn·bùliǎo)

RC: **cannot manage, handle, supervise**

十個孩子，我一個人管不了。

管ㄍㄨㄢˇ不ㄅㄨˋ著ㄓㄠˊ (guǎn·bùzháo)

RC: **no authority to manage, handle, or interfere**

這是我家的事，你管不著。

35. 私ㄙ 立ㄌㄧˋ (sīlì) *AT*: **privately run**

公ㄍㄨㄥ 立ㄌㄧˋ (gōnglì)

AT: **established and maintained by the government**

這附近有一所公立大學，是州政府辦的。

國立 (guólì) *AT*: **nationally run**
州立 (zhōulì) *AT*: **state run**
市立 (shìlì) *AT*: **municipally run**

36. 公平 (gōngpíng)
SV: **to be fair, just, impartial, equitable**
為什麼你給他的錢比較多？我覺得不公平。

37. 國內 (guónèi) *N*: **inside the country , domestic**
國外 (guówài)
N: **outside the country, overseas, abroad**
國內風景好的地方，他都去過了，下次他打算到國外去看看。

38. 論文 (lùnwén)
N: **thesis, dissertation, treatise (M：篇)**
他的畢業論文很長，一共有七百多頁。

39. 學位 (xuéwèi) *N*: **academic degree**
在這個地方，沒有學位很難跟別人競爭。

40. 博士 (bóshì) *N*: **PhD degree, doctorate**
張教授是加州大學的中文博士。

專有名詞 Proper Names

1. 洛杉磯 (Luòshānjī) Los Angeles

注釋

1. In 2001 Taiwan discontinued the use of the Joint Examination for high school. The reason was that many people felt that it was unfair and unobjective for the fate of the students to be decided by a single exam, after having studied diligently in junior high school for three years. Therefore the Ministry of Education of the R.O.C., after having researched the problem

thoroughly, decided to adopt a multi-faceted admission policy. Students may be admitted by several different methods, e.g.「推薦甄選」、「申請入學」and「登記分發」. The admission criteria includes grades, leadership, performing skills etc., in addition to the scores of the Basic Aptitude Test（基本學力測驗）taken twice during the last semester of junior high school. In the year 2002 the use of the Joint Examination for university was also discontinued.

2.人人都想念大學 means "Everyone wants to go to college." As stated in Note 3 of Lesson 1, study is of primary importance in Taiwan. The purpose of study in high school is to get into a college and obtain a degree, thereby assuring one of a good job and future career.

3.義務教育 means "compulsory education". In 1922, the Chinese government decided to adopt an educational system similar to the American system. However, only the six years of elementary school was made compulsory at that time and everyone had to pass an exam to go to a junior high school. In 1968, compulsory education was extended to nine years, thereby including junior high school.

4.SAT stands for Scholastic Aptitude/Achievement/Assessment Test. Everyone in the States must take this test in order to apply to college.

5.錄取三萬多人 refers to the rate of students who pass the Joint Examination of Universities and are admitted to a college. This figure used to be around 30% of all examinees, but has been gradually increasing. In 1991, 41% of those who took this exam were admitted to college.

6.小留學生的問題 Some parents do not want their children to receive their education in Taiwan because of the difficulty in getting into high school and college. Therefore they take their children to be educated in other countries, often to the States. Boys formerly could not go abroad after age 16 due to regulations concerning the compulsory military service. According to these old regulations, young children were not allowed to have their own passports either. So some of the parents simply left their children with relatives or friends in the States while they went back to Taiwan to work or care after other members of the family. These children left in the U.S. lacked proper identification papers and often had no immediate family. They encountered many problems and sometimes went astray. The number of these 小留學生 in the States has been estimated to be approximately 50 thousand. In 1988, the Taiwanese government changed the law so that children now can have their own passports. Boys under 18 are now also allowed to study abroad first, then come back to serve in the army.

7. 專科學校 is a junior college. A junior high school graduate can go to a five-year junior college（五年制專科學校）by passing an examination. A senior high school graduate can go to a three-year college（三年制專科學校）. There are also two-year programs（二年制專科學校）for graduates of vocational high school. The course work under all three of these programs is practical and vocation-oriented, useful for finding work.

8. 當兵 Military service in Taiwan is compulsory for all healthy males. The average service is two years, which must be served between the ages of 18-45. Students can request a draft deferment while they are in an accredited college or graduate program.

9. 學費都沒有美國那麼高. For the 1991-92 school year the average tuition at public universities in Taiwan was NT$ 12,837 per semester. The average tuition at private universities was NT$ 38,456 per semester.

文法練習

☞ 一 才 (V) NU M (N)，就…… only V NU M (N) and......

⊙才一個小考就讓你有這麼大的壓力。

Only one small test and you're so stressed-out.

用法說明：「才」在這裡強調數量「少」，而「就」的後面則強調程度比期望的高。前後兩句做相對鮮明的比照。

Explanation: In this usage, 才 emphasizes the relatively small quantity of N which produces a result (preceded by 就) greater than one would expect. The two parts of the sentence express a clear contrast.

練習：請用「才(V) NU M (N)，就……」完成下面對話。

Exercise: Please complete the following dialogues using the "才(V) NU M (N)，就……" pattern.

1. 張：昨天晚上她做了二十道菜，可是我們只有五個客人。

   Chang: Last night she made 20 dishes, but we only had 5 guests.

   李：<u>才五個客人，就做了二十道菜！怎麼吃得完？</u>

   Li: Only five guests and she made 20 dishes?! How could you eat it all?

2. 張：我吃飽了，不吃了。

   李：你才＿＿＿＿＿＿，你平常吃兩碗的啊？

3. 張：這兩個句子我是用三個小時翻完的。

   李：才＿＿＿＿＿＿，太慢了吧！

4. 張：今天是我第一次上中文課，我學了三十個中國字。

   李：才＿＿＿＿＿＿，不錯嘛！

5. 張：我買了一個鳳梨，四塊半。

   李：才＿＿＿＿＿＿，好貴啊！

☞ 二 才

(used to refute or top the previous speaker's statement)

⊙這才是壓力。

Now, this is what you call pressure.

用法說明：這個「才」是用來反駁別人的意見。

Explanation: In this usage, 才 indicates that the speaker is refuting or topping the previous speaker's statement.

練習：請用「才」完成下面對話。

Exercise: Please use 才 to complete the dialogues below.

1. 張：今天的地震好大啊！

   Chang: The earthquake today was really big!

   李：今天的不算什麼，上次的才大呢！

   Li: Today's was nothing, but last time's, that was really big!

2. 張：請隨便坐！對不起，我的房間很亂。

   李：哪裡，________________。

3. 張：我記得你很喜歡背書，不喜歡寫報告。

   李：我才________________，你弄錯了。

4. 張：不要叫我請客，我沒錢。

   李：________________，大家都知道你有很多房子。

5. 張：你這麼晚回家，不怕你爸爸生氣嗎？

   李：我才________________，他自己也很晚回家。

☞ 三 幸虧／幸好／還好／好在……，要不然……

Fortunately......, otherwise......

⊙幸虧我們家移民了，要不然我一定念不了大學。

Fortunately, our family immigrated; otherwise, I definitely wouldn't be able to go to college.

用法說明： 表示慶幸，「幸虧」的後面是已成的事實，如果這個事實沒發生的話，「要不然」後面的情形就會發生。

Explanation: This pattern indicates that the speaker is happy that the fact stated after 幸虧 has occurred or is true. If this were not the case, the undesirable situation following 要不然 would have occurred.

練習： 請用「幸虧……，要不然……」改寫下面句子。

Exercise: Please rewrite the following sentences using the "幸虧……，要不然……" pattern.

1. 要是他坐了那班飛機，他也死了。
   If he had been on that flight, he would have died too.
   →幸虧他沒坐那班飛機，要不然也死了。
   Fortunately, he didn't take that flight; otherwise, he would have died too.
2. 要是你上次考試不及格，今天就得補考了。
   ……………………………………………………………
3. 要是昨天下雨，我們搬家就有問題了。
   ……………………………………………………………
4. 要是丟了的那個東西很值錢，他一定很著急。
   ……………………………………………………………
5. 要是附近沒有洗手間，就麻煩了。
   ……………………………………………………………

☞ 四 會……的 will, should

⊙他會慢慢適應的。 He will be able to slowly adjust.

用法說明： 「會」在這裡表示「將來很可能」。「的」表示肯定，語氣較婉轉。

Explanation: Here, 會 indicates that the future situation indicated is likely, and 的 indicates that it is definite, so the tone, while definite,is relatively mild and tactful.

練習： 請用「會……的」完成下面對話。

Exercise: Please use “會……的” to complete the dialogues below.

1. 張：你哥哥明天一定來嗎？

   Chang: Is your older brother definitely coming tomorrow?

   李：你放心，他一定會來的。

   Li: Don’t worry, he should definitely come.

2. 張：這件事情不告訴爸爸，行不行？

   李：不行，如果你不告訴他，他會＿＿＿＿＿＿＿。

3. 張：我妹妹的男朋友離開她了，她不吃也不喝，怎麼辦？

   李：別擔心，她會＿＿＿＿＿＿＿。

4. 張：你出國以後，大概就不容易再見到你了。

   李：沒關係，我＿＿＿＿＿＿。

5. 張：怎麼辦？我的病恐怕好不了了。

   李：你想得太多了，只要你聽醫生的話，不會＿＿＿＿＿＿＿。

☞ 五 滿

(I) 滿 NU-M-(N)　　to reach or fully attain NU M (N)

⊙……，可是男孩子滿了十八歲就得先去當兵了。

......, but when boys reach 18 years of age, they first have to serve in the army.

用法說明：「滿 NU-M-(N)」表示已達到某種「實足」的程度。

Explanation: This pattern expresses a state of having reached or fully attained a specified quantity.

練習：請用「滿 NU-M-(N)」完成下面對話。

Exercise: Please use “滿 NU-M-(N)” to complete the following dialogues.

1. 張：你今年二十歲了吧？

   Chang: You’re 20 years old this year, aren’t you?

   李：我的生日是下個月三號，還差一個多星期才滿二十歲。

   Li: My birthday is the 3rd of next month, so I still have a little over a week until I’m twenty.

2. 張：你說這家商店送香水 (perfume)，他們怎麼沒送我？

李：買東西滿＿＿＿＿＿＿＿，才送一瓶香水。

3. 張：選這門課的人才三個，學校還讓王教授教嗎？

李：如果不滿＿＿＿＿＿＿＿，恐怕就有問題。

4. 張：你怎麼有這麼多的時間去旅行？不必上班嗎？

李：我到公司已經滿了＿＿＿＿＿＿＿，可以有兩個星期的假。

5. 張：你兒子今年要上小學了吧？

李：不行啊！他還沒滿＿＿＿＿＿＿＿。

（II）V滿　something is filled by the action

用法說明：「滿」在此為結果動詞語尾，Actual Type 跟 Potential Type 都可以。

Explanation: This 滿 is a RE (resultative verb ending). The RC can be used in either Actual Type form or Potential Type form.

練習：請填上合適的「V滿」結果動詞形式。

Exercise: Please fill in the blanks with an appropriate "V滿" in RC form.

1. 先把這個箱子裝滿，再裝另外一個。
   First, fill this suitcase then the other one.
2. 那家旅館還＿＿＿＿＿＿，還有空房間。
3. 對林教授的課有興趣的人不多，教室總是＿＿＿＿＿＿。
4. 老師要我們寫五頁的報告，我查的資料才這麼一點，怎麼＿＿＿＿＿＿？
5. 他房間的牆上＿＿＿＿＿＿他自己的畫。

☞ 六　只好

to have no alternative but to. . . . . ., can only, cannot but

⊙這些人只好當完兵再考大學嘍？

Then these people have to first do military service before taking he exam for college?

用法說明：「只好」表示「只能這麼做」，所以「只好」的後面是此刻唯一能行的辦法。語氣有稍許無奈。

Explanation: 只好 indicates that something is the only alternative. This alternative always follows 只好. The tone implies that this final alternative is not necessarily ideal either.

練習：請用「只好」完成下面句子。

Exercise: Please complete the following sentences which contain 只好.

1. 我買不到蘋果，只好買葡萄.
   I can't buy apples, so I had better buy grapes.
2. 明天的考試，我還沒準備好，只好＿＿＿＿＿＿。
3. 我們不出產小麥，只好＿＿＿＿＿＿。
4. 他的成績太爛了，只好＿＿＿＿＿＿。
5. 我說了半天，他還是不了解，我只好＿＿＿＿＿＿。

☞ 七 不管／不論／無論……都……
regardless of whether......(all), no matter whether...... (all)

⊙臺灣的大學，不管公立的私立的，學費都沒有美國那麼高。

Universities in Taiwan, (regardless of) whether they are public or private, all have lower tuition than in America .

用法說明：「不管」的後面可加疑問詞 (QW)、選擇式 (A/ not A) 或兩個相對的詞，表示不同的情況。雖然有不同的情況，「都」後面的事實都不受影響。

Explanation: You can place a Question Word, a Choice Type structure (A/ not A), or two opposites after 不管 to indicate possible situations. This pattern indicates that even if this situation (or situations) occurs, it will not influence the fact expressed after 都.

練習：請用「不管……都……」完成下面對話。

Exercise: Please use the "不管……都……" pattern to complete the dialogues below.

1. 張：如果明天下雨，你還去不去？
   Chang: If it rains tomorrow, will you still go?

李：不管天氣怎麼樣，我都要去。

Li: I'll be going no matter what the weather is like.

不管天氣好不好，我都要去。

I'll be going whether it rains or not.

不管天氣好壞，我都要去。

I'll be going whether the weather is good or bad.

2. 張：我看你別去了，那個地方太遠了。

李：不管＿＿＿＿＿＿＿＿＿＿＿。

3. 張：你喜歡吃法國菜，還是中國菜？

李：不論＿＿＿＿＿＿＿＿＿＿＿。

4. 張：下星期，你哪天有空？

李：不論＿＿＿＿＿＿＿＿＿＿＿。

5. 張：每個人都得買票嗎？

李：無論＿＿＿＿＿＿＿＿＿＿＿。

☞ 八 像……這樣／那樣…… ......like...... (similar to)

⊙像你這樣出國留學的人多不多？

Are there many people like you who study abroad?

用法說明： 這個句型跟第五課的「像……什麼的」不同。「像」後面指出特定的對象，「這樣」的後面是兩件事物相同的特點。

Explanation: This sentence pattern is not the same as the pattern "像……什麼的" (Chapter 5). Here, the word or phrase following 像 points out a specific object, and the word or phrase following 這樣 refers to a specific trait shared by that object and the subject.

練習： 請用「像……這樣／那樣……」改寫下面句子。

Exercise: Please rewrite the sentences below using the "像……這樣／那樣……" pattern.

1. 跟她一樣漂亮的女孩子多不多？

   Are there many girls as pretty as her?

   →像她那樣漂亮的女孩子多不多？

Are there many pretty girls like her?

2. 我從來沒看過跟我弟弟房間一樣髒的地方。

……………………………………………………………………………

3. 跟宮保雞丁一樣的菜，我都覺得太辣了。

……………………………………………………………………………

4. 柳橙這一類的水果，在美國到處都買得到。

……………………………………………………………………………

5.「不敢當」這一類的客氣話，我們還沒學過。

……………………………………………………………………………

☞ 九 不是……，就是……　If not......, then......

⊙……不是在國內念研究所，就是出國留學。

......they either go to graduate school within the country or they study abroad.

用法說明：「不是」後面的情況跟「就是」後面的情況，兩者當中一定有一種成立。

Explanation: This pattern indicates that of the two situations mentioned after 不是 and 就是 one of them is certain to occur or is certain to be true.

練習：請根據提示用「不是……就是……」回答下面問題。

Exercise: Please answer the following questions using the “不是……就是……” pattern and the information in parentheses.

1. 老張到哪裡去了？（辦公室、女朋友家）

   Where did old Chang go?

   →不是在辦公室，就是在女朋友家。

   He's either at the office or at his girlfriend's house.

2. 你在這家餐廳吃飯都吃什麼？（宮保雞丁、青豆蝦仁）

……………………………………………………………………………

3. 這裡冬天的天氣怎麼樣？（颳風、下雨）

……………………………………………………………………………

4. 他這兩天忙什麼？（查資料、寫報告）

....

5. 這是誰的書？（哥哥的、姐姐的）

....

☞ 十 V得差不多了　almost finished (via V)

⊙寫得差不多了。

I'm almost finished writing it.

用法說明：「V得差不多了」表示某件事情在進行中，而且快要達到預期中的目標。

Explanation: This pattern indicates that some action is in progress and that the desired goal will soon be reached or attained.

練習：請用「V得差不多了」回答下面問題。

Exercise: Please answer the following questions using the pattern "V得差不多了".

1. 明天的考試，你準備好了沒有？

   Have you finished preparing for tomorrow's test?

   →準備得差不多了。

   I'm pretty much done.

2. 王先生要買你們公司的電腦，這件事談得怎麼樣了？

....

3. 野餐要吃的東西都買了嗎？

....

4. 你衣服洗好了沒有？我們該走了！

....

5. 客人都來了嗎？可以開始了吧？

....

課室活動

Role playing:

1. Three students. One student acts as a teacher, the second acts as a student who got the highest score on a recent test, and the third as a classmate who accuses the other student of having cheated on his test. The actors should try to express the lively discussion one might expect in such a situation. Some useful supplementary words include: 作弊 (zuò//bì; to cheat on an exam, in a contest, or in gambling), 懶(lǎn; to be lazy), 偷看 (tōukàn; to peek), 答案 (dá'àn; answer), 侮辱 (wǔrù; to insult; humiliate), 忌妒 or 嫉妒 (jìdù or jídù; to be jealous of).

2. Two students : One acts as a parent who is visiting the U.S. from Taiwan. The other acts as his/her friend who has been living in the States for a long time. The parent wants his/her child to study in the States and is asking about the education system. The parent should ask questions such as: 怎麼選學校？怎麼申請？大概的教育制度 (zhìdù; system) 怎麼樣？Some useful supplementary words include: 以上 (yǐshàng ; more than; over; above), 學區 (xuéqū; school district), 設備 (shèbèi; facilities; equipment).

短文

小留學生的問題

在台灣，每個男人都有當兵的義務。從前政府規定，16歲到18歲的男孩，不能隨便出國，得等當完兵才可以。

台灣的聯考競爭激烈，有些父母擔心小孩子受不了聯考的壓力，所以想辦法在兒子16歲以前，把他送到國外念書。可是父母還得在台灣工作，只能在放假的時候，去國外看孩子。這些小孩子有的住在父母的朋友家，有的一個人住在父母給他們買的房子裏。他們大部分英文並不好，除了功課的問題以外，還要適應環境。碰到問題，不管是心理的、身體的、生活的，都沒有父母在旁邊幫忙，當然覺得很怕、很孤單。不少孩子就這樣學壞了，像打人、考試作弊什麼的。這時候父母想把孩子接回來，恐怕孩子也很難再回到台灣的學校念書了。

Vocabulary:

1. 規定 (guīdìng) : to regulate; here, to restrict
2. 作弊 (zuò//bì) : to cheat on a test

第八課

你也打工嗎

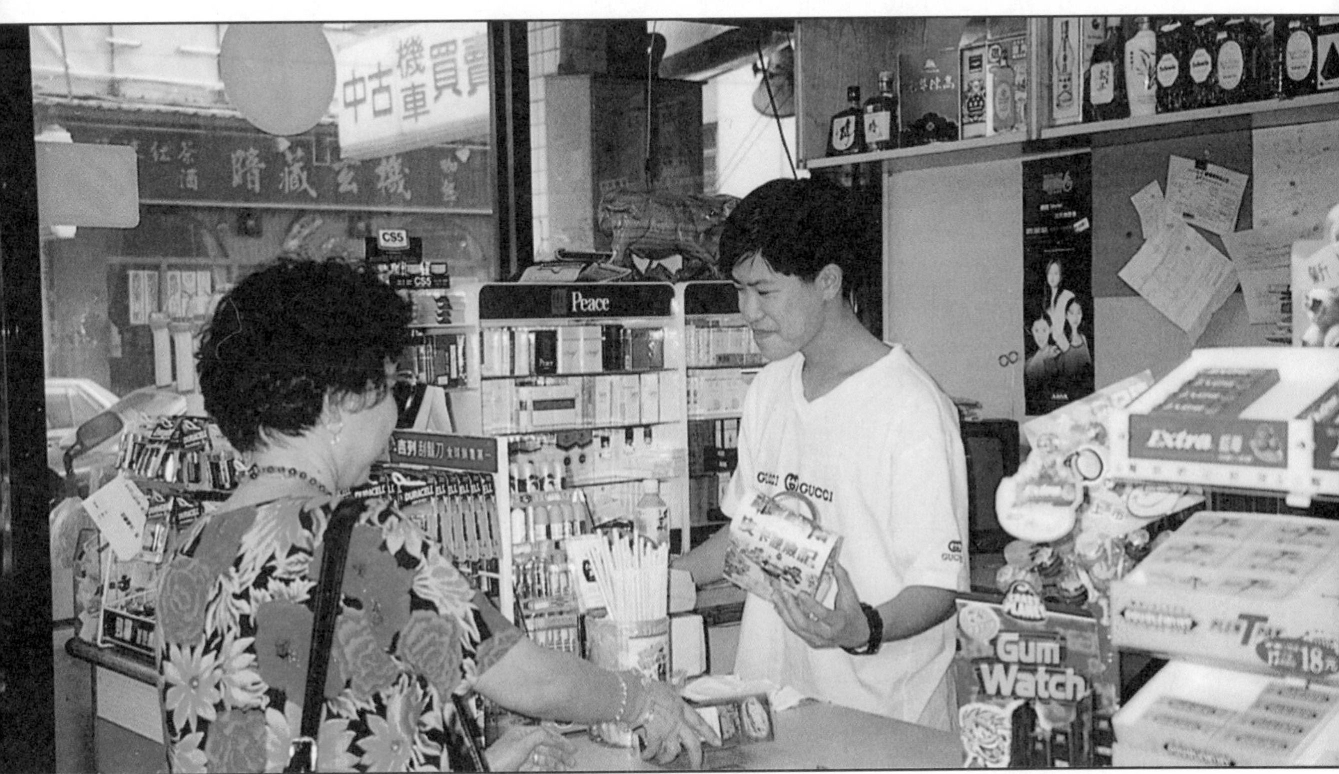

・在便利商店打工的高中生（劉咪咪提供）

（學校湖邊）

偉立：天晴了，真好。（拿出口香糖）要不要？

美真：好啊。（拿了一片）前幾天一直下雨，又濕又冷。

台麗：今天不冷不熱，風也不大，這種天氣很舒服，出來野餐最好了。

建國（拿出可樂）：來，一個人一罐，我請客，別客氣。

美真：你今天**可**真大方[1]！

偉立：那是因為他昨天剛拿到第一次打工賺的錢。

台麗：哦？！那是該好好兒地慶祝**一下**。

美真：才請我們喝一罐可樂，太小氣了吧？該請吃大餐**才**對。

建國：你忍心把我辛苦賺來的錢一次就吃**光**啊？

偉立：他是很辛苦，每次都很晚才回來，累得一躺下就睡著了。早上不但聽不見鬧鐘的聲音，我叫他也叫不醒。

美真：你**到底**打什麼工啊？**怎麼這麼**累？

建國：我在一家小酒館[2]做服務生，越晚客人越多。

台麗：你為什麼不找個輕鬆一點的工作？

建國：我什麼經驗都沒有，而且酒館的小費也多，我想存點錢去旅行。這裡還有麵包、蘋果，誰要吃，自己來。

美真：（拿起一個麵包）你一個星期去幾次？

建國：星期三、星期六，晚上八點到十二點。有時候還要替別人代班。

台麗：（拿了一個蘋果）老闆怎麼樣？

建國：（又開了一罐可樂）大家都說他是小氣鬼。每個鐘頭只給我們兩塊錢。有一次我不小心打破了一個杯子，他不但扣我錢，還罵我笨手笨腳。

偉立：那是常有的事情，老闆總是這樣的。我第一次在餐廳打工的時候送錯了菜，老闆把我罵了一頓，就叫我走路[3]

了。

美真：你現在在哪裡打工？

偉立：我每星期在圖書館打六個小時的工。

美真：做些什麼？

偉立：有人來借書、還書的時候，我登記**一下**。

台麗：那很輕鬆嘛！

偉立：也不一定，得看什麼時候。要是沒人來的話，我可以看點書，這是最大的好處。

建國：下一次我也要去申請在圖書館工讀，有錢賺，可以看書，還可以欣賞漂亮的女生[4]。

偉立：你們兩個呢？也打工嗎？

美真：我上個週末**才**去替一個中國人看孩子[5]。我從來沒有帶小孩的經驗，孩子一哭，我就手忙腳亂，不知道怎麼辦才好了。

台麗：我剛來，想先適應**一下**環境，而且我這學期有獎學金，所以沒有打工。不過，在臺灣我一直當家教[6]。

偉立：（拿起一個蘋果）你教什麼？

台麗：我到一些中學生家去教他們英文。有些父母很客氣，每次去都有點心吃；有些學生不用功，教起來很累，這個錢也不好賺。

美真：現在臺灣學生打工的情形很普遍，送報**啊**，做店員**啊**，到公司做小妹[7]**啊**，到速食店去當服務生**啊**，還有人去擺地攤，做什麼的都有。

偉立：真的嗎？我以為中國父母都只要孩子念書，不讓他們打工。

美真：那是從前，臺灣社會改變了。現在很多人覺得打工是一種很好的經驗，不但可以學到課本裡沒有的東西，還可以賺零用錢。

建國：哎呀！我不能忍了，喝太多了，我得去上廁所[8]了。

・在工廠打工的高中生（劉咪咪提供）

生詞及例句

1.湖ㄏㄨˊ (hú) *N*: **lake**

2.口ㄎㄡˇ香ㄒㄧㄤ糖ㄊㄤˊ (kǒuxiāngtáng)

N: **chewing gum**（**M**：片／包）

3.一ㄧˋ直ㄓˊ (yìzhí) *A*: **always, all along, continually**

我一直不明白他為什麼要移民。

4.可ㄎㄜˇ樂ㄌㄜˋ (kělè) *N*: **cola (the beverage)**（**M**：罐／瓶）

5.請ㄑㄧㄥˇ客ㄎㄜˋ (qǐng//kè)

VO: **to host, to invite, to treat someone (to dinner, etc.)**

他說他要請客，不知道他要請我吃飯，還是看電影。

6.大ㄉㄚˋ方ㄈㄤ (dàfāng) *SV*: **to be generous ; natural and poised**

(1)他真大方，送你這麼貴的禮物。

(2)你表妹又漂亮又大方，難怪這麼多人喜歡她。

7.賺ㄓㄨㄢˋ (zhuàn) *V*: **to earn; to make a profit**

他念大學的學費都是自己打工賺來的。

8.小ㄒㄧㄠˇ氣ㄑㄧˋ (xiǎoqì) *SV*: **to be stingy, mean**

他幫你拿了兩件行李，你只給一塊錢，太小氣了吧？

小ㄒㄧㄠˇ氣ㄑㄧˋ鬼ㄍㄨㄟˇ (xiǎoqìguǐ)

N: **cheapskate , tightwad, miser**

王先生從來不請客，大家都說他是小氣鬼。

鬼ㄍㄨㄟˇ (guǐ) *N*: **ghost; spirit; demon; devil**

酒ㄐㄧㄡˇ鬼ㄍㄨㄟˇ (jiǔguǐ) *N*: **heavy drinker, drunkard**

9.忍ㄖㄣˇ心ㄒㄧㄣ (rěnxīn)

VO: **to be hardhearted enough to, to have the heart to, to bear to**

他正在生病，你忍心告訴他那個壞消息嗎？

忍ㄖㄣˇ (rěn) *V*: **to put up with, tolerate, bear, endure**

我忍了很久，最後還是跟他說了。

忍ㄖㄣˇ住ㄓㄨˋ (rěn//zhù)

RC: **to control oneself, to keep oneself from doing something**

他聽說他母親死了，忍不住哭了起來。

10. 光ㄍㄨㄤ (guāng)　*RE*: **used up, exhausted**

我帶來的錢很快就用光了。

11. 鬧ㄋㄠˋ鐘ㄓㄨㄥ (nàozhōng)　*N*: **alarm clock**

鬧ㄋㄠˋ (nào)

V: **to create a disturbance, to agitate, to trouble, to disturb**

(1) 孩子一生病，就鬧得全家都睡不好。

(2) 他兒子沒申請到獎學金，他就來辦公室鬧，把東西都打壞了。

(3) 這個房子聽說鬧鬼 (be haunted)，所以沒人敢住。

12. 叫ㄐㄧㄠˋ醒ㄒㄧㄥˇ (jiào//xǐng)　*RC*: **to wake someone up**

已經九點半了，他還在睡，你為什麼還不叫醒他？

醒ㄒㄧㄥˇ (xǐng)　*V*: **to be awake**

他醒了，可是還躺在床上不想起來。

13. 到ㄉㄠˋ底ㄉㄧˇ (dàodǐ)

A: **in the end, at last, finally; to completion, to the end, in the final analysis (used in an interrogative sentence to indicate an attempt to get to the bottom of the matter)**

你昨天說要去，今天又說不要去，你到底要不要去？

14. 經ㄐㄧㄥ驗ㄧㄢˋ (jīngyàn)　*N/V*: **experience**

這種工作，我沒做過，一點經驗也沒有，可是我一定會好好地學。

有ㄧㄡˇ經ㄐㄧㄥ驗ㄧㄢˋ (yǒu jīngyàn)　*SV*: **to be experienced**

我們需要一位有經驗的醫生，你剛畢業，不行。

對ㄉㄨㄟˋ……(X) 有ㄧㄡˇ經ㄐㄧㄥ驗ㄧㄢˋ (duì......(X)......yǒu jīngyàn)

PT: **has experience in...... (X)**

我表姐是小學老師，對教小孩子很有經驗。

15. 小ㄒㄧㄠˇ費ㄈㄟˋ (xiǎofèi)　*N*: **a tip, pourboire**

要是他們的服務很好，我就多給一點小費。

16. 存ㄘㄨㄣˊ錢ㄑㄧㄢˊ (cún//qián) *VO*: **to deposit money, to save up**

(1)我爸爸給我的錢，我還用不著，先存在銀行裡吧！

(2)我哥哥說他要存錢買一個照像機。

存ㄘㄨㄣˊ (cún) *V*: **to deposit, to keep**

我打工賺的錢還沒用，都存起來了。

17. 代ㄉㄞˋ班ㄅㄢ (dài//bān)

VO: **to fill in for someone's shift at work**

張大年病了，不能去打工，今天晚上我得代他的班。

代ㄉㄞˋ課ㄎㄜˋ (dài//kè) *VO*: **to substitute teach**

林教授明天不能來，誰代他那門心理學的課呢？

18. 老ㄌㄠˇ闆ㄅㄢˇ (lǎobǎn)

N: **the boss, the owner of a shop or business**

19. 罵ㄇㄚˋ (mà) *V*: **to scold**

他今天被老師罵了，因為又忘了做功課。

20. 笨ㄅㄣˋ手ㄕㄡˇ笨ㄅㄣˋ腳ㄐㄧㄠˇ (bèn shǒu bèn jiǎo) *IE*: **to be clumsy**

我真是笨手笨腳，這個月我已經打破了七個盤子了。

笨ㄅㄣˋ (bèn) *SV*: **to be stupid**

腳ㄐㄧㄠˇ (jiǎo) *N*: **foot**

21. 頓ㄉㄨㄣˋ (dùn) *M*: **(used for meals , scoldings)**

我生日那天，朋友們請我吃了一頓大餐。

22. 叫ㄐㄧㄠˋ／請ㄑㄧㄥˇ…… 走ㄗㄡˇ路ㄌㄨˋ (jiào/qǐng... zǒulù)

PT: **to fire someone, to dismiss someone from a job**

他三天沒來上班了，是不是老闆請他走路了？

23. 還ㄏㄨㄢˊ (huán) *V*: **to repay, give back, return**

有借有還，再借不難。

24. 登ㄉㄥ記ㄐㄧˋ (dēngjì)

V: **to register, to enter one's name, to sign up**

誰要參加這個活動，請來系辦公室登記。

25. 一ㄧˊ下ㄒㄧㄚˋ (yíxià) a little, a while

(1)你頭髮的樣子改變一下，也許會好看一點。

(2)你要不要進來坐一下？

下ㄒㄧㄚˋ (xià) *M*: **(for downward actions of the hand)**

他說了不該說的話以後，馬上敲了三下桌子。

26. 好ㄏㄠˇ處ㄔㄨˋ (hǎochù) *N*: **advantage, benefit**

在臺灣學中文的好處是可以天天練習。

壞ㄏㄨㄞˋ處ㄔㄨˋ (huàichù) *N*: **disadvantage, harm**

27. 工ㄍㄨㄥ讀ㄉㄨˊ (gōngdú)

V: **work-study, work arranged for students by the school**

念大學的時候，我在圖書館工讀了兩年。

讀ㄉㄨˊ (dú) *V*: **to read; to go to / attend school or college**

讀ㄉㄨˊ書ㄕㄨ (dú//shū) *VO*: **to study, to read**

28. 女ㄋㄩˇ生ㄕㄥ (nǚshēng) *N*: **school age girl, female student**

男ㄋㄢˊ生ㄕㄥ (nánshēng) *N*: **school age boy, male student**

臺灣的學生宿舍，男生、女生是分開的。

29. 週ㄓㄡ末ㄇㄛˋ (zhōumò) *N*: **weekend**

30. 看ㄎㄢ (kān) *V*: **to look after, to take care of, to watch for**

錢先生跟他太太要去旅行，請我去替他們看房子。

看ㄎㄢ家ㄐㄧㄚ (kān//jiā) *VO*: **to mind the house**

31. 帶ㄉㄞˋ (dài) *V*: **take care of (a child), to bring up the young**

我沒想到把孩子帶大這麼不容易。

32. 手ㄕㄡˇ忙ㄇㄤˊ腳ㄐㄧㄠˇ亂ㄌㄨㄢˋ (shǒu máng jiǎo luàn)

IE: **to be in a great flurry, to be in a frantic rush**

那幾個男生在廚房裡手忙腳亂地給我們做飯。

亂ㄌㄨㄢˋ (luàn)

SV/A/RE: **to be messy, disordered, confused / disorderly, groundlessly / disordered, untidy, rumpled**

(1)小弟，你的房間真亂，桌上、地上、床上都有書。你怎麼知道我借你的那本書在哪裡？

(2)你說我拿了你的書，我沒有！你沒看見我拿，怎麼可以亂說？

(3) 我桌上的資料是要交給老師的，你別弄亂了。

33. 家ㄐㄧㄚ 教ㄐㄧㄠˋ (jiājiào)　　*N*: **a private tutor**

他的成績不好，所以他媽媽給他請了個家教。

34. 普ㄆㄨˇ 遍ㄅㄧㄢˋ (pŭbiàn)　　*SV*: **to be widespread, common, universal**

學生在考試以前開夜車是很普遍的情形。

普ㄆㄨˇ 通ㄊㄨㄥ (pŭtōng)　　*SV*: **common, mediocre, ordinary**

我們只是普通朋友，沒有特別的關係。

35. 店ㄉㄧㄢˋ 員ㄩㄢˊ (diànyuán)

N: **shop assistant, sales person (in a shop)**

你一直在那家鞋店當店員嗎？

36. 擺ㄅㄞˇ 地ㄉㄧˋ 攤ㄊㄢ (băi//dìtān)

VO: **to display goods for sale on a mat out on the street**

在紐約擺地攤的都賣些什麼東西？

擺ㄅㄞˇ (băi)　　*V*: **to display, spread out, place**

請你把那個書架擺在書桌右邊。

地ㄉㄧˋ 攤ㄊㄢ (dìtān)

N: **a mat on which to display goods for sale outdoors**

地攤上的東西雖然便宜，可是不一定好。

37. 社ㄕㄜˋ 會ㄏㄨㄟˋ (shèhuì)　　*N*: **society**

現在社會上女人上班的情形很普遍。

社ㄕㄜˋ 會ㄏㄨㄟˋ 學ㄒㄩㄝˊ (shèhuìxué)　　*N*: **sociology**

38. 改ㄍㄞˇ 變ㄅㄧㄢˋ (găibiàn)　　*V*: **to change, alter, transform**

我本來想找工作，現在計畫改變了，想念研究所了。

39. 課ㄎㄜˋ 本ㄅㄣˇ (kèbĕn)　　*N*: **textbook**

你們心理學，用什麼課本？

課ㄎㄜˋ 文ㄨㄣˊ (kèwén)　　*N*: **text in a school book**

這本會話 (conversation) 書，每一課都分三部分：生字、句型 (jùxíng, sentence pattern) 跟課文。

40. 零ㄌㄧㄥˊ 用ㄩㄥˋ 錢ㄑㄧㄢˊ (língyòngqián)

N: **pocket money, money for incidental expenses, allowance**

每個月除了房錢、飯錢，我還需要二十塊零用錢看電影、喝飲料。

41. 上ㄕㄤˋ廁ㄘㄜˋ所ㄙㄨㄛˇ (shàng//cèsuǒ)

VO: **to go to the toilet , to use the restroom**

我不敢喝太多水，就是怕要上廁所，太麻煩！

廁ㄘㄜˋ所ㄙㄨㄛˇ (cèsuǒ) *N*: **toilet, lavatory**

這是男廁所，你不要走錯了。

注釋

1. "你今天可真大方！" means: "You are really generous today!". "太小氣了吧?!" means: "Aren't you stingy!". This kind of joking can be used among good friends, however, in other situations it is considered to be very rude.
2. 小酒館 refers to a "pub". These are getting more popular in Taiwan. Many people just call them by their English name--pub.
3. 叫……走路 means "to tell (somebody) to leave". In other words, to fire someone. The slang expression 炒魷魚 (chǎo//yóuyú) was derived from Cantonese and has the same meaning, and it is used as follows: 他被老闆炒魷魚了 (He was fired by the boss.), 老闆想炒我魷魚 (The boss wants to fire me.) This expression literally means "to stir-fry squids". It came to represent getting fired because squid curls up when it is fried, and there is an expression for leaving a job 捲鋪蓋 (juǎn//pūgài, to roll up one's bedding). Thus the curling, rolled up fried squid evokes the idea of firing someone from a job. The formal expression for being fired is 解雇 (jiěgù), e.g. 他被老闆解雇了 and 老闆想解雇我.
4. 男生 / 女生 is short for 男學生 / 女學生. In Taiwan, these are general terms referring to any young person or anyone who looks young, since most

young people are students. Sometimes the young people are called 男孩/女孩, because Chinese consider unmarried young people to still be children (孩子). Most Chinese are not used to referring to a person as 男人/女人, because these terms imply a certain air of disapproval. The terms 那個男的/女的 would be used instead.

5. 看孩子, i.e. baby sitting, is not popular in Taiwan. Most Chinese parents do not feel comfortable hiring an acquaintance or a stranger to care for their children. They either leave the children with their parents, take the children out with them, or choose not to go out.

6. 家教 is short for 家庭教師. It refers to a private tutor or teacher. People hire 家庭教師 to help their child with his/her studies, especially if the child's scholastic record indicates that he/she may not be able to pass the 聯考. 家教 usually go to the child's house once or twice a week for two or three hours each time.

7. 在公司做小妹 means "to work at a company as an office helper". 小妹 literally means "little sister". Some companies hire girls who attend school in the evening as daytime office helpers. Office helpers perform simple tasks such as delivering documents, answering phone calls, receiving visitors, etc. Boys who do this job are called 小弟, however, they are far less common.

8. 上廁所 means "to go to the toilet". It is more polite to say 去/用 洗手間, meaning "to use the washroom". Many students use the slang expression 上一號. Another more subtle expression is 去方便一下.

文法練習

不 SV_1 不 SV_2

neither SV_1 nor SV_2 (somewhere in between)

⊙今天不冷不熱……

Today is neither hot nor cold......

用法說明：兩個 SV 都是單音節，意思相對。「不 SV_1 不 SV_2」表示 介於兩者之間的程度 。

Explanation : This pattern is used with two single-syllable stative verbs with opposite meanings. "不 SV_1 不 SV_2" indicates that the actual situation is somewhere between the two stated extremes.

練習：請用「不 SV_1 不 SV_2 」改寫下面各句。

Exercise: Please use "不 SV_1 不 SV_2" to rewrite the following sentences.

1. 這條褲子不太長也不太短，你穿正合適。

   This pair of pants is neither too long nor too short; it fits you perfectly.

   →這條褲子不長不短，你穿正合適。

   This pair of pants is just right in length; it fits you perfectly.

2. 我準備的菜不太多也不太少，剛夠四個人吃。

   ....

3. 十五、六歲的小孩，不算大也不算小，問題比較多。

   ....

4. 那個桌子不太高也不太矮，正合我的需要。

   ....

5. 這件衣服穿了幾年了，不新了，可是也不算舊，丟了可惜，留著也不想穿，真麻煩。

   ....

☞ 二 可 (used to emphasize the tone of the speaker)

⊙你今天可真大方!

You really are generous today!

用法說明：多用於口語，放在副詞、動詞、SV……等前面，表示強調語氣。可表示 a. 不以為然，b. 強調程度，c. 事情好不容易完了。可如跟 SV一起用，SV 之前應有真、太等副詞，要不然 SV 後面應有了或呢。

Explanation : This is used more often in informal speech. It is placed in front of an Adverb, a V, a SV, etc, to express a stronger tone. Sometimes it is used to indicate a. disagreement with the previous speaker, b. to emphasize degree, c. to show that matter is very difficult to resolve. If 可 is used with a SV, the adverbs 真 or 太 should be placed before the SV; otherwise a 了 or 呢 should be used after the SV.

練習：Exercise:

㈠請把「可」放在句中合適的地方。

Please place 可 in the appropriate place in the following sentences.

例：我等了那麼久，你來了。

I've waited so long. you've arrived.

→我等了那麼久，你可來了。

I've waited so long; you're finally here.

a. 1. 我不像你這麼有錢，想買什麼就買什麼。

....

2. 老張不是小孩子，你以為他會聽你的嗎？

....

b. 1. 李小姐真愛看電影，她每天都要看一場。

....

2. 這裡的房子不便宜，我們還是去別的地方買吧！

....

3. 誰說這個孩子什麼都不懂，他知道的事情多呢！

....

4. 這個藥每四個鐘頭吃一次，你別忘了。

....

c. 1. 這一個月的衣服，我洗完了。

....

2. 這麼多的課，我都上完了。星期天要好好地休息休息了。

....

㈡請根據提示，用「那可」或「可」完成下面對話。

1. Please use 那可 or 可 to complete the following dialogues according to the information provided in parentheses.

例：張：怎麼辦？我寫好的報告丟了。（麻煩）

Chang: What should I do? I've lost the report that I finished.

李：那可麻煩了。

Li: What a pain!

a. 1. 張：在加油站打工，小費一定很多。（不一定）

李：那可＿＿＿＿＿＿，得看哪一區。

2. 張：小王那麼笨手笨腳的，一定不會跳舞。（會跳）

李：你錯了，他可＿＿＿＿＿＿。

b. 1. 張：這個週末我哥哥姐姐的孩子都要到我家來。（熱鬧）

李：那可＿＿＿＿＿＿。

2. 張：我打破盤子的事，老闆知道了嗎？（不得了）

李：怎麼能告訴他?!要是他知道了，那可＿＿＿＿＿＿。

3. 張：我有車，可以幫你搬家。（太好了）

李：那可＿＿＿＿＿＿。

4. 張：我這學期的學費都被偷走了！（怎麼辦）

李：那可＿＿＿＿＿＿。

c. 1. 張：老陳的博士論文寫了四年，昨天交出去了。（寫完）

李：他可＿＿＿＿＿＿。

☞ 三 V 一下　V one time, V once , V a bit

⊙那是該好好地慶祝一下。

In that case , we should do some proper celebrating.

⊙有人來借書、還書的時候，我登記一下。

When people come to borrow and return books, I check them in and out.

用法說明：「下」是動量詞 (Mv)。「一下」是「一會兒」的意思。「V 一下」表示一次短促的動作。「V一下」使語氣比較婉轉，感覺不那麼嚴肅。

Explanation: 下 serves as a measure word for verbs. 一下 means 一會兒 (for a moment, for a very brief time). V 一下 indicates one short action. However, V 一下, should not always be taken literally. It often serves to simply lighten the tone of a statement or request to make it more polite.

練習：請用「V一下」改寫下面句子。

Exercise: Please use "V一下" to rewrite the sentences below.

1. 你新買的公寓，我們可不可以參觀參觀？
   Can we take a tour of your new apartment?
   →你新買的公寓，我們可不可以參觀一下？
   Can we take a quick tour of your new apartment?
2. 這裡風景不錯，我們下車欣賞欣賞吧！
   ………………………………………………………………………………
3. 考完了，我們開個舞會輕鬆輕鬆。
   ………………………………………………………………………………
4. 這兩件衣服，我比較了以後，覺得還是綠的好。
   ………………………………………………………………………………
5. 來、來、來，我給你們介紹。
   ………………………………………………………………………………

☞ 四 才 (indicator of prerequisite)

⊙該請我們吃大餐才對。

It's only fitting that you should treat us to eat a big meal.

⊙孩子一哭，我就手忙腳亂，不知道怎麼辦才好了。

As soon as a child cries, I get in a fluster; I don't know what to do (to properly resolve the situation).

用法說明：這個「才」跟第三課一樣，也是強調「條件」，但「才」後面常是「好」、「對」、「行」、「可以」等字。

Explanation: Here, 才 is used in the same way as in Chapter 3, indicating the conditions required to achieve a desired state or outcome. However, in this use of 才, the words 好, 對, 行, or 可以 are often placed after it.

練習：請用「才對」、「才好」改寫下面句子。

Exercise: Please rewrite the following sentences using 才對 or 才好.

1. 這篇報告很難寫，我不知道應該怎麼開始。

This report is very difficult to write; I don't know how to start.

→這篇報告很難寫，我不知道怎麼開始才好。

This report is very difficult to write; I don't know how to start (in order to get good results).

2. 他幫了我很多忙，我不知道應該怎麼謝謝他。

....

3. 學生考壞了，罵沒有用，應該多鼓勵。

....

4. 跟人約會，一定要準時到。

....

5. 借了錢，一定要還。

....

☞ 五 V光　V up (use up, exhaust), V till it is used up

⊙你忍心把我辛苦賺來的錢一次就吃光啊？

You would have the heart to take my hard-earned money and swallow it up in one shot?

用法說明：「光」在此是 RE，是「完」、「盡」、「一點不剩」的意思，使用時均為 Actual Type。可跟「把」一起用。

Explanation: Here, 光 serves as a RE, meaning that some thing is finished, used up, exhausted, or done to the greatest extent possible. It is used in the Actual Type form, and can be used together with 把.

練習：Exercise:

㈠請用「把」跟「V光」改寫下面句子。

Please rewrite the following sentences using 把 and V 光.

1. 冰箱裡的啤酒，老闆都喝完了。

The boss drank all of the beer in the refrigerator.

→老闆把冰箱裡的啤酒都<u>喝光了</u>。

The boss drank up all of the beer in the refrigerator.

2. 我給他的錢，他都用完了。

....

3. 他值錢的東西，小偷都偷走了。

....

4. 天氣太熱，這個孩子就把身上的衣服全脫了。

....

5. 老師說的話，我全忘了。

....

㈡請根據提示，用「V 光」完成下面對話。

Using the verbs in parentheses, please use “V 光” to complete the dialogues below.

1. 張：這部電影真難看。（走）

   Chang: This movie is really bad.

   李：難怪看到一半，人都走光了。

   Li: No wonder everybody walked out halfway through the movie.

2. 張：你怎麼不願跟他約會？（死）

   李：他太小氣，全世界的男孩子都 ________________ ，我也不要跟他出去。

3. 張：我做的炸雞味道怎麼樣？（搶）

   李：好極了。你看，一拿出來就 ________________ 。

4. 張：我要去圖書館借心理學。（借）

   李：別去了，最近大家都要交報告，這一類的書都 ___________ 。

5. 張：他們的花真好看！（賣）

   李：是啊！好快就 ________________ 。

☞ 六 到底 after all, in the final analysis

⊙你到底打什麼工啊？

So what work do you actually do?

用法說明：用於疑問句，表示追究事情的真相，是「究竟」的思。「到底」可在主語前，也可在主語後。主語是疑問詞時，應在「到底」後面。「到底」句尾不可有「嗎」，但可用「呢」或「嘛」。

Explanation: 到底 is used in questions to indicate an attempt to find out the truth or get to the bottom of a matter. 到底 can be placed either in front of or behind the subject, unless the subject is a QW, in which case 到底 must always come first. If 到底 is used, do not place 嗎 at the end of the sentence. Instead, use the particle 呢 or 嘛.

練習：Exercises:

㈠請用「到底」完成下面各句。

Please use 到底 to complete the following sentences.

1. 他昨天說要去中國大陸，今天說要去歐洲，他到底要去哪裡啊？
   Yesterday he said he wanted to go to mainland China, and today he said he wants to go to Europe. Where does he really want to go?
2. 你說你的女朋友很漂亮，可是我們都沒見過，到底＿＿＿＿＿＿＿？
3. 你說這個字對，他說那個字對，到底＿＿＿＿＿＿＿？
4. 你不喜歡運動，也不喜歡看電影、看書，你到底＿＿＿＿＿＿＿？
5. 我幫他，他不高興，我不幫他，他也不高興，他到底＿＿＿＿＿＿＿＿＿＿＿＿＿＿？

㈡改錯

Correct the errors.

1. 你到底去不去嗎？
2. 誰到底有這個門的鑰匙？

☞ 七 怎麼這麼……

Why so......? (used in a question or a rhetorical question)

⊙怎麼這麼累？

Why are you so tired?

用法說明：「怎麼」的意思是「為什麼」。「怎麼這麼……」可表示疑問或感歎。如果表示感歎，可以不必回答。「這麼」的後面通常加 SV，但少數動詞或助動詞 (AV) 亦可使用。

Explanation: 怎麼 means "why" or "how". "怎麼這麼……", can be used to express a question or make an exclamation through a rhetorical question, depending on the speaker's tone. The word or phrase following "怎麼這麼……" is usually a SV, but certain verbs and auxillary verbs can be used also.

練習： 請根據所給情況，用「怎麼這麼……」表示疑問或感歎。

Exercise: Please use "怎麼這麼……" to indicate doubt, frustration, or exasperation toward the given situations.

1. 今天的氣溫有九十多度。

   The temperature today is higher than 90 degrees.

   →怎麼這麼熱?!

   How did it get so hot?!

2. 弟弟這次小考只考了二十五分。

   ……………………………………………………………………

3. 室友說昨天吃了一天水餃，今天還想吃。

   ……………………………………………………………………

4. 哥哥說他女朋友叫他做什麼他都願意，要他死也可以。

   ……………………………………………………………………

5. 看見朋友什麼舞都會跳，而且跳得非常好。

   ……………………………………………………………………

☞ 八 TW 才 just or only TW (indicating not long ago)

⊙我上個週末才去替一個中國人看孩子。

Just last weekend I went to baby-sit for a Chinese person.

用法說明： 「才」放在時間詞 (TW) 或表示時間的短語後面。強調說話者覺得事情發生在「不久以前」，即使十年、八年前的事亦可。

Explanation : In this usage 才 is placed after a TW or a phrase indicating time . It emphasizes the speaker's feeling that something occurred relatively recently, even if it was eight or ten years ago.

練習：請把「才」放在句中合適的地方。

Exercise: Please place 才 in the appropriate place in the following sentences.

1. 我昨天吃過北京烤鴨，今天不想再吃了。
   I ate Peking Duck yesterday; I don't want to have it again today.
   →我昨天才吃過北京烤鴨，今天不想再吃了。
   I just ate Peking Duck yesterday; I don't want to have it again today.
2. 他上個月告訴你這件事，你怎麼就忘了？
   ....
3. 這篇論文是一年以前寫成的，資料還算很新。
   ....
4. 他十年前畢業，所以還不到四十歲。
   ....
5. 你出門以前上過廁所，怎麼現在又要上了？
   ....

☞ 九 ……啊，……啊，……啊，…… (used in lists for pauses)

⊙現在臺灣學生打工的情形很普遍，送報啊，做店員啊，到公司做小妹啊，……

In Taiwan today the occurrence of students doing part-time work is very common; they deliver papers. . . work in stores. . . work as errand girls in companies......

用法說明：在列舉人、地、事、物時，「啊」在每一項後面，表示停頓的語氣。

Explanation: Here, when listing people, places, events, objects, times, etc., 啊 is placed after each item to indicate a pause, often as the speaker thinks of the next item on the list.

練習：請把「啊」放在句中合適的地方。

Exercise: Please place 啊 in the appropriate place in the following sentences.

1. 媽媽剛剛上街買了一大袋東西，雞蛋、麵包、水果，什麼都有。
   Mom just went out and bought a big bag of things: eggs, bread, fruit, etc.

→媽媽剛剛上街買了一大袋東西，雞蛋啊，麵包啊，水果啊，什麼都有。

Mom just went out and bought a big bag of things: eggs, bread, fruit, etc.

2. 這裡的春天風景很好，山、水、花，都特別美。

....

3. 昨天野餐去的人很多，張先生、李小姐，都去了。

....

4. 弟弟真像爸爸，不管眼睛、鼻子、頭髮的顏色，都像得不得了。

....

5. 他去過的地方可多了，像紐約、波士頓、洛杉磯，這些大城他當然都去過。

....

課室活動

Role playing:

1. Two students: One acts as a manager of a McDonald's fast food restaurant. The other is a student who wants to get a part-time job (打工) there. The manager has advertised for someone to help in the restaurant, so the student has come for an interview. The two should try to develop a spirited discussion of the job requirements, job benefits, and the student's qualifications as an employee so the manager can reach a decision. Some useful supplementary words include: 工錢 (wages), 薪水 (xīnshuǐ; salary), 個性 (gèxìng; personality), 職務 (zhíwù; official duties), 職位 (zhíwèi; position in a job).

2. Four students : The four work in the same office. Person A has an MBA and is serious and hard-working. He/she was hired only two weeks ago. Person B, an average employee who also tends to be a bit emotional, has been working here

for ten years. Person C, an easy-going guy who studies part-time at college in the evening, has been working here for four years. Person D is the director of the office. A has to finish an assignment today but is unable to concentrate because B and C are chattering and laughing loudly. A asks them to quiet down and tells them to take work a little more seriously. This causes an argument to break out amongst the three. A few minutes later the director walks in. How does he handle this, and how do the other three respond? Each student should appropriately act out his/her role. Some useful supplementary words include: 企管碩士 (qìguǎn shuòshì; Master of Business Administration), 神氣 (shénqì; putting on airs; to be cocky; overweening), 認真 (rènzhēn; to be serious, conscientious), 吵架 (chǎo//jià; to quarrel, wangle), 教訓 (jiàoxùn; to lecture somebody for wrongdoing), 主任 (zhǔrèn; director of an office or department).

我念高中的時候就半工半讀了。

我念大學的時候也半工半讀。

我現在上班了，還是半工半讀。

半天工作、半天讀報。

短文

我的中文履歷表

月　日

今天到系辦公室交作業，看到助教正在填一張表，我從來沒看過那樣的東西，她告訴我是中文履歷表①。原來她計畫畢業後回台灣工作。她說：在台灣找工作，不管是別人介紹，自己看報上的廣告②，還是大公司去學校找，都應該填好履歷表跟照片③一起寄去，等接到通知再去面談④。我也想看看自己會不會填，就跟助教要了一張。沒想到表上很多字我都不認識，原來「性別⑤」是問你是男的還是女的，「學歷⑥」是問哪個學校畢業的，「通訊處⑦」就是地址，「曾任職務⑧」就是從前做過什麼事。我剛剛把會填的都填了，明天拿給助教看看對不對，也許明年去台灣找工作的時候，就用得著了。

姓名	高偉立
性別	男
年齡	20歲　民國⑨1972年7月4日生
出生地	美國紐約州水牛城
學歷	
通訊處	
電話	
曾任職務	1. 餐廳服務生　2. 圖書館工讀生　3. 送報生
身份證字號⑩	
應徵職務⑪	
希望待遇⑫	
貼相片處	

Vocabulary:

1. 履歷表 (lǚlìbiǎo): curriculum vitae
2. 廣告 (guǎnggào): advertisement
3. 照片 (zhàopiàn): photo
4. 面談 (miàntán): interview
5. 性別 (xìngbié): sex
6. 學歷 (xuélì): educational background
7. 通訊處 (tōngxùnchù): one's address
8. 曾任職務 (céngrèn zhíwù): work experience
9. 民國: the year based on the establishment of the R.O.C. in 1912, e.g. 民國一年 is 1912.
10. 身分證字號 (shēnfènzhèng zìhào): National I. D. card number
11. 應徵職務 (yìngzhēng zhíwù): position for which one is applying
12. 希望待遇 (dàiyù): desired pay

第九課

誰最漂亮

・中國小姐選美（《中國時報》江妙瑩攝）

（林建國的表姐站在宿舍門口）

表姐：怎麼回事？你們怎麼現在才來？我等得急**死了**[1]。

建國：對不起，來晚了。來參加你們學校園遊會的人太多，路上**都**塞車了。

美真：就是啊！路上都是車，半天都動不了。

表姐：哦？真沒想到，我們這裡從來不塞車的。這幾位是……？

建國：噢！我**來**介紹一下，這是我表姐丁小青，他是高偉立。(用手指著說)謝美真，李平。

表姐：大家好！

李平、美真、偉立：你好！

建國：你們宿舍好難找啊！

表姐：是嗎？怎麼會呢[2]？

建國：你們校園很大。每一棟大樓都離得很遠，而且名字都看不清楚。所以，我們就迷路了。

表姐：**早知道**我**就**去車站接你們了。

李平：沒關係。這樣我們正好有機會欣賞一下你們美麗的校園。

偉立：我們先走一走，運動運動，等一下可以多吃一點兒。

建國：你們學校環境真好，還是私立學校有錢。

李平：這些房子不但漂亮，而且各有各的特色。

美真：這裡秋天的樹好美，什麼顏色都有。

表姐：春天的花更美呢！走吧！我們到湖邊去。現在恐怕人已經很多了。

※ ※ ※ ※ ※ ※

(四人下車)

李平：你們餓嗎？

美真：餓**倒是**不餓，**可是**可以吃一點東西。

偉立：**既然**不怎麼餓，我們**就**去吃pizza[3]吧！

李平、美真、建國：好啊！

※ ※ ※ ※ ※ ※

（四人邊吃邊說）

偉立：今天的園遊會真熱鬧！

美真：是啊！林建國，你表姐好漂亮！那雙眼睛好像會說話。我好羨慕她那頭又黑又亮的長頭髮。

李平：嗯，你表姐很大方。

建國：很多人都這麼說。追她的人多得不得了。

偉立：我擲飛鏢的時候，旁邊收錢的那個女孩子，你們注意到沒有？

建國：對，對，對，那個女生身材真是好**得沒話說**[4]，尤其是那雙長腿。笑起來也很迷人。難怪那個攤位前面擠了那麼多人。

美真：你們男生就注意女生的身材。

李平：她笑起來很甜，可惜近看皮膚不夠細。

偉立：你來美國幾年了，你覺得美國女孩跟中國女孩比起來怎麼樣？

李平：大部分的中國人都覺得眼睛大，鼻子高，嘴巴小，皮膚細白，才好看[5]。一般說來，美國女孩比較高大，沒有中國女孩秀氣。但是美國女孩的活潑、大方，中國女孩就**比不上**了。

美真：你去買冰淇淋的時候，我們在熱狗攤位看見一個很帥的男生，像電影明星那麼英俊。

建國：英俊**是**英俊，**可是**我不喜歡他那種態度，自以為比別人有魅力。

偉立：對！我最討厭這種人。我覺得我雖然醜，可是我很溫柔，怎麼沒有人發現呢？

建國：**誰叫**你總是不修邊幅?!其實你一點也不醜。如果你把鬍子刮乾淨，打扮一下，還可以算帥哥[6]呢！

・園遊會（吳俊銘攝）

生詞及例句

1. 園ㄩㄢˊ遊ㄧㄡˊ會ㄏㄨㄟˋ (yuányóuhuì)　*N*: **an outdoor fair**

2. 塞ㄙㄞ車ㄔㄜ (sāi//chē)　*VO*: **to be jammed with traffic**

　我今天上、下班的時候，路上塞車，塞了二十分鐘，車子都動不了。

3. 校ㄒㄧㄠˋ園ㄩㄢˊ (xiàoyuán)　*N*: **campus, school yard**

　放假了，校園裡一個人也沒有。

4. 棟ㄉㄨㄥˋ (dòng)　*M*: **(used for buildings)**

5. 迷ㄇㄧˊ路ㄌㄨˋ (mílù)

　V: **to lose one's way / bearings, to get lost**

　他給我的地址不對，所以我迷路了。

6. 正ㄓㄥˋ好ㄏㄠˇ (zhènghǎo)　*A*: **happen to, chance to, as it happens**

　我去找他的時候，他正好要出門。

7. 美ㄇㄟˇ麗ㄌㄧˋ (měilì)　*SV*: **beautiful**

　這條路開好了以後，大家都可以欣賞到臺灣東部美麗的風景了。

8. 特ㄊㄜˋ色ㄙㄜˋ (tèsè)　*N*: **special or distinctive characteristic**

　校園大，學生少，是我們學校的一個特色。

9. 樹ㄕㄨˋ (shù)　*N*: **tree（M：棵 kē）**。

10. 倒ㄉㄠˋ是ㄕˋ (dào·shì)

　A: **yet, nevertheless, contrary to expectations**

　張：走了半天了，你累不累？

　李：我累倒是不累，可是很渴。

11. 既ㄐㄧˋ然ㄖㄢˊ (jìrán)　*A*: **since, now that**

　既然他非吃西餐不可，我們就吃西餐吧。

12. 雙ㄕㄨㄤ (shuāng)

　M: **(used for pairs of objects, e.g. chopsticks, shoes, etc.)**

13. 羨慕 (xiànmù) *V/SV*: **to admire, to envy envious**

(1)他的工作又輕鬆又能賺很多錢，我們都很羨慕他。

(2)你的女朋友真漂亮，大家都羨慕得不得了。

14. 追 (zhuī) *V*: **to pursue, chase after**

那個女孩子很好，如果你想追她，就約她去看電影吧！

15. 擲飛鏢 (zhí//fēibiāo) *VO*: **to throw darts**

擲 (zhí) *V*: **to throw, cast, fling**

飛鏢 (fēibiāo) *N*: **a dart（M：支 zhī）**

16. 收 (shōu) *V*: **to collect, gather, receive, put away**

時間到了，不要再寫了，我要收考卷了。

收到 (shōu//dào) *RC*: **to receive, get, obtain**

他剛剛收到一封母親寄來的信。

收起來 (shōu//qǐ·lái) *RC*: **to put away, gather**

你快把錢收起來，小心丟了。

17. 身材 (shēncái) *N*: **figure, build, physique**

她每天慢跑、游泳，難怪身材這麼好。

18. 腿 (tuǐ) *N*: **leg（M：條）**

腿短的人跑得比較慢嗎？

19. 迷人 (mírén) *SV*: **to be charming, enchanting, spellbinding**

他的聲音很迷人，讓人忍不住想跟他多聊聊。

迷 (mí)

V/N: **to be fascinated, spellbound or charmed by, to be infatuated with / a (sports, etc.) fan, enthusiast**

(1)他很迷籃球，沒事就去打。

(2)他是一個電影迷，只要有好電影，他一定去看。

20. 攤位 (tānwèi) *N*: **a stall, a booth**

在這個市場裡，樓上的攤位都是賣水果的。

攤子 (tān·zi) *N*: **a stand, a street stall**

這兩天大學聯考，老王就在學校門口擺了個攤子賣飲料。

21. 擠 (jǐ)

V/SV: **to squeeze, to press, to force in / crowded, crammed, packed**

(1)車上的人太多，我擠不上去。

(2)市場裡人很多，擠得不得了。

22. 皮ㄆㄧˊ膚ㄈㄨ (pífū) *N*: **skin, epidermis**

皮ㄆㄧˊ (pí) *N*: **leather, hide（M：張／塊）**

這雙鞋是真皮做的，價錢當然貴。

皮ㄆㄧˊ包ㄅㄠ (píbāo) *N*: **handbag, briefcase**

23. 細ㄒㄧˋ (xì) *SV*: **to be fine, delicate**

我的頭髮又細又少，怎麼弄都不好看。

24. 嘴ㄗㄨㄟˇ巴ㄅㄚ (zuǐ·bā) *N*: **mouth（M：張）**

他嘴巴很甜，你得小心他說的不是真的。

25. 秀ㄒㄧㄡˋ氣ㄑㄧˋ (xiù·qì) *SV*: **to be delicate, refined, graceful**

你 弟弟寫的字像女孩兒寫的一樣，好秀氣！

26. 活ㄏㄨㄛˊ潑ㄆㄛ (huópō) *SV*: **to be lively, vivacious, vigorous**

他上課討論的時候，話很多，很活潑。

27. 冰ㄅㄧㄥ淇ㄑㄧˊ淋ㄌㄧㄣˊ (bīng·qílín) *N*: **ice cream**

28. 熱ㄖㄜˋ狗ㄍㄡˇ (règǒu) *N*: **hot dog**

狗ㄍㄡˇ (gǒu) *N*: **dog**

29. 電ㄉㄧㄢˋ影ㄧㄥˇ明ㄇㄧㄥˊ星ㄒㄧㄥ（影ㄧㄥˇ星ㄒㄧㄥ）(diànyǐng míngxīng) (yǐngxīng)

N: **movie star**

明ㄇㄧㄥˊ星ㄒㄧㄥ (míngxīng) *N*: **a (movie, t.v., music, etc.) star**

30. 英ㄧㄥ俊ㄐㄩㄣˋ (yīngjùn) *SV*: **to be good-looking, handsome, dashing**

他的男朋友很英俊，可是腿太短。

31. 態ㄊㄞˋ度ㄉㄨˋ (tàidù) *N*: **attitude**

他的態度很不客氣，我們都很生氣。

32. 魅ㄇㄟˋ力ㄌㄧˋ (mèilì) *N*: **glamour, enchantment, attractiveness**

他很有魅力，不管男的、女的都很迷他。

33. 討ㄊㄠˇ厭ㄧㄢˋ (tǎoyàn)

V/SV: **to dislike, to loathe, to hate/to be disgusting, repugnant,**

disagreeable, annoying

(1)我最討厭又濕又冷的天氣。

(2)他又嘮叨了，真討厭。

34. 醜ㄔㄡˇ (chǒu) *SV*: **to be ugly**

我小時候不好看，哥哥姐姐都叫我「醜小鴨」。

35. 溫ㄨㄣ柔ㄖㄡˊ (wēnróu) *SV*: **gentle and soft**

他那雙眼睛看人的時候很溫柔。

36. 不ㄅㄨˋ修ㄒㄧㄡ邊ㄅㄧㄢ幅ㄈㄨˊ (bù xiū biānfú)

IE: **untidy / untidy in dress**

我舅舅穿得很隨便，總是不修邊幅。

37. 鬍ㄏㄨˊ子˙ㄗ (hú·zi) *N*: **mustache, beard, whiskers**

我女兒說我留鬍子看起來像壞人。

38. 刮ㄍㄨㄚ (guā) *V*: **to shave**

39. 打ㄉㄚˇ扮ㄅㄢˋ (dǎbàn) *V*: **to get dressed up, to put on make-up**

明天是我男朋友的生日，我一定要打扮得漂亮一點。

40. 帥ㄕㄨㄞˋ哥ㄍㄜ (shuàigē) *N*: **handsome young man**

帥ㄕㄨㄞˋ (shuài) *SV*: **to be handsome, elegant in appearance**

王先生雖然不年輕了，可是很會打扮，所以還是很帥。

注釋

1. 我等得急死了 means "I've waited so long that I died of anxiety." This is an exaggeration of course. This expression is used mostly by women.
2. "怎麼會呢？" means "How could this be?" It is short for "怎麼會這樣呢？" It indicates that a situation is contrary to a person's expectations.
3. Pizza. The full translation is 義大利脆餅, (Yìdàlì cuìbǐng), which means "crispy Italian pastry". Many people just say "pizza", written 披薩 (pīsà).
4. 好得沒話說 is used in positive situations. For negative situations other expressions are used, such as 不是普通的 SV (e.g. 笨) (extraordinarily stu-

pid) or SV (e.g. 笨) 得離譜 (stupid even beyond the rule book). These phrases, however, would be considered impolite by anyone other than very close friends.

5. This reflects the Chinese standard of beauty. Chinese do not consider dark skin to be beautiful. Most Chinese women like to keep their skin light, so they often carry parasols under the sun.

6. 帥哥 came into popular use in the middle of '80s. It means "handsome young man". 帥 means "dashing", or "smart-looking". A 帥哥 not only has a good looking face but also has a good build and stylish clothes .

文法練習

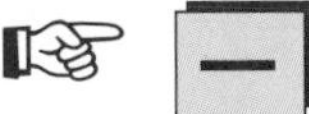

一 SV 死了 SV to death, extremely SV,

⊙我等得急死了。

I got extremely anxious waiting.

用法說明：「SV死了」跟「SV極了」、「SV得不得了」意思差不多，但程度更強。是一種誇張的語氣。大部分表示不好的意思。

Explanation: "SV 死了" means almost the same thing as "SV極了", "SV 得不得了", but the tone is even stronger. It expresses exaggeration and usually has negative connotations.

練習：根據所給提示，用「SV 死了」完成下面對話。

Exercise: Following the provided hints, please use "SV 死了" to complete the dialogues below.

1. 張：那家飯館的菜怎麼樣？（難吃）

   Chang: How's the food at that restaurant?

   李：難吃死了！我從來沒吃過那麼難吃的菜。

   Li: Awful! I've never eaten anything so disgusting.

2. 張：你房東對你這麼壞，你為什麼不搬家？（麻煩）

李：搬家＿＿＿＿＿＿＿＿＿＿，我寧願看他的臉色。

3. 張：明天期中考，你今天應該早一點睡。（緊張）

李：我＿＿＿＿＿＿＿＿＿＿，怎麼睡得著呢？

4. 張：申請獎學金的人那麼多，小王能申請到真不容易。（高興）

李：是啊！他＿＿＿＿＿＿＿＿＿＿！他說要請客。

5. 張：老林的女朋友不但漂亮，身材好，還很溫柔。(羨慕)

李：就是嘛！大家都＿＿＿＿＿＿＿＿＿＿。

☞ 二 都 even

⊙來參加你們學校園遊會的人太多，路上都塞車了。

So many people came to your school fair that even the road was jammed with traffic.

用法說明：「都」表示情況「甚至達到這種程度」，放在要強調的事情之前，說話時應輕讀。

Explanation: 都 shows that conditions have reached such an extreme level that even a certain situation has occurred. 都 is placed in front of that situation and should be spoken with no emphasis.

練習：請把「都」放在句中合適的地方。

Exercise: Please place 都 in the appropriate place in the following sentences.

1. 今天是媽的生日，我才買蛋糕的。你怎麼忘了？

I bought a cake because today is Mom's birthday. How could you forget?

→今天是媽的生日，我才買蛋糕的。你怎麼都忘了？

I bought a cake because today is Mom's birthday. How could you forget?

2. 我才打破一個杯子，老闆就罵了半個小時，我被氣哭了。

………………………………………………………………

3. 老陳真小氣！病得那麼重還不願意看醫生。

………………………………………………………………

4. 林小姐越來越漂亮了，兩年沒見我差一點不認識了。

歐陽泰

① 我上課的時候順便去7-11買麵包.

② 他說他是英國人，難道他這麼不客氣。

③ 這裡沒什麼可看的。

④ 這個電影很好。一方面導演很好。一方面男主角演技很好。

⑤ 他說他要幫我買新筆，可是我說算了。

....

5. 我男朋友一直說我胖，說得我不敢再吃了。

....

☞ 三 來 V let (S) V

⊙我來介紹一下，……

Let me introduce you......

用法說明：這個「來」表示要做某件事，並不真正向說話者移動，由「來」前面的主語進行「來」後面的「要做的事」。有緩和語氣的作用。

Explanation: When used this way, 來 does not express the action "come". Instead, it shows that the subject before 來 is about to perform the action indicated in the verb following 來. It serves to give the statement a casual, friendly tone.

練習：請用「來 V」完成下面對話。

Exercise: Please use 來 to complete the dialogues below.

1. 媽媽：我累了，今天我可不要洗碗了。

   Mom: I'm tired. I really don't want to wash dishes today.

   女兒：我來洗吧！

   Daughter: I'll wash them!

2. 張：車票我買，旅館誰訂？

   李：旅館，我來__________。

3. 張：這個桌子太重，我一個人搬不動。

   李：我來__________。

4. 張：我們去哪兒吃飯，決定了沒有？

   李：你常在外面吃，還是你來__________吧！

5. 張：這條山路我沒走過，不敢開車去。

   李：小王正好在這兒，他走過好幾次，讓他來__________吧！

☞ 四 早知道（……）（我／我們）就……了。
If (I) had known beforehand that......then......

⊙早知道我就去車站接你們了。

If I had known beforehand, I would have gone to meet you at the train station.

用法說明：「早知道」的後面是已成的事實，但並不是說話者所期望的，語言環境清楚時，可省略。「就」的後面是說話者遺憾（或後悔）應做而未做的事。

Explanation: The words following 早知道 show a fact or situation that exists, but that the speaker had not expected to occur. When the context is clear, then the fact or situation can be omitted. Following「就」is something that the speaker should have and would have done if he had known about the situation beforehand. This pattern expresses the speaker's regret.

練習：請根據所給情況，用「早知道（……）（我／我們）就……了。」表示遺憾。

Exercise: In accordance with the provided hints, please use the "早知道（……）（我／我們）就……了。" pattern to express the speaker's regret.

1. 本來要選張教授的課，後來沒選，現在聽說他的課非常有趣。

   Originally, I wanted to take Professor Chang's class, but I didn't. Now I hear that his class is really interesting.

   →早知道我就選了。

   If I had known, then I would have taken it.

2. 從前不知道有這個獎學金，現在才聽說這個獎學金，而且申請的人都申請到了。

   ……………………………………………………………………

3. 留在家做功課，沒跟朋友去看電影。後來聽朋友說電影非常好看。

   ……………………………………………………………………

4. 地理系畢業以後，一直找不到合適的工作。

   ……………………………………………………………………

5. 幫妹妹搬家，可是她不但不謝謝我，還說我把她的東西弄丟了。

……………………………………………………………………………………

☞ 五 ……倒是……，可是（不過／就是）……

Well, it is......however......

⊙餓倒是不餓，可是可以吃一點東西。

I'm not really hungry, but I could eat a little something.

用法說明：「倒是」前面是重覆對方的問題或說法，「倒是」後面才是真正的回答。說「倒是」的目的是說話者可利用這個時候考慮如何回答，亦可使語氣較婉轉。「倒是」後面肯定、否定都可以。「是」可省略，但大部分的人省略「倒」。

Explanation: Preceding 倒是 is the opening response to the other party's question or comment, but following 倒是 is the speaker's real answer. 倒是 allows the speaker some time while deciding upon an answer and also serves to soften the tone of the reply. The words following 倒是 can be either positive or negative. Either 倒 or 是 can be omitted, but usually it is 倒 which is omitted.

練習：請用「……倒是……，可是（不過／就是）……」回答下面問題。

Exercise: Please use the pattern "……倒是……，可是（不過／就是）……" to answer the questions below.

1. 這個花瓶好漂亮，你買吧！

   This flower vase is beautiful ; you should buy it!

   →漂亮是漂亮，可是價錢太貴，我買不起。

   It may be beautiful, but it's too expensive: I can't buy it.

2. 你為什麼不跟他們一起去，你不喜歡游泳嗎？

   ……………………………………………………………………………………

3. 你想不想看電影？

   ……………………………………………………………………………………

4. 你為什麼不坐公車去？車票不貴啊！

   ……………………………………………………………………………………

5. 你會說法文啊？我以為你沒學過。（請用否定句回答）

....

☞ 六 既然……，就……　Since......, then......

⊙既然不怎麼餓，我們就去吃 pizza 吧！

Since you're not that hungry, then let's go eat pizza!

用法說明：「既然」的後面是已發生或認定會發生的事實，「就」的後面是說話者因為這個事實而表示的意見。

Explanation: Following 既然 is an existing fact, or something that is considered to happen, and following 就 is a position that the speaker takes using this fact as a basis.

練習：請用「既然……，就……」完成下面對話。

Exercise: Please use the "既然……，就……" pattern to complete the following dialogues.

1. 張：小王沒什麼經驗，做這件事恐怕有問題。

   Chang: Little Wang has no experience, I'm afraid that he'll have trouble doing this.

   李：既然他沒什麼經驗，就另外找人做吧！

   Li: Since he doesn't have any experience, then let's look for somebody else to do it!

2. 張：週末出去玩的人多，我怕塞車。

   李：你既然____________________。

3. 張：那個女孩又大方又活潑，我好欣賞她！

   李：既然____________________。

4. 張：我想吃冰淇淋，可是這個攤位的已經賣完了。

   李：既然____________________。

5. 張：我頭疼，不想去參加園遊會了。

   李：既然____________________。

☞ 七 SV得沒話說 undescribably, beyond words

⊙那個女生身材真是好得沒話說。

That girl's figure is absolutely amazing.

用法說明：強調程度很高，高到沒有合適的話可以形容。大部分用在好的情況，若用在不好的情況，似乎說話者並不在乎。

Explanation: This pattern emphasizes that the level of something is so high that no words can properly describe it. Usually it is used in positive situations, but sometimes it is used to describe negative situations and gives the impression that the speaker really does not care.

練習：請用「SV得沒話說」完成下面對話。

Exercise: Please use "SV得沒話說" to complete the dialogues below.

1. 張：小王的成績好棒，每一科都是A.

   Chang: Little Wang's grades are excellent ; he has an A in every class.

   李：是啊！他的成績真是<u>棒得沒話說</u>。

   Li: That's right! His grades are really amazing.

2. 服務生A：我沒看過這麼大方的人，我每次幫他開門，他都給我二十塊。

   服務生B：這個人真是＿＿＿＿＿＿＿＿＿＿。

3. 張：你的房子真便宜！房租跟水電費加起來才一百塊錢。

   李：是啊！這房子真的＿＿＿＿＿＿＿＿＿＿。

4. 張：那個女孩真漂亮，學校裡每個男生都很迷她。

   李：她是＿＿＿＿＿＿＿＿＿＿。

5. 張：那個人的衣服髒得好像幾年沒換了。

   李：那是＿＿＿＿＿＿＿＿＿＿。

☞ 八 比不上

cannot compare to, cannot compete with, is no competition for

⊙……但是美國女孩的活潑、大方，中國女孩就比不上了。

......but Chinese girls can't compare to American girls in terms of vivaciousness and natural poise.

用法說明：「上」表示達到一定的水準。這個 RC 僅使用 Potential Type。

Explanation: 上 indicates that the subject has reached a certain level (of quality, accuracy, standard, etc.) This RC is used in Potential Type form (not Actual Type).

練習：請用「比不上」完成下面對話。

Exercise: Please use 比不上 to complete the dialogues below.

1. 張：你跟小王，誰的打工經驗多？
   Chang: Between you and Li'l Wang, who has more work experience?
   李：他的經驗比較多，我比不上他。
   Li: He has more experience than I. I am no competition for him.
2. 張：東方小孩獨立，還是西方小孩獨立？
   李：西方小孩獨立多了，＿＿＿＿＿＿＿＿＿。
3. 張：美國葡萄酒比法國葡萄酒好喝嗎？
   李：法國葡萄酒世界有名，＿＿＿＿＿＿＿＿＿。
4. 張：這家旅館雖然便宜，可是服務不好。
   李：小旅館的服務當然＿＿＿＿＿＿＿＿＿。
5. 張：林教授上課，每一次教室裡都坐得滿滿的。
   李：是啊，他的魅力＿＿＿＿＿＿＿＿＿。

九 誰叫……?!

Who told (asked) you to......? (rhetorical question)

⊙誰叫你總是不修邊幅?!

Who asked you to always be so sloppily dressed?

用法說明：不是問句。「誰叫」的後面是說明某件事情發生的原因，而此原因是有道理的，不該埋怨的。

Explanation: Sentences like these are rhetorical questions. Following 誰叫 is an explanation that some bad situation is due to the other party's own shortcoming. It implies that the other party has no right to complain.

練習：請用誰叫完成下面對話。

Exercise: Please use 誰叫 to complete the dialogues below.

1. 張：你們為什麼不等我，先走了？

   Chang: Why did you leave and not wait for me?

   李：誰叫你不準時?!

   Li: Who told you to be late?

2. 張：沒想到他這次考這麼爛！

   李：誰叫他＿＿＿＿＿＿＿＿＿＿＿?!

3. 張：真倒楣，老闆又扣我錢了！

   李：誰叫你＿＿＿＿＿＿＿＿＿＿＿?!

4. 張：我不好意思讓你哥哥請客。

   李：有什麼不好意思，誰叫他＿＿＿＿＿＿＿＿＿＿＿?!

5. 張：你男朋友對你這麼不好，你為什麼不離開他？

   李：沒辦法，誰叫我＿＿＿＿＿＿＿＿＿＿＿?!

課室活動

1. 遊戲：猜 (cāi; to guess) 猜我是誰？（你知道我是誰嗎？）

Before class, the teacher prepares cards with people's names on them, one per student. The names should be of people well known to the class such as celebrities, classmates, professors etc. Each student is given a card and is asked to describe the person on their card to the class. They can even liven it up by using body language and mannerisms typical of the person. Their description may begin with statements such as: "我是男的。我很高，我有六呎高。我的頭髮……" The rest of the class is to guess the identity of this person. The game can be made more exciting by dividing the class into two teams which compete against each other.

Some useful supplementary words include: 禿頭 (tūtóu; bald-headed person), 肚子 (dù·zi; belly; abdomen), 金頭髮藍眼睛的 (blonde-haired and blue-eyed), 戴眼鏡 (dàiyǎnjìng; wear glasses), 胸部 (xiōngbù; chest, bosom), 安靜(ānjìng; to be quiet), 屁股 (pì·gǔ; buttocks, rear end).

2. Read the following narrative and discuss or debate with the class: the pros and cons of beauty contests. Some useful supplementary words include: 贊成 (zànchéng, to agree, approve), 反對 (con, against), 外表 (appearance), 內在美 (inner beauty), 三圍 (sānwéi, measure of figure).

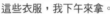

這些衣服，我下午來拿。

老闆，我來拿衣服。

已經洗好了，小姐。早上送衣服來的是你媽吧？！

短文

報上的短評[1]

今天是「X州[2]小姐」選美[3]報名[4]的最後一天，已有三十二位小姐填好報名表。這次參加的小姐，年齡[5]都比以前小了很多，大部分高中都還沒有畢業。她們雖然看起來活潑、大方，可是都打扮得太老，並不適合她們的年紀。很多人擔心像她們這麼年輕，生活經驗跟常識[6]都不夠，如果選她們來代表[7]美國的現代[8]美女，合適嗎？而且以前選出來的美國小姐也鬧過不少新聞：不是生過孩子，就是照過裸照[9]，要不然就是跟別人的先生有不正常[10]的關係。這也是為什麼每年都有人在討論這個活動還要不要再辦。

到底什麼才是『美』？我們又為什麼要選美？我覺得政府有義務教育年輕人：不要以為有漂亮的臉，迷人的身材就是美。腦子[11]裡面有沒有東西才是更值得注意的。

Vocabulary:

1.短評 (duǎnpíng): short critique

2.X 州: “a certain” state in the U.S. “X” is used to represent the name of an exisiting person, place, time or thing, whose exact identity or date cannot either be remembered or be revealed, such as "Mr. X in X city......." It should be pronounced as "mǒu".

3.選美 (xuǎnměi): beauty contest

4. 報名 (bào//míng): to enroll

5.年齡 (niánlíng): age

6.常識 (chángshì): common sense

7.代表 (dàibiǎo): to represent

8.現代 (xiàndài): modern

9.裸照 (luǒzhào): nude photos

10.不正常 (búzhèngcháng): abnormal; here, illicit

11.腦子 (nǎo·zi): brain; here, mind

第十課

你選誰

・投票（新聞局提供）

（活動中心）

偉立：那邊有位子，我們坐那兒吧！（兩人過去坐下）

錢太太：我的英文不好，每次語言交換你都很辛苦，真抱歉！

偉立：沒什麼！只要對你有幫助，我就很高興了。

錢太太：你真好，謝謝你！剛剛外面那些人在說什麼？我就聽懂了幾句話，好像是選舉參議員的事，對嗎？

偉立：對了，我們十一月初舉行期中選舉[1]，所以最近有很多政見發表會，也有人到處幫他們的黨拉票[2]。

錢太太：就選參議員嗎？

偉立：有的州除了選參議員，還選眾議員、州長，和市長。

錢太太：多久選一次？

偉立：眾議員**每**兩年選一次；參議員任期六年，每兩年輪流改選三**分之**一。州長、市長有的兩年選一次，有的四年選一次。

錢太太：你是民主黨，還是共和黨？

偉立：我是民主黨。

錢太太：你幫民主黨拉票了嗎？你一定希望他們贏吧？！

偉立：那還用說嗎[3]？我大哥這次就幫紐約州長候選人助選。

錢太太：那一定很忙嘍？

偉立：是啊，每天**為了**競選經費跑來跑去，不是安排政見發表會、布置場地，就是發傳單。忙得吃飯都沒時間。

錢太太：你大哥怎麼那麼熱心？

偉立：他念研究所的時候，在國會工讀，認識了一些國會議員，學了很多，很有興趣往政治這**方面**發展。

錢太太：**這麼說**，也許有一天你會是美國總統的弟弟呢！

偉立：（笑）到白宮的路可不好走啊！你們怎麼選總統？

錢太太：我們跟你們不一樣，我們要先選國民大會代表，**由**他們**來**選舉。以後也許會改成直接選舉。

偉立：也是四年選一次嗎？

錢太太：不是，我們是六年選一次[4]。

偉立：那你們的國會議員怎麼選的呢？

錢太太：我們的國會包括立法院[5]跟國民大會[6]。怎麼選的，我以後再告訴你吧。（看錶）

偉立：是啊！時間不早了，我們該學英文了。

※ ※ ※ ※ ※ ※

（公車站）

助教：嗨！高偉立，等車啊[7]？

偉立：是啊，我剛投完票，想回宿舍吃飯。你買東西啊[7]？

助教：嗯，買了些雞蛋、鮮奶[8]跟洗衣粉。我**正要**去學校，要不要我送你[9]？我的車就停在前面。

偉立：好啊，謝謝。（兩人過去上了車）

助教：投票的人多不多？

偉立：不少，我等了好久才輪到。

助教：你投過幾次票了？

偉立：兩年前的大選，我還**不到**十八歲，沒有選舉權，所以這次是第一次。

助教：你的票投給誰了？

偉立：我當然支持民主黨的候選人，我覺得他們競選時答應選民的事情，比較容易做到。

助教：**你看**，你支持的人有希望當選嗎？

偉立：誰敢說？這一次競爭很激烈。你呢？你投過幾次票？

助教：兩次。我們是滿了二十歲，在一個地方住滿六個月，才可以投票。

偉立：哦，原來是這樣。宿舍到了，我要下車了，謝啦，再見。

・政見發表會（吳俊銘攝）

生詞及例句

1. 抱歉 (bàoqiàn)　　*IE/SV*: **sorry / to be sorry, to regret**

　(1) 抱歉！路上塞車，所以來晚了。

　(2) 不能幫他的忙，我覺得對他很抱歉。

　抱 (bào)

　V: **to hug, to embrace, to hold or carry in one's arms**

　　孩子哭了，媽媽把他抱起來，他就不哭了。

　道歉 (dào//qiàn)　　*VO*: **to apologize**

　　這件事情是我錯了，我跟你道歉。

2. 選舉權 (xuǎnjǔquán)　　*N*: **the right to vote**

　選舉 (xuǎnjǔ)　　*N*: **election**

　　找什麼人做這件事，選舉是最公平的辦法。

　權 (quán)　　*N*: **a right ; power, authority**

　人權 (rénquán)　　*N*: **human rights**

　改選 (gǎixuǎn)　　*V*: **to re-elect**

　　這些人已經做了很多年了，應該改選了。

　助選 (zhùxuǎn)

　V: **to help elect, to assist a campaign effort**

　　他有很多幫別人助選的經驗。

　大選 (dàxuǎn)　　*N*: **general election**

3. 競選 (jìngxuǎn)

　V: **to enter an election, to run for office, to campaign for office, to enter a beauty contest**

　　他姐姐很漂亮，很多人都說她可以出來競選美國小姐。

4. 候選人 (hòuxuǎnrén)　　*N*: **candidate (for office)**

　　這一次出來競選的候選人都很年輕。

5. 當選 (dāngxuǎn)　　*V*: **to be elected**

　　這次競選的人太多，要當選不容易。

6. 選民 (xuǎnmín) *N*: **voter, elector**

這個地方的選民，好像對這次的選舉都不太關心。

7. 參議員 (cānyìyuán) *N*: **senator**

8. 眾議員 (zhòngyìyuán)

N: **member of the House of Representatives (U.S.); Member of Parliament (M.P.)(U. K.)**

議員 (yìyuán) *N*: **member of a legislative assembly**

市議員 (shìyìyuán)

N: **member of a municipal assembly**

議會 (yìhuì) *N*: **council, assembly, parliament**

9. 月初 (yuèchū) *TW*: **the beginning of the month**

下個月初，二號到六號我們要舉行這學期的期中考。

月底 (yuèdǐ) *TW*: **the end of the month**

年底 (niándǐ) *TW*: **the end of the year**

10. 政見發表會 (zhèngjiàn fābiǎohuì)

N: political convention

政見 (zhèngjiàn) *N*: **political views**

那個候選人的政見並不合選民的需要。

發表會 (fābiǎohuì)

N: **convention or exhibition of new ideas or products**

發表 (fābiǎo)

V: **to make public, make known, express an idea**

他的研究報告是在上個月的國家地理雜誌上發表的。

11. 黨（政黨）(dǎng)(zhèngdǎng) *N*: **political party**

12. 拉票 (lā//piào) *VO*: **to solicit votes**

最近他到處替這一州的參議員候選人拉票。

拉 (lā) *V*: **to pull, to tug**

這個門太重，我拉不動，打不開。

13. 州長 (zhōuzhǎng) *N*: **governor (of a state)**

市長 (shìzhǎng) *N*: **mayor (of a city)**

校ㄒㄧㄠˋ長ㄓㄤˇ (xiàozhǎng)

N: **principal / head of a school, head-master**

班ㄅㄢ長ㄓㄤˇ (bānzhǎng)　　*N*: **class leader**

14. 和ㄏㄢˋ（ㄏㄜˊ）(hàn, hé)　　*CONJ*: **and**

因為她有漂亮的臉和迷人的身材，追她的人多得不得了。

15. 任ㄖㄣˋ期ㄑㄧˊ (rènqí)　　*N*: **term of office, tenure of office**

任ㄖㄣˋ (rèn)　　*M*: **(for the terms of an office)**

州長的四年任期快滿了，你要選誰做下一任的州長？

16. 輪ㄌㄨㄣˊ流ㄌㄧㄡˊ (lúnliú)　　*V/A*: **to take turns, by turns, in turn**

(1) 這個星期的衣服你洗，下個星期我來洗，大家輪流。

(2) 我舅媽生病，我舅舅跟我表弟輪流去醫院照顧她。

17. X 分ㄈㄣ之ㄓ Y (X fēn zhī Y)　　*IE*: **the fraction Y of X**

(1) 全世界人口有五分之一是中國人。

(2) 中國人口是世界人口的五分之一。

18. 贏ㄧㄥˊ (yíng)　　*V*: **to win**

我們來比比誰跑得快，贏的人請客，好不好？

19. 為ㄨㄟˋ了˙ㄌㄜ (wèi·le)

CV: **so as to, in order to, for the purpose of**

為了讓他高興，我唱了一首歌給他聽。

為ㄨㄟˋ (wèi)

CV: **on someone's behalf, for someone's sake**

今天是你的生日，這些菜都是為你做的。

20. 經ㄐㄧㄥ費ㄈㄟˋ (jīngfèi)

N: **operating funds of an organization（M：筆）**

系裡的經費不夠，只能買兩部電腦。

21. 安ㄢ排ㄆㄞˊ (ānpái)　　*V*: **to arrange matters, to plan**

他安排了一個很好的機會，讓我們見面。

排ㄆㄞˊ (pái)

V/M: **to line up, arrange in order / M. for rows, lines**

(1) 買票的時候，他排在我後面。

(2)你把教室裡的桌子排好，就可以回去了。

(3)我看電影的時候，都喜歡坐在最後一排。

22. 布置（佈置）(bùzhì)　　*V*: **arrange, set-up**

你把房子布置一下，就像新的一樣。

23. 場地 (chǎngdì)　　*N*: **place, site**

這個新歌發表會的場地很大，坐得下一萬人。

場 (chǎng)　　*M*: **(used for an event or happening)**

這場雨下了兩個鐘頭。

24. 發傳單 (fā//chuándān)

VO: **to issue a handbill / leaflet**

他們發傳單，是為了讓大家注意孩子的教育問題。

發 (fā)　　*V*: **to distribute leaflets, to issue a handbill**

考卷發完了，誰沒拿到的，請舉手。

傳 (chuán)　　*V*: **to pass, pass on**

我說「停」的時候，這個球傳到誰手裡，誰就得唱歌。

傳單 (chuándān)　　*N*: **handbill, leaflet**

25. 熱心 (rèxīn)

SV/A: **to be warmhearted, enthusiastic / zealously, enthusiastically**

不管是誰的事，他都很熱心幫忙。

26. 國會 (guóhuì)　　*N*: **parliament, congress**

27. 政治 (zhèngzhì)　　*N*: **politics**

我對政治完全沒有興趣，我不想競選。

28. 方面 (fāngmiàn)　　*N*: **aspect, position, side, party**

學中文，聽、說、讀、寫，哪一方面最困難？

29. 總統 (zǒngtǒng)　　*N*: **president (of a republic)**

30. 代表 (dàibiǎo)

V/N: **to represent, to stand for / representative, delegate**

(1)我們代表中文系，歡迎你們來參觀。

(2)這幾位都是今年選出來的學生代表。

31. 由ㄧㄡˊ (yóu)　　*CV*: **by, up to (someone)**

考試時間由老師決定。

32. 直ㄓˊ 接ㄐㄧㄝ (zhíjiē)　　*A*: **directly**

下了課，我不回家，要直接去餐廳吃飯。

33. 投ㄊㄡˊ 票ㄆㄧㄠˋ (tóu//piào)　　*VO*: **to vote, to cast a ballot**

去年的總統選舉，你的票投給誰了？

34. 包ㄅㄠ 括ㄎㄨㄛˋ (bāokuò)　　*V*: **to include, consist of, comprise of**

特餐包括一個菜、一個湯，還有一杯咖啡。

35. 鮮ㄒㄧㄢ 奶ㄋㄞˇ (xiānnǎi)　　*N*: **fresh milk**

牛ㄋㄧㄡˊ 奶ㄋㄞˇ (niúnǎi)　　*N*: **(cow's) milk**

36. 洗ㄒㄧˇ 衣ㄧ 粉ㄈㄣˇ (xǐyīfěn)　　*N*: **laundry detergent (powder)**

奶ㄋㄞˇ 粉ㄈㄣˇ (nǎifěn)　　*N*: **powdered milk**

37. 支ㄓ 持ㄔˊ (zhīchí)

V/N: **to support, to back / support, backing**

張：你的做法很對，我完全支持。

李：謝謝你對我的支持。

38. 答ㄉㄚ 應ㄧㄥˋ (dāyìng)

V: **to promise, to agree ; to answer, to reply, to respond**

(1)這件事，我真的做不到，所以沒辦法答應你。

(2)媽媽叫你，你為什麼不答應？

39. 你ㄋㄧˇ 看ㄎㄢˋ (nǐ kàn)　　*IE*: **in your opinion**

他今天沒來，你看他會不會生病了？

專有名詞 Proper Names

1. 民ㄇㄧㄣˊ 主ㄓㄨˇ 黨ㄉㄤˇ (Mínzhǔ Dǎng)　　Democratic Party
2. 共ㄍㄨㄥˋ 和ㄏㄜˊ 黨ㄉㄤˇ (Gònghé Dǎng)　　Republican Party
3. 白ㄅㄞˊ 宮ㄍㄨㄥ (Bái Gōng)　　White House (Washington, D. C.)
4. 國ㄍㄨㄛˊ 民ㄇㄧㄣˊ 大ㄉㄚˋ 會ㄏㄨㄟˋ (Guómín Dàhuì)　　National Assembly

5. 立ㄌㄧˋ法ㄈㄚˇ院ㄩㄢˋ (Lìfǎ Yuàn)　　Legislative Yuan

注釋

1. 期中選舉 is midterm election. Sometimes congressional, gubernatorial, and/or mayoral elections coincide with presidential election years, sometimes they don't. Those elections held in the middle (two years into) of a presidential term are called midterm elections. A senator's term of office is six years; elections are staggered with one third of the seats up for election every two years. House elections are held every two years. Terms of office for governors and mayors vary from state to state, depending on each state's constitution.
2. 拉票 means "to solicit votes", but not necessarily on a formal basis. 助選 means to solicit votes formally.
3. "那還用說嗎？" means "Does one even need to mention it?!" " Of course," "Certainly." It is casual and should not be used in speaking to elders or superiors.
4. According to the revised Constitution of the Republic of China, the president is elected every four years by the citizens, not by the 國民大會 as prior to 1996. This revision was made in 1992.
5. 立法院 is the Legislative Yuan, the body of the national government which proposes and debates bills and passes laws. The legislators are known as 立法委員. They are elected by the people every three years. The number of seats varies with the population. The first legislators were elected in 1948.
6. 國民大會 is the National Assembly. Members of the National Assembly are known as 國民大會代表. They are elected by the people every six years. They are authorized to vote for the President and Vice President, and revise the Constitution. The number of seats in the National Assembly

varies with the population. Formerly included in Parliament were the following three groups: 立法院、監察院、國民大會. The 立法委員, members of the 監察院 (Control Yuan), and 國民大會代表 who came to Taiwan with Chiang Kai-shek were allowed to retain their seats until December 1991. Their continued presence represented the legitimate rule of the government of the Republic of China over all of China. Members of the 監察院 (Jiānchá Yuàn), or Control Yuan, are known as 監察委員. They are elected by provincial assemblymen and city councilors every six years. Their responsibilities include impeachment and censoring of officials. The first members of the Control Yuan were elected in 1948. A constitutional change enacted in 1992 removed the 監察委員 from Parliament.

7. "等車啊？" and "你買東西啊？" are greetings. See Note 4 of Lesson 1.

8. 鮮奶 means "fresh milk". Many Chinese people are not used to drinking cold milk. They often buy powdered milk and make warm milk themselves. If you mention 牛奶, the first idea that comes to most Chinese is warm milk made from powder. Many people do not drink fresh milk because they have an allergy to it which causes gastric disorders.

9. "要不要我送你？" means "Do you want me to give you a lift?" (Literally : "Do you want me to send you there?") Another way to say this is "要不要搭個便車？" 搭便車 (dā//biànchē) means to get a lift from someone or to hitchhike, e.g. 我要搭別人的便車去紐約。

文法練習

☞ 一 每 Nu + M_1(N) + V + 一 + M_2

Vonce/have one every Nu – M

⊙ 眾議員每兩年選一次。

Members of the House of Representatives are elected once every two years.

用法說明：說明某個動作發生的規律。

Explanation: This pattern explains the rate of occurrence for some action.

練習：請用「每 Nu + M_1 (N) + V + 一 + M_2」改寫下面各句。

Exercise: Please rewrite the following sentences using the pattern "每 Nu + M_1 (N) + V + 一 + M_2".

1. 我們念完六課就考一次。

   After we finish going over 6 chapters then we have a test.

   →我們每六課考一次。

   We have a test once every six chapters.

2. 這個機場，五分鐘就有一架飛機起飛。

   ……………………………………………………………………………………

3. 這個園遊會有很多攤位，二十公尺就有一個。

   ……………………………………………………………………………………

4. 在這個國家，兩個人就有一輛汽車。

   ……………………………………………………………………………………

5. 奧林匹克運動會 (Àolínpīkè Yùndònghuì, Olympic Games) 四年就舉行一次。

   ……………………………………………………………………………………

☞ 二 X 分之 Y (fraction)Y / X

⊙參議員每兩年輪流改選三分之一。

One third of the senators run for election every two years.

用法說明：表示把某個整體分成 X 份，取其中 Y 份。

Explanation: This pattern refers to y parts out of a total of X parts. ("X 分之 Y" in simple fraction form = Y / X)

練習：請用「X 分之 Y」改寫下面句子。

Exercise: Please rewrite the sentences below using "X 分之 Y".

1. 這個學校，五個學生當中只有一個是女的。

Only one out of every five students in this school is female.

→這個學校的學生只有五分之一是女的。

Only 1/5th of this school's students are female.

2. 我星期六買了六個蘋果，才兩天，就壞了兩個。

....

3. 他做生意的錢有一半是他爸爸給的。

....

4. 我弟弟念高中，上學期的期末考一共考了八科，有兩科不及格。

....

5. 你成績這麼好，申請獎學金一定沒問題。(100%)

....

☞ 三

（Ⅰ）為了　for the purpose of, so as to, in order to

⊙每天為了競選經費跑來跑去。

He runs around every day seeking out campaign funds.

用法說明：「為了」後面是目的或目的物，再後面是要達成此目的的做法或手段。如果先說做法或手段，後面應該說「是為了」。

Explanation: Following 為了 is a purpose or a desired object. After this , the method through which the goal is to be attained is given. When the positions of the method and goal are inverted, then 為了 is changed to 是為了 and placed between them.

練習：請根據提示，用「為了」及「是為了……」回答下面問題。

Exercise: Following the provided hints, please use "為了" and "是為了……" to answer the questions below.

1. 他為什麼每個週末都去圖書館？（查資料）

Why does he go to the library every weekend?

→他為了查資料，所以每個週末都去圖書館。

In order to look up information, he goes to the library every weekend.

→他每個週末都去圖書館是為了查資料。

The reason he goes to the library every weekend is to look up information.

2. 林建國為什麼到酒館打工？（多賺小費）

....

3. 你哥哥怎麼每天開夜車？（通過博士班的考試）

....

4. 那個參議員怎麼這麼早就開始跟選民拉票？（競選總統）

....

5. 他為什麼一個人到那麼遠的地方去工作？（理想）

....

6. 你搬了好幾次家了，到底是為什麼？（孩子）

....

(II) 為＋N / PN＋V

for, in order to benefit (a person, group, organization, etc.)

用法說明：「為」的前面有主語，後面是名詞或代名詞 (PN)，再後面是動詞，表示做某事是特別給該名詞或代名詞做的。

Explanation: Here 為 is preceded by the subject and followed by a noun (or pronoun) and verb. It indicates that the action is performed by the subject particularly for the benefit of the noun (or pronoun) mentioned. The difference between 為 and 為了 is that following「為了」is a reason or goal, whereas, following 為 is the recipient of the benefits of an action.

練習：請把「為 N/PN」放在句中合適的地方。

Exercise: Please place "為 N/PN" in the appropriate place in the following sentences.

1. 今天是你的生日，所以我做了一個蛋糕。

Today is your birthday, so I made a birthday cake.

→今天是你的生日，所以我為你做了一個蛋糕。

Today is your birthday, so I made a birthday cake for you.

2. 他競選的時候，答應做的事都沒做到。

....

3. 做父母的總想在家裡布置一個舒服的生活環境。

....

4. 你每天忙到這麼晚才回家，老闆應該對你好一點才對。

....

5. 張校長辛苦了很多年了。

....

☞ 四 方面 aspect, direction, field, area

⊙……很有興趣往政治這方面發展。

...... very interested in going into the field of politics.

用法說明：「方面」有「範圍」、「範疇」的意思。前面可用名詞、數字，或「這」、「那」、「哪」、「每」、「各」、「別的」。

Explanation: 方面 means field, scope or category, but in translation this often remains unspoken. One can place a noun, a numeral, or a demonstrative 這、那、哪、每、各, or 別的 in front of 方面.

練習：請把「方面」放在句中合適的地方。

Exercise: Please place 方面 in the appropriate place in the sentences below.

1. 他剛到美國，吃的、住的都不習慣。

When he first arrived in America, he was neither accustomed to the food nor the lifestyle.

→他剛到美國，吃的、住的（各）方面都不習慣。

When he first arrived in America, he was uncomfortable both from the standpoint of food and lifestyle.

2. 小張念研究所是為了研究社會的問題。

....

3. 那個人只會念書，追女朋友，完全沒有經驗。（可以加「這」）

....

4. 法國話，我只會說，文法我一點都不懂。

……………………………………………………………………………………

5. 如果你參加競選，只要發表政見就行了，別的都由我們來替你安排。

……………………………………………………………………………………

☞ 五 這麼說 If you put it that way, then...... / If so , then ......

⊙這麼說，也許有一天你會是美國總統的弟弟呢！

If it's as you say it is, then maybe someday you'll be the younger brother of the American president!

用法説明：「這麼說」意思是「如果按照你說的」，後面是說話者根據對方說的話做的推測。如果並不確定自己所做的推測，可在句尾加「嘍」。

Explanation: 這麼說 means "If things are as you say, then......" After 這麼說 the speaker states his or her conclusion or prediction based on what the other party has said. If the speaker is not so confident about his conclusion 嘍 can be added at the end of the sentence.

練習：請用「這麼說」完成下面對話。

Exercise: Please complete the dialogues below using 這麼說.

1. 張：如果你真的找不到人幫忙，就打電話給我吧！

   Chang: If you really can't find anybody to help, then give me a call!

   李：這麼說，你答應了。

   Li: If you put it that way, then I guess you've agreed to do it.

2. 張：冰淇淋、蛋糕，我都愛吃。

   李：這麼說，＿＿＿＿＿＿＿＿＿＿＿＿＿＿＿＿。

3. 張：我先生念大學的時候，我才念小學。

   李：這麼說，＿＿＿＿＿＿＿＿＿＿＿＿＿＿＿＿。

4. 張：小林從來沒生過病，連感冒都很少。

   李：這麼說，＿＿＿＿＿＿＿＿＿＿＿＿＿＿＿＿。

5. 張：謝教授教書已經教了二十年了。

李：這麼說，＿＿＿＿＿＿＿＿＿＿＿＿＿＿＿＿。

☞ 六 由 N / PN 來 V (O) up to N to V

⊙我們要先選國民大會代表，由他們來選舉。

First we choose the representatives for the National Assembly, then they are responsible for voting.

用法說明：「由」的後面是施行動作者，「來」的後面是要做的事。（請參看第九課文法練習三）這個句型表示做這件事的責任或權利歸施行動作者。賓語放在句首或句尾都可以。語言環境清楚時可省略。

Explanation: After 由 is the performer of the action, and after 來 is the necessary action. (Please refer to sentence pattern 3 in Chapter 9) This pattern shows that this person has the responsibility or right to perform the given action. The object can be placed either at the beginning or the end of the sentence. When the context is clear, 由 can be omitted.

練習：請用「由 N / PN 來 V(O)」完成下面句子。

Exercise: Please complete the sentences below using the pattern "由 N / PN 來 V(O)".

1. 我媽說我只要把書念好就行了，學費的事由她來想辦法。
   My mother said all I have to do is concentrate on doing well in school. She will be responsible for dealing with the tuition.
2. 氣候，我已經介紹完了，這裡到底出產什麼，由＿＿＿＿＿＿＿＿。
3. 張教授教文法，說話練習由＿＿＿＿＿＿＿＿。
4. 我們家的小事，我可以決定，可是大事就由＿＿＿＿＿＿＿＿。
5. 明天的舞會，我布置場地，飲料由＿＿＿＿＿＿＿＿。

☞ 七 正要 just about to, on the verge of

⊙我正要去學校。

I'm just about to go to school.

用法說明：強調「剛準備做」某件事，雖然還沒做，可是幾乎已經開始做了。

也可以說「正想」或「正打算」。

Explanation: This emphasizes that one is just about to do something, and although you have not done it yet, you have, for all practical purposes, started. You could also say 正想 (just thinking about) or 正打算 (just planning to).

練習：請用「正要」改寫下面句子。

Exercise: Please use "正要" to rewrite the sentences below.

1. 他剛拿起刮鬍刀，你就打電話來了。
   He had just picked up the razor when you called.
   →他正要刮鬍子，你就打電話來了。
   He was just about to shave when you called.
2. 老張來找我的時候，我剛準備出門。
   ……………………………………………………………………
3. 我剛準備問老師這個問題，沒想到老師先問我了。
   ……………………………………………………………………
4. 真倒楣！我剛準備回家，就下起雨來了。
   ……………………………………………………………………
5. 我媽剛準備上車，就聽到我爸在叫她。
   ……………………………………………………………………

☞ 八 不到 not yet, under, less than

⊙我還不到十八歲，沒有選舉權。

I still hadn't reached 18 yet; I didn't have the right to vote.

用法說明：「不到」的後面加「數字」，表示尚未達到那個程度，但相差不多。

Explanation: When 不到 is placed before a number it indicates that one has not yet arrived at that point. However, it also implies that it is not very far off.

練習：請用「不到」完成下面句子。

Exercise: Please use 不到 to complete the sentences below.

1. 這麼多衣服，他不到半個小時就洗完了，好快啊！
   He washed all these clothes in less than half an hour, that's fast!

2. 這個電影大人才能看，你不到＿＿＿＿＿＿＿，不可以看。
3. 我搬到這兒才五個月，還不到＿＿＿＿＿＿＿，所以認識的人不多。
4. 這個冰箱好便宜，只要九十多塊，還不到＿＿＿＿＿＿＿。
5. 他們學校很小，每班學生才十幾個，還不到＿＿＿＿＿＿＿。

☞ 九 你／我看 in your/my opinion

⊙你看，你支持的人有希望當選嗎？

In your opinion, does the candidate you support have a chance of winning the election?

用法說明：「看」在此處是「想」或「認為」的意思，「我看」的後面是說話者的看法或建議，「你看」的後面都是問句，詢問對方的看法。

Explanation: Here, 看 means "think" or "believe". Following 我看 is the speaker's own thought or opinion, and following 你看 is a solicitation for another's opinion.

練習：請用「我看」回答下面問題。

Exercise: Please answer the following questions using 我看.

1. 你看，明天會不會下雨？
   What do you think, will it rain tomorrow?
   → 我看，一定不會。一般來說，這個時候很少下雨。
   In my opinion, it definitely won't rain. Generally speaking, it seldom rains during this period.
2. 你看，法文難學還是中文難學？
   ……………………………………………………………………
3. 你看，我什麼時候去看張老師比較好？
   ……………………………………………………………………
4. 你看，小張跟小王，誰可能申請到獎學金？
   ……………………………………………………………………
5. 你看，王先生的政見發表會在哪兒舉行才合適？
   ……………………………………………………………………

課室活動

1. Role playing

Two students: One student acts as a curious Chinese 小留學生, the other as his/her tutor. The 小留學生 saw someone distributing leaflets concerning the upcoming presidential campaign. So he/she has come to the tutor with such questions as: 美國人怎麼選總統？是不是直接選舉？要不要選代表？為什麼要選代表？什麼人可以做候選人？什麼人可以投票？沒有參加政黨的人也可以競選嗎？Some useful supplementary words include: 家世背景 (family background), 聲望 (popularity, prestige, reputation), 學歷 (xuélì; record of formal schooling), 資格 (qualifications), 承諾 (chéngnuò; promise to undertake, undertake to do something), 條件 (conditions, requirements).

2. 遊戲

This game can be played by paired students or by a larger group. First, have the students memorize the following names: 額頭 (é tóu, forehead), 下巴 (xiàbā, chin), 耳朵 (ěr·duo, ear), 眼睛, 鼻子, 嘴巴. Then have the students make fists with both hands and touch their noses（鼻子）. The leader, usually the teacher on the first round, then says: 鼻子, 鼻子, 鼻子——耳朵 (or another facial part from the list above). The third time that 鼻子 is repeated, it should be spoken more slowly, tipping off the other players that he is about to change. Everyone must move both their fists at the same time the new part is called out（in this case, 耳朵）. All players, including the leader, must quickly move both fists from the 鼻子 to 耳朵. Anyone who touches any part of the face part other than 耳朵 loses, including the leader himself. The loser then must take over as leader. But before he does so, he must share with the class, in Chinese, his views on what issues should be emphasized in a presidential campaign.

短文

幫同學助選

各位同學：

大家好！你們都知道Peter Johnson這次要競選學生聯合會[1]代表，就像傳單上說的，Peter是個關心校園問題，瞭解同學需要，而且又熱心服務的人。各位一定還記得，上次放假的時候，小偷到學生宿舍來偷東西，Peter為了追小偷，不管外面下著大雨，也不怕小偷手裏拿著刀子，追了十幾分鐘，才把同學的東西追回來。從這件事情，我們也發現校園安全[2]已經成了問題。只要Peter當選了代表，一定會跟學校一起來想辦法，讓大家可以放心地在校園裏活動。除了安全問題，Peter也會請學校多準備經費買書、買電腦、辦活動；另外像補助學費，安排工讀機會，學校餐廳價錢什麼的，也都是他特別注意的問題。如果您願意給他一個為您服務的機會，就請您別忘了下禮拜一把票投給最理想的學聯會代表候選人：3號[3] Peter Johnson！3號 Peter Johnson！謝謝您的支持。

Vocabulary:

1. 學生聯合會 (xuéshēng liánhéhuì)：students association
2. 安全 (ānquán)：security / safety
3. 三號：No. 3. In Taiwan each election candidate carries a special personal number through the election campaign. This is so that the voters can identify and remember

them more easily. These numbers are all decided by drawing lots. Most of the candidates hope to be "number one."

你看，這是我上次的傳單，這次競選我恐怕沒希望了！

因為我答應選民的事一件也沒做到。

哇！好極了，這些傳單，這次還可以再用。

第十一課

歷史是怎麼說的

・中華民國國慶日的活動：舞龍（新聞局提供）

（演講廳）

偉立：你覺得他的演講怎麼樣？你同意他的看法嗎？

李平：這位教授講的是中國大陸的民主運動，我們臺灣的情形不太一樣。

偉立：有什麼不同？

李平：大陸實行的是共產主義。

偉立：那你們到底實行什麼主義呢？

李平：這**就要從**孫中山先生**說起**了。孫中山，你聽說過嗎？

偉立：是 Dr. Sun Yet-sen嗎？

李平：對了！他在一九一一年革命成功，推翻了腐敗的清朝政府，建立了中華民國。想要建設一個三民主義[1]的新中國，沒想到不久就發生了內戰[2]。然後又是世界大戰。

偉立：第二次世界大戰的時候，中國不是跟日本打仗嗎？

李平：是啊！我們跟他們打了八年[3]。就**因為**長時間打仗**的關係**，社會一直沒辦法安定，人民的生活很苦，毛澤東領導的共產黨就在這個時候發展起來了。

偉立：你們那個時候的政府，是不是蔣介石領導的？

李平：是。戰爭結束以後，國民政府[4]的力量弱了很多，**再加上**共產黨的勢力越來越大，控制了中國大部分的地方。因為情形越來越嚴重，蔣介石就決定**先**把政府遷到臺灣，想**等**有了力量**再**回大陸去。

偉立：這是哪一年的事？

李平：一九四九年，這是中國歷史上很重要的一年。**從**這個時候**起**，中華民國在臺灣，實行三民主義；中華人民共和國在大陸，實行共產主義。因為各有各的制度，就有了不同的發展。

偉立：你們也希望將來能**像**東、西德**一樣**統一嗎？

・雙十節慶祝大會（新聞局提供）

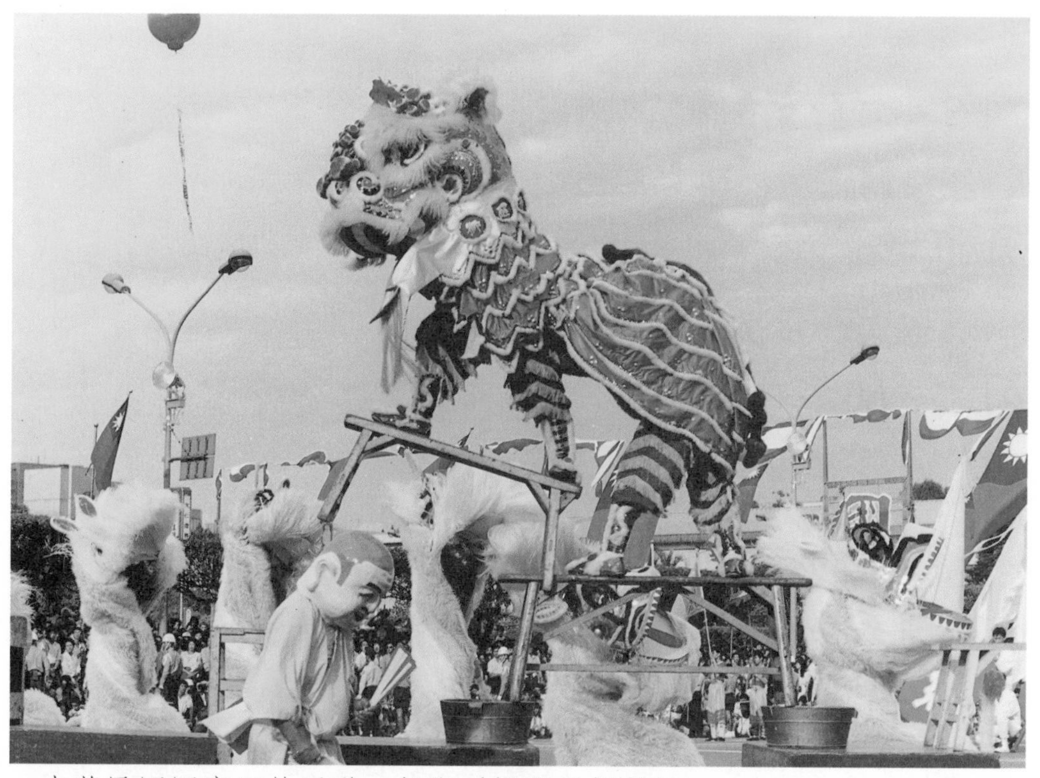

・中華民國國慶日的活動：舞獅（新聞局提供）

李平：我們當然希望有一天會統一。東歐有些國家已經放棄了共產主義，這就證明共產主義並不適合人類社會。你說對不對？

偉立：對啊！我認為民主化才是最好的辦法。

※ ※ ※ ※ ※ ※

（高偉立敲門）

錢太太：嗨！高偉立。歡迎，歡迎。來，這雙拖鞋給你穿[5]。

偉立：噢！謝謝。錢先生呢？還沒下班嗎？

錢太太：快了。他公司最近比較忙。同同[6]，高哥哥[7]來了！

大同（過來）：高哥哥，你好。

偉立：嗨！大同，生日快樂，這個送給你。

大同：謝謝。

偉立：你不打開看看嗎？（大同看看媽媽）

錢太太：沒關係，打開看看吧[8]！

大同：哇！印第安人！謝謝高哥哥。

偉立：沒什麼，小東西[9]。大同真有禮貌。

錢太太：哪裡，應該的。他最喜歡看漫畫書了。謝謝你的禮物。

大同：我看過好多印第安人的電影，現在他們到哪裡去了？

偉立：歐洲人移民過來以後，印第安人就**一**天**比一**天少了。你們的歷史課教到哪兒了？

大同：剛剛念到獨立戰爭，殖民地的代表們決定要建立一個獨立的國家，由華盛頓領導軍隊跟英國打仗，在一七七六年宣布獨立。

錢太太：不錯嘛！**多少**學了**一點**[10]。

偉立：是啊！記得很清楚。還有一個「南北戰爭」，美國歷史上只有這一次內戰，你們以後一定也會學到。

錢太太（聽見開門聲）：好了，爸爸回來了，我們吃飯吧！

生詞及例句

1. 歷ㄌㄧˋ史ㄕˇ (lìshǐ) *N*: **history**

2. 演ㄧㄢˇ講ㄐㄧㄤˇ廳ㄊㄧㄥ (yǎnjiǎngtīng) *N*: **auditorium, lecture hall**

   演ㄧㄢˇ講ㄐㄧㄤˇ (yǎnjiǎng)

   V/N: **to deliver a speech, give a lecture / lecture, speech**

   講ㄐㄧㄤˇ (jiǎng) *V*: **to speak, explain**

   政治系昨天請總統來演講，他講的是「政黨跟政府的關係」。

   講ㄐㄧㄤˇ價ㄐㄧㄚˋ (jiǎng//jià) *VO*: **to bargain , to haggle over prices**

   我跟他講了半天的價，他只願意便宜一塊錢。

3. 同ㄊㄨㄥˊ意ㄧˋ (tóngyì)

   V/N: **to agree, give consent / agreement, consent**

   (1)他不是好人，所以我不同意把房子租給他。

   (2)沒有他的同意，你不可以進他的房間。

4. 民ㄇㄧㄣˊ主ㄓㄨˇ運ㄩㄣˋ動ㄉㄨㄥˋ (mínzhǔ yùndòng)

   N: **democratic movement**

   民ㄇㄧㄣˊ主ㄓㄨˇ (mínzhǔ) *N/SV*: **democracy / to be democratic**

   這個國家非常不民主，連搬家都得政府同意才行。

   運ㄩㄣˋ動ㄉㄨㄥˋ (yùndòng)

   N: **movement, campaign, drive (political, social, etc.)**

參加這次學生運動的大部分是男學生。

5. 實行 (shíxíng)

V: **to carry out, to implement, to put into practice**

如果經費不夠，這個計畫實行起來就有困難。

6. 共產主義 (gòngchǎnzhǔyì) *N*: **communism**

主義 (zhǔyì) *N*: **doctrine, "-ism"**

美國是不是最早實行民主主義的國家？

共產黨 (gòngchǎndǎng) *N*: **communist party**

7. 革命 (gémìng) *V/N*: **to revolt, to overhaul / a revolution**

(1) 這個國家的政府不民主，人民才起來革命的。

(2) 法國大革命的時候，死了多少人？

8. 成功 (chénggōng) *N/SV*: **success / to be successful**

(1) 成功是每一個人都希望的。

(2) 他生意做得很大，很成功。

9. 推翻 (tuīfān) *V*: **to overthrow, overturn, topple**

牛頓 (Newton) 這個說法，到現在還沒有人能推翻。

推 (tuī) *V*: **to push, to shove**

那個門他推了半天都推不開，後來才發現應該往裡拉。

10. 腐敗 (fǔbài) *SV*: **rotten, decayed; corrupt**

這個政府裡的人只關心怎麼讓自己賺更多的錢，真腐敗。

11. 建立 (jiànlì) *V*: **to establish, to set up, to found**

亞洲最早建立的民主國家是哪一國？

12. 建設 (jiànshè) *V/N*: **to build, to construct / construction**

(1) 他答應選民一定要把這個城市建設好。

(2) 這個地方的建設，完全沒有計畫。

13. 內戰 (nèizhàn) *N*: **civil war**

14. 打仗 (dǎ//zhàng)

VO: **to go to war, to engage in combat, to battle**

美國跟別的國家打過仗嗎？

15. 安定 (āndìng) *N/SV*: **stability / to be stable, to be settled**

(1) 社會的安定是每一個人都希望的。

(2) 他搬好家以後，就可以安定了。

16. 人民 (rénmín) *N*: **the people, citizen**

這個國家的人民都支持他們的政府嗎？

17. 領導 (lǐngdǎo) *N/V*: **leadership, guidance / to lead, guide**

(1) 有了他的領導，我們一定會打贏。

(2) 這次的民主運動是誰領導的？

18. 戰爭 (zhànzhēng) *N*: **war, combat**

男人跟女人的戰爭，誰都贏不了。

19. 結束 (jiéshù) *V*: **to end, finish, conclude**

期末考一考完，學期就結束了。

20. 力量 (lìliàng) *N*: **strength, power**

我一個人的力量不夠，得大家一起做才行。

力氣 (lì·qì) *N*: **energy, power**

他在山上迷了路，餓了三天。我們發現他的時候，他連走路的力氣都沒有了。

21. 弱 (ruò) *SV*: **to be feeble, weak, frail**

他病剛好，所以身體還很弱。

22. 勢力 (shìlì) *N*: **force, power, influence**

用這種電腦的人越來越多，所以這家公司在市場上的勢力也越來越大。

23. 控制 (kòngzhì)

N/V: **control, command / to control, manipulate, dominate**

(1) 在共產國家，人民的生活都受到政府的控制。

(2) 演講的時候，得控制好時間。

24. 嚴重 (yánzhòng) *SV*: **to be serious, grave, critical**

他這次感冒很嚴重，病了一個月才好。

嚴 (yán) *SV*: **to be strict, severe**

這個老師很嚴，一個字寫錯了，就要扣兩分。

25. 遷 (qiān)　　*V*: **to move to another place**

辦公室太小了，他想遷到附近的新大樓去。

26. 制度 (zhìdù)　　*N*: **system**

這是一個新公司，制度都還沒建立。

27. 將來 (jiānglái)　　*MA/N*: **in the future / the future**

(1) 他現在替別人助選，將來自己要出來競選。

(2) 為了孩子的將來，她覺得非搬家不可。

28. 統一 (tǒngyī)

N/V: **unification / to unify, unite, integrate, make uniform**

這個國家的語言一直沒辦法統一。

29. 放棄 (fàngqì)　　*V*: **to abandon, give up, renounce**

我看沒有希望了，我們放棄吧！

30. 證明 (zhèngmíng)

N/V: **proof, evidence / to prove, to confirm**

(1) 你一直說你是對的，請證明給我看。

(2) 他生病，不能去上課，他應該拿一張醫生證明給老師看。

31. 人類 (rénlèi)　　*N*: **humankind, the human race**

人類學 (rénlèixué)　　*N*: **anthropology**

32. 認為 (rènwéi)　　*V*: **to believe that, consider that**

這個候選人沒有什麼經驗，我認為他不會當選。

33. 民主化 (mínzhǔhuà)

N/V: **democratization / to democratize**

(1) 人人都希望早一點看到那個國家的民主化。

(2) 你們想要民主化，一定要改變制度。

西化 (xīhuà)　　*N/V*: **westernization / to westernize**

制度化 (zhìdùhuà)

N/V: **systematization / to systematize**

電腦化 (diànnǎohuà)

N/V: **computerization / to computerize**

自ㄗˋ動ㄉㄨㄥˋ化ㄏㄨㄚˋ (zìdònghuà) *N/V*: **automation / to automate**

34. 拖ㄊㄨㄛ鞋ㄒㄧㄝˊ (tuōxié) *N*: **slippers, thongs（M: 雙）**

拖ㄊㄨㄛ (tuō)

V: **to pull, drag, haul; to drag on, delay; to mop**

(1) 箱子太重了，我拿不動，只好拖回家。

(2) 這篇報告上星期就該交了，你怎麼拖到今天才交？

(3) 地上有水，請你拖一拖。

35. 禮ㄌㄧˇ貌ㄇㄠˋ (lǐmào) *N*: **courtesy, manners, social etiquette**

別人說話的時候，你應該注意聽，這是禮貌。

有ㄧㄡˇ禮ㄌㄧˇ貌ㄇㄠˋ (yǒu lǐmào)

SV: **to be courteous, to have good manners, to be polite**

客人還在喝咖啡，你就一直看錶，真沒禮貌。

36. 漫ㄇㄢˋ畫ㄏㄨㄚˋ書ㄕㄨ (mànhuàshū) *N*: **comic book**

漫ㄇㄢˋ畫ㄏㄨㄚˋ (mànhuà) *N*: **caricature, cartoon**

他們每天搶報紙，就是為了看漫畫。

37. 殖ㄓˊ民ㄇㄧㄣˊ地ㄉㄧˋ (zhímíndì) *N*: **colony**

38. 軍ㄐㄩㄣ隊ㄉㄨㄟˋ (jūnduì) *N*: **army, troops, armed forces**

聯合國沒有自己的軍隊。

軍ㄐㄩㄣ人ㄖㄣˊ (jūnrén) *N*: **soldier, serviceperson**

陸ㄌㄨˋ軍ㄐㄩㄣ (lùjūn) *N*: **ground forces, land forces, army**

海ㄏㄞˇ軍ㄐㄩㄣ (hǎijūn) *N*: **naval forces, navy**

空ㄎㄨㄥ軍ㄐㄩㄣ (kōngjūn) *N*: **air force**

39. 宣ㄒㄩㄢ布ㄅㄨˋ (xuānbù) *V*: **to declare, proclaim, announce**

大家請注意，我現在要宣布一個消息。

布ㄅㄨˋ (bù) *N*: **cloth（M：塊／尺）**

40. 多ㄉㄨㄛ少ㄕㄠˇ (duōshǎo)

A: **(in this chapter) more or less, somewhat**

他說了半天，你多少借給他一點吧！

專有名詞 Proper Names

1. 孫中山 (Sūn Zhōngshān) Sun Yat-sen (1866 -1925)
2. 清朝 (Qīng Cháo) Ch'ing Dynasty (1644 - 1911)
3. 中華民國(Zhōnghuá Mín'guó)
   Republic of China (1912 - present) (government in Taiwan since 1949)
4. 三民主義 (Sānmín zhǔyì) Three Principles of the People
5. 第二次世界大戰 (Dì'èr cì Shìjiè Dàzhàn)
   World War II
6. 毛澤東 (Máo Zédōng) Mao Tse-tung (1893- 1976)
7. 蔣介石 (Jiǎng Jièshí) Chiang Kai-shek (1887-1975)
8. 國民政府 (Guómínzhèngfǔ) National Government
9. 中華人民共和國 (Zhōnghuá Rénmín Gònghéguó)
   The People's Republic of China (1949 - present) (government in Mainland China)
10. 東德 (Dōng Dé) (the former) East Germany
11. 西德 (Xī Dé) (the former) West Germany
12. 東歐 (Dōng Ōu) East Europe
13. 印地安人 (Yìndì'ān rén) American Indians
14. 華盛頓(Huáshèngdùn)
    George Washington.
15. 南北戰爭(Nánběizhànzhēng)
    the American Civil War (1861-1865)

注釋

1. 三民主義 ：the Three Principles of the People. Dr. Sun Yat-sen (1866-1925) authored this three-part theory in 1898 as an ideal for shaping the Chinese nation and as a means to promote the political and economic status

of Chinese people. The three parts consist of 民族主義 (Mínzú Zhǔyì; racial rights), 民權主義 (Mínquán Zhǔyì; political rights), and 民生主義 (rights for life and the pursuit of happiness). 民族主義 establishes equal rights to all races in the Chinese nation , and declares that Chinese citizens have rights equal to other citizens of the world. 民權主義 asserts that everyone has an equal right to participate in politics and the running of government. According to 民生主義 everyone should have equal access to daily necessities of life, including education, food, housing, clothing, transportation and recreation.

2. 內戰 means "civil war". The Republic of China, established in 1912, was the first republic in Asia. Democracy was a new concept to the Chinese and therefore faced some opposition at the beginning. In 1915 袁世凱 (Yuán Shìkǎi) claimed that he was the emperor and tried to restore imperialism. 雲南, Yunnan Province declared itself independent. Military factions appeared in various places throughout the country, resulting in many local battles. In 1928 Chiang Kai-shek (1887 - 1975) and his troops succeeded in carrying out the Northern Expedition, clearing out all the warlords and once again unifying the country.

3. "我們跟他們（日本）打了八年". The Japanese invaded northeastern China in 1931. The war against Japan formally began in 1937, after they attacked 宛平 (Wǎnpíng), a county close to 北平 (Běipíng), the capital. The war ended eight years later in 1945 with the surrender of Japan. As part of the war settlement, Taiwan was returned to China. It had been governed by Japan for fifty years as the result of a previous treaty signed during the Ching Dynasty.

4. 國民政府 refers to The National Government of the Republic of China, before the Constitutional Central Government was formed in 1948. During that time 國民黨, the Kwomintang (KMT) or Nationalist Party, had full control of the government.

5. 這雙拖鞋給你穿 means "Here, you can wear these slippers." Most people

living in Taiwan have adapted this Japanese custom of leaving one's shoes at the doorway in order to keep the interior of the house clean.

6. 同同, the child's given name is 大同, but here the first syllable has been eliminated and the last syllable has been duplicated. Many parents like to address their children, especially young ones, in this manner as a term of endearment.

7. 高哥哥 means "Brother Gao." In Chinese society, children usually address older people of the same generation as 哥哥 or 姐姐, whether they are related or not. This expresses a feeling of closeness and familiarity.

8. "沒關係，你打開看看吧！" means: "It's all right, go ahead and open it." As a custom, Chinese people do not usually open gifts in front of the person who has presented the gift. This avoids giving the impression that the recipient is more concerned about the gift than about the giver or his goodwill.

9. "沒什麼，小東西。" means: "It's nothing, just a small token." Chinese often say this when presenting a gift as a form of courtesy. Some people say 小意思 instead of 小東西.

10. 多少學了一點 means "so you have learned something." Statements such as this may imply two intentions. On one hand it might be 客氣話, a polite remark, resulting because 錢太太 does not want to make a big issue of her son's achievements before a guest. On the other hand it might be a joking statement which subtly contains some encouragement for her son.

文法練習

一

(I) 從……起 to start from……

⊙這就要從孫中山先生說起了。

In order to explain this, we need to begin by talking about Sun Yat-sen.

⊙從這個時候起，中華民國在臺灣，實行三民主義……

Starting from this year, the Republic of China on Taiwan has been practising the Three Principles of the People......

用法說明：「起」表示「開始」。「從」的後面常用時間詞，有時也可用表示地方的詞。

Explanation: 起 means "to start". This pattern means "to start from......" 從 is often followed by a TW, or sometimes, a PW

練習：請用「從……起」改寫下面句子。

Exercise: Please rewrite the following sentences using the "從……起" pattern.

1. 我媽說我六歲以後就很少生病了。

   My mother says that after I turned six I hardly ever got sick.

   →我媽說我從六歲起就很少生病了。

   My mother says that starting from the time I turned six years old I hardly ever got sick .

2. 小王找到了新工作，明天就不來這兒上班了。

   ....

3. 他搬進來的那天，我們就成了好朋友。

   ....

4. 第十一課開始，我要改變教法。

   ....

5. 七號房開始，每一間都要好好兒地查一查。

   ....

(II) 這就要從……說起了

to explain this one must begin by talking about…

⊙這就要從孫中山先生說起了。

In order to explain this, we need to begin by talking about Sun Yat-Sen.

用法說明：「這」表示「這件事」，「就要」是「就得」的意思。說話者要說明某件事，但這件事不是一兩句話可以說清楚的，現在打算從某一點開始談。因為「起」的意思是「開始」，所以前面還可以用其他動詞，如「找」、「做」、「寫」、「看」……等，表示開始做那件事。

Explanation: 這 refers to 這件事. 就要 means "then one must". The speaker wants to explain something cannot be clearly described in a brief statement, so he uses this pattern to introduce his explanation and indicate his starting point. Since 起 means "to start", other verbs, such as 找, 做, 寫, 看 ......, etc., can be placed in front of 起 to show what action one is starting.

練習：請用「這就要從……說起了」回答下面問題，並再加以說明。

Exercise: Please answer the questions below using the "這就要從……說起了" pattern.

1. 張先生為什麼會競選州長？

   Why is Mr. Chang running for governor?

   →這就要從他的政治理想說起了。他從小就對政治有興趣、關心社會問題。他一直在找機會證明自己政治方面的看法是對的。

   To explain this one must begin by talking about his political ideals. Ever he was young, he has been interested in politics and concerned about social issues. He has always been looking for a chance to prove that his political views are correct.

2. 你為什麼想學中文？

   ....

3. 我們學校離你家這麼遠，你為什麼要來這兒念大學呢？

   ....

4. 你跟你的女朋友怎麼好起來的？

   ....

5. 你怎麼會到××（地方）去打工的？

   ....

☞ 二 因為……的關係 Due to......

⊙就因為長時間打仗的關係，社會一直沒辦法安定，……

Due to the length of the war, society never had a chance to stabilize, ...

用法說明：「因為」的後面大部分是名詞或簡單的短語。說話者不欲詳細說明原因，或覺得原因不必交代那麼清楚，就用「因為……的關係」表示。

Explanation: Usually, the word following 因為 is a noun or a simple clause. The speaker does not want to or does not think it is necessary to give an elaborate explanation for his/her statement; the connection between the first clause and the second clause is obvious and requires no further explanation.

練習：請根據提示，用「因為……的關係」回答下面問題。

Exercise: Please answer the questions below using the "因為……的關係" pattern and the information in parentheses.

1. 你們為什麼不租大點兒的場地？（經費）

   Why don't you rent a larger site?

   →因為經費的關係，我們租不起大點兒的場地。

   Due to funding, we cannot rent a larger site.

2. 你們怎麼準備了那麼多吃的東西？（颱風）

   ....

3. 你今天怎麼只教了生詞？（時間）

   ....

4. 昨天這附近為什麼塞車？（學校開園遊會）

   ....

5. 小王怎麼這麼獨立？（從小住校）

   ....

☞ 三 再加上 furthermore; additionally

⊙國民政府的力量弱了很多，再加上共產黨的勢力越來越大，控制了中國大部分的地方……

The power of the National Government was much weakened. Furthermore, the Communist Party became increasingly powerful. Therefore, they controlled most of mainland China......

用法說明：「再加上」的前後都是造成後面事件的原因，可是「再加上」後面的原因比前面的更有決定性。

Explanation: The situations before and after 再加上 are all factors that contribute to the result that follows, but the factor stated after 再加上 is usually the final, determining factor which leads to the result.

練習：請用「再加上」完成下面句子。

Exercise: Please use 再加上 to complete the sentences below.

1. 今天是週末，天氣又好，再加上期中考也考完了，所以出來玩的學生特別多。

   It's the weekend, the weather is beautiful, and besides that, the mid-term exams are over; so there are especially many students outside today.
2. 這份工作很輕鬆，錢也多，再加上＿＿＿＿＿＿＿＿，所以他非常喜歡。
3. 那個地方颱風多，地震也多，再加上＿＿＿＿＿＿＿＿，不適合人住。
4. 我最近工作很忙，壓力很大，再加上＿＿＿＿＿＿＿＿，就病倒了。
5. 他不但醜，而且不修邊幅，再加上＿＿＿＿＿＿＿＿當然沒有女孩子會喜歡他。

☞ 四 先……，等……，再……。 first......, wait until......, and then ......

⊙蔣介石就決定先把政府遷到臺灣，想等有了力量再回大陸去。

Chiang Kai Shek decided to first move the government to Taiwan, wait until it had more strength, and then return to the mainland.

用法說明：指出做三件事的順序。用於說話或動作當時及後來的情況。（請參看第三課文法練習五、六）

Explanation: This pattern shows the sequence of three actions, starting with the time a statement is made or an action is performed, and then moving into the situations that follow. (Please refer to sentence patterns 5 and 6 in Chapter 3.)

練習：請用「先……，等……，再……」回答下面問題。

Exercise: Please answer the following questions using the "先……等……再……" pattern.

1. 在臺灣的中國人都願意跟大陸統一嗎？
   Do the Chinese people in Taiwan all want to unite with the mainland China?
   →他們說中國大陸得先放棄共產主義，等一切民主化以後，再談統一。
   They say that mainland China must first give up communism. After they've fully democratized, then unification can be discussed.
2. 你下了課就直接回家嗎？
   ....
3. 我想工讀，要怎麼申請？
   ....
4. 他借給你的錢，你這個月要還嗎？
   ....
5. 你有了錢，要先買房子，還是先買車子？
   ....

☞ 五 像……一樣 like...... / similar to......

⊙你們也希望將來能像東、西德一樣統一嗎？

Do you hope that in the future you'll also be able to unite like East and West Germany have?

用法說明：「像……一樣」表示兩個人、地、事物有類似之處，如果要說明類似之處，就加在「一樣」的後面。

Explanation: "像……一樣" indicates that two people, places or things have similar characteristics. To further explain how they are similar, a characteristic or condition can be placed after 一樣.

練習：請用「像……一樣」完成下面句子。

Exercise: Please use the "像……一樣" pattern to complete the following sentences.

1. 我們學校各國學生都有，像聯合國一樣。
   Our school has students from all countries; it's just like the United Nations.
2. 這裡怎麼這麼亂，像__________一樣。
3. 我妹妹的皮膚像__________一樣，又白又細。
4. 他什麼都學不會，像__________一樣笨。
5. 張小姐打扮得好漂亮，像__________一樣。

六 一M比一M

more and more / less and less /......er and ......er (every) ......

⊙……印地安人就一天比一天少了。

The Indian population is getting smaller and smaller every day.

用法說明：表示程度逐漸加深。

Explanation: This pattern indicates that the degree of something is gradually intensifying.

練習：請用「一M比一M」改寫下面句子。

Exercise: Please use the "一M比一M" pattern to rewrite the sentences below.

1. 夏天到了，天氣就熱起來了。
   Summer has arrived, so the weather has started to get hotter and hotter.
   →夏天到了，天氣就一天比一天熱了。
   Summer has arrived, so the weather has been getting hotter and hotter every day.
2. 這幾次的考試都很難，而且越來越難。

....

3. 每年大學聯考競爭都很激烈，以後會更激烈。

....

4. 這幾課書越到後面越難教。

....

5. 我這幾個朋友都很會說話，小王比小李會說話，小張比小王更會說話，小陳比他們都會說話。

....

☞ 七 多少V一點／一些／幾M (more or less) V a little

⊙多少學了一點。

You've learned a little something.

用法說明：「多少」是「或多或少」，「不管是多少，總……」的意思。多用作建議或對所提到的事故意表示不予重視的意思。

Explanation: 多少 means "more or less" or "no matter how much or how little, it's always ......". This pattern is mostly used to offer a suggestion or to downplay the thing mentioned in the conversation.

練習：請用「多少V一點／一些／幾M」完成下面對話。

Exercise: Please complete the dialogues below using "多少V一點／一些／幾M".

1. 張：他跟我借錢，我真不想借他。

   Chang: He wants to borrow money from me. I really don't want to lend it to him.

   李：不借不好吧？多少借給他一點嘛！

   Li: I don't think it's a good idea not to lend him anything. Give him a little something.

2. 張：你在美國住了兩年，英文說得不錯了吧？

   李：還說得不太好，不過多少＿＿＿＿＿＿＿＿。

3. 張：這個課真無聊，我不想去上。

李：你應該去上課，多少＿＿＿＿＿＿＿＿。

4. 張：我不舒服，不想吃東西。

李：這些菜都是為你做的，多少＿＿＿＿＿＿＿＿。

5. 張：這個工作是你爸爸幫你找的嗎？

李：是我自己找的，不過我爸爸多少＿＿＿＿＿＿＿＿。

課室活動

1. Role playing:

The students select and play the role of one of the following political figures: 孫中山，蔣介石，毛澤東，現任美國總統，前任美國總統, or 現任中華民國總統. The teacher acts as a moderator for a televised discussion panel in which each of the five historical personalities participate . The moderator begins the discussion by asking them what they think about 中國的將來. Supplementary words include: 改革 (reform), 改善 (gǎishàn; to improve), 經濟 (jīngjì; economy), 進步 (jìnbù; to progress, advance), 資本主義 (zīběn zhǔyì; capitalism), 自由經濟 (free market economy), 思想 (sīxiǎng; thoughts), 和平 (hépíng; peace), 相處 (xiāngchǔ; to get along with one another).

2. 遊戲：Musical Chairs

Find out if the students know any Chinese songs. If they do not, teach them a simple one such as: 兩隻老虎，兩隻老虎，跑得快，跑得快。一隻沒有眼睛，一隻沒有尾巴 (wěi·bā, tail), 真奇怪，真奇怪！Then have the students form a circle with their chairs. There should be one chair less than the total number of students. The game starts with the students circling around the chairs, singing the song they have just learned. When the teacher says 停, every student should quickly take a seat. The one who has no chair loses. He must describe in Chinese to the class some important event in

American history, then he is removed from the game. Then one chair is removed and the game starts again. This is repeated until only one player is left.

短文

爸爸的信

建國：

最近功課忙吧？上個月我回台灣，看了很多朋友，參觀了不少地方。

十月是台灣最快樂的一個月，天氣好，假日[1]多，活動也多。第一個好日子就是雙十節[2]，中華民國的國慶日[3]。這是為了紀念[4]一九一一年十月十日國父[5]孫中山先生推翻清朝，革命成功。每年的這一天都有很多慶祝活動，像遊行[6]、放煙火[7]什麼的。跟美國七月四日的獨立紀念日[8]一樣熱鬧。像我這樣回國參加慶祝活動的華僑[9]非常多。

十月二十五日是台灣光復節[10]，是二次大戰結束那年，日本政府把台灣還給中國的日子。三十一日是蔣中正總統的生日，這兩天也有不少的紀念活動。

這些年台灣各方面的發展非常快，改變了很多，等明年一月我們全家回去的時候，你也會發現一切都跟你小時候不一樣了。好了，我們下次再談吧！

父字

11月15日

AEROGRAMME•VIA AIRMAIL•PAR AVION

Vocabulary:

1. 假日 (jiàrì): holiday
2. 雙十節 (Shuāngshí Jié): Doubl T nth, a holiday c l brating th formation of th R public of China
3. 國慶日 (Guóqìng Rì): dat of a nation's formation
4. 紀念 (jì'niàn): to comm morat
5. 國父 (guófù): fath r of a nation
6. 遊行 (yóuxíng): parad
7. 放煙火 (fàng//yānhuǒ): to s t off fir works
8. 獨立紀念日 (Dúlì Jì'niànrì): Ind p nd nc Day
9. 華僑 (huáqiáo): Ov rs as Chin s
10. 光復節 (Guāngfù Jié): R troc ssion Day, day in which a t rritory is r turn d to its moth r-nation

第十二課

看球賽

・棒球賽（新聞局提供）

（體育館看臺上）

建國：哇！剛才的球賽好精彩。我們七號打得真棒，他一個人就得了二十八分。

美真：對呀！他投籃投得好準，防守也不錯，**要不是**後來犯規太多，他還可以得更多分。

台麗：他投籃的動作很漂亮。人也帥，好多女生都很迷他。

建國：是啊！給他加油的都是女生。

偉立：我覺得十五號也很好，每次搶到球都能得分。

美真：他那麼高，只要他站在籃下，誰都搶不到球。

建國：他跟隊友的默契也很好。他拿到球，**就是**沒機會投籃，**也**不會把球傳丟了，從來沒有出過錯！

台麗：上半場十三號打得不錯，不知道下半場教練為什麼不**讓**他打了？

偉立：可能因為他太愛出鋒頭，沒有團隊精神。你知道，比賽的時候，最重要的是合作。

建國：今天那個禿頭裁判不公平，好幾次對方犯規，他都假裝沒看見。幸虧我們有實力，要不然比數一定差得更多，不會只是九十八比九十三。

美真：所以好多人噓[1]他。

建國：真不知道他們從哪裡找來的爛裁判！我好幾次想進場把他拉出來。

偉立：我看見九號也**被**他氣得要打人了。

建國：九號，我認識。他常跟女朋友到我打工的酒館來玩。這個人很容易生氣，**動不動就**罵人。哎喲！**說到**打工，我得走了。今天John有事，我得去代班。再見啦！

美真：談**得正**高興，你就要走了。

建國：那有什麼辦法，誰叫我答應他的呢？我非走不可了。去

・籃球賽
（新聞局提供）

晚了，又要看老闆的臉色[2]。

台麗：那我們也走吧！

※　※　※　※　※　※

（在餐廳）

台麗：剛剛看大家這麼興奮，讓我想到以前在臺灣看棒球賽的情形。

偉立：在臺灣很多人看棒球賽嗎？

美真：我們最喜歡看的就是棒球賽跟籃球賽。

台麗：我還記得我們的棒球隊第一次到美國比賽[3]，大家寧可不睡覺，也要看電視轉播[4]。打贏了，就放鞭炮慶祝[5]，大家都興奮得不得了。

美真：對啊！對啊！每次看轉播的時候，我老爸[6]都準備好多吃的、喝的，我們一邊看，一邊吃，真有意思。

偉立：我們家也一樣。尤其是我老爸，他不但一邊看，一邊吃，看到緊張的時候還又叫又罵。好像自己是教練一樣。

美真：我老哥[6]也總以為自己是教練。要是中華隊投手**一連**投了幾次四壞球，他就會對著電視大叫「換投手！」。

台麗：你老哥真有意思！

美真：還有一次，中華隊在最後一局打了一支再見全壘打，他興奮得跳起來，把桌上的杯子都打破了。

偉立：他跟我老爸一起看球賽一定很熱鬧。

美真：我老哥在佛羅里達念博士。有機會應該介紹他們認識認識。他還是很迷棒球。每次中華隊來比賽，他一定開幾個小時的車去當啦啦隊，給他們加油。

偉立：像他這樣的棒球迷，臺灣有不少吧？

台麗：是啊！臺灣棒球運動的發展越來越制度化了，幾年前已經有了職業球隊[7]，都是由大公司的老闆支持的。

偉立：我們職業球隊的球員大部分是從大學選出來的，很多校友捐錢給自己的大學發展校隊，打得好的球員就有機會參加職業球隊。

美真：欸，這麼說，要是書念不好，會打球也不錯[8]。

生詞及例句

1. 球賽 (qiúsài)　　*N*: **ballgame, match**

　　你喜歡看哪一種球賽？籃球賽，網球賽，還是…？

　比賽 (bǐsài)　　*N/V*: **competition, match / to compete**

　　(1) 你要不要參加這次的演講比賽？

　　(2) 我們來比賽，看誰跑得快。

2. 體育館 (tǐyùguǎn)　　*N*: **gym, gymnasium**

　體育 (tǐyù)

　N: **physical training, sports, physical education**

　　我很愛運動，可惜我們一個星期只有兩個鐘頭的體育課。

3. 看臺（台）(kàntái)　　*N*: **grandstand**

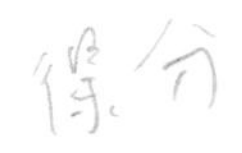

　　比賽還沒開始，看臺上已經坐滿了人。

　月臺（台）(yuètái)　　*N*: **railway platform**

4. 精彩 (jīngcǎi)　　*SV*: **brilliant, excellent, splendid**

　彩色 (cǎisè)　　*AT*: **multicolored, colored**

　　彩色電視的價錢比黑白的貴多了。

5. 得分 (dé//fēn)

　VO: **to score points (in sports competitions, contests, tests, etc.)**

　　這次考試，他得了一百分。

得 (dé) *V*: **to get, obtain, receive, gain**

得到 (dé·dào) *RC:* **to get, obtain, receive, acquire**

他去年打工，得到不少經驗。

6. 投籃 (tóu//lán) *VO*: **to shoot a basket (basketball)**

他投籃投了三次都沒進。

籃 (lán) *M*: **basket**

他來看我的時候，送了我一籃蘋果。

籃子 (lán·zi) *N*: **basket**

7. 準 (zhǔn) *SV*: **accurate**

我的錶很準，一分都不差。

8. 防守 (fángshǒu) *N/V*: **defense / to defend, guard**

(1)他們在防守方面比較差，難怪贏不了。

(2)這個地方很重要，所以有很多軍隊防守。

9. 犯規 (fàn//guī) *VO*: **to commit a foul**

他傳球的時候帶球走，所以犯規了。

10. 動作 (dòngzuò) *N*: **movement, action**

她又拉頭髮了，每次我看到這個動作，就知道她又緊張了。

11. 隊友 (duìyǒu) *N*: **teammate**

他只管防守，所以拿到球一定傳給隊友，很少投籃。

隊 (duì) *M*: **team, squad**

參加這次比賽的，一共有五隊，法國隊打得最好。

校友 (xiàoyǒu) *N*: **alumni, alumnus**

每年有一千多人從這個學校畢業，所以他們的校友很多。

12. 默契 (mòqì) *N*: **tacit agreement or understanding**

我們兩個很有默契，我心裡想什麼，我敢說他都知道。

13. 出錯 (chū//cuò)

VO: **to make a mistake, to blunder, to err**

他打工的時候老出錯，不是送錯菜，就是打破盤子，所以老闆叫他走路了。

14. 上半場 (shàngbànchǎng) *N*: **first half (of a game)**

下半場 (xiàbànchǎng) *N*: **second half (of a game)**

昨天那場籃球賽打得真爛，上半場結束人都走光了，下半場就沒人看了。

球場 (qiúchǎng) *N*: **playing field, court, ball field**

15. 教練 (jiàoliàn) *N*: **coach, trainer**

16. 出鋒頭 (chū//fēng·tóu)

VO: **to show off, to seek the limelight**

他穿這麼奇怪的衣服，就是為了出鋒頭。

17. 團隊精神 (tuánduì jīngshén) *N*: **team spirit**

你幫幫他吧！我們都是同一家公司的人，應該有團隊精神。

精神 (jīngshén) *N*: **spirit, vigor, drive**

他最喜歡籃球，一說到籃球，精神就來了。

18. 合作 (hézuò) *N/V*: **cooperation / to cooperate**

(1) 請大家把書放回書架上再走，謝謝各位的合作！

(2) 你是病人，得跟醫生合作，病才會好。

19. 禿頭 (tūtóu) *N*: **"baldhead", bald -headed person**

禿 (tū) *SV*: **to be bald**

禿頭的人，才三十歲就禿了。

20. 裁判 (cáipàn) *N*: **a referee**

籃球比賽，每一場都有一個裁判。

判 (pàn) *V*: **to judge, to decide**

他在籃下的時間太長，所以裁判判他犯規。

21. 對方 (duìfāng) *N*: **opposing side, the other side**

你們買房子的事談得怎麼樣了？對方怎麼說？

22. 假裝 (jiǎzhuāng)

V: **to pretend, make believe, simulate, feign**

我問他什麼時候還我錢，他就假裝睡著了。

假 (jiǎ) *SV*: **to be false, fake, a sham, phony**

我記得他是禿頭，所以他的頭髮是假的吧！

23. 實力 (shílì)

N: **strength (including resources and potentialities)**

這次考試沒時間準備，就看你的實力了。

24. 比數 (bǐshù) *N*: **score (in a competition, contest, etc.)**

這兩隊的實力差很多，所以比數差很多。

25. 噓 (xū)

V/ON: **to hiss (off a court, field, or stage) / Hiss! Boo!**

(1)他的歌唱得好爛，還沒唱完，大家就把他噓下來了。

(2)噓！小聲一點，小心別人聽到！

噓聲 (xūshēng) *N*: **sound of hissing or booing**

他上次演講，準備得不夠，得到的只有噓聲。

26. 動不動就 (dòng·búdòngjiù)

PT: **with little provocation, with out provocation, at the drop of a hat**

他很討厭我，動不動就找我麻煩。

27. 看臉色 (kàn//liǎnsè)

VO: **to watch the facial expressions of others (literal meaning). Refers to paying attention to the mood of superiors and adjusting ones behavior accordingly**

自己當老闆，就不必看別人的臉色了。

28. 興奮 (xīngfèn) *SV*: **to be excited**

明天要去旅行，他今天晚上興奮得睡不著。

29. 棒球 (bàngqiú) *N*: **baseball**

球隊 (qiúduì) *N*: **ball team（M：支）**

那支球隊剛剛從國外比賽回來。

校隊 (xiàoduì) *N*: **school team**

下學期我希望能參加棒球校隊。

球員 (qiúyuán) *N*: **ball player**

30. 轉播 (zhuǎnbò)

V: **(of radio or TV broadcast) to relay, to broadcast from on site**

這次的亞洲運動會，電視要不要轉播？

播出 (bòchū)　　*V*: **to broadcast, transmit**

電視上已經播出他昨天的演講了。

31.放鞭炮 (fàng//biānpào)　　*VO*: **to set off firecrackers**

新年的時候，中國人一定放鞭炮。

放 (fàng)　　*V*: **to let go, set free, release ; to place, put**

鞭炮 (biānpào)　　*N*: **firecracker**

32.投手 (tóushǒu)　　*N*: **pitcher**

這個投手在這場比賽一共投了幾個球？

33.一連 (yìlián)　　*A*: **in succession, one after another**

一連吃了幾天的漢堡，我真吃膩了。

34.壞球 (huàiqiú)

N: **"ball" (a pitch outside the "strike" zone in baseball)**

好球 (hǎoqiú)　　*N*: **"strike" (in baseball)**

他投了兩好球、三壞球了，只有一次機會了。

35.局 (jú)

M: **(for time periods in sports games: "set" in tennis, "inning" in baseball, etc.)**

你昨天那場網球賽，前兩局都打得不錯。

出局 (chūjú)　　*V*: **to be "out" (in baseball)**

已經兩人出局了，得分的機會不大了。

36.支 (zhī)

M: **(used for stick-like things, also for army units, etc.)**

37.再見全壘打 (zàijiàn quánlěidǎ)

N: **game ending home run（M：支）**

他打了一支再見全壘打，大家高興得不得了。

全壘打 (quánlěidǎ)　　*N*: **home run（M：支）**

安打 (āndǎ)　　*N*: **base hit, safe hit（M：支）**

一壘 (yīlěi)　　*N*: **1st base**

二壘 (èrlěi)　　*N*: **2nd base**

三壘 (sānlěi) *N*: **3rd base**

本壘 (běnlěi) *N*: **home base**

38. 啦啦隊 (lālāduì) *N*: **cheerleaders**

你比賽的時候，我們去做啦啦隊，給你加油！

39. 職業 (zhíyè)

N/AT: **occupation, profession / professional**

(1) 這班學生的父母做什麼職業的都有，像醫生、老師、生意人什麼的。

(2) 他兩個哥哥都是職業軍人。

40. 捐錢 (juān//qián) *VO*: **to contribute, donate money**

我們想給那些沒有父母的孩子捐一點錢。

捐 (juān) *V*: **to contribute, to donate**

她決定移民以後，把家裡的書都捐給圖書館了。

專有名詞 Proper Names

1. 中華隊 (Zhōnghuá Duì) Chinese team

注釋

1. 噓 means "to hiss or boo as an expression of hatred or disapproval." A slang term meaning the same thing is 開汽水, as in: 裁判不好，很多人開汽水。
2. 看老闆的臉色 means "to watch the boss's expression" and to act according to his/her mood. In this chapter 建國 means, "If I am late, I'll have to watch my boss's expression." or stated another way, "If I am late, I'll have to watch my boss express his displeasure."
3. 中華隊第一次到美國比賽. The first time that a baseball team from

Taiwan competed in the United States was in 1969. The team traveled to Williams Port, Pennsylvania, to participate in the Little League Baseball World Series, and won the championship.

4. 大家不睡覺也要看電視上的轉播. Because of the difference in time zones, when the Chinese team began playing in the afternoon in the United States, it was midnight in Taiwan. Many people stayed up late to watch the televised games.

5. 放鞭炮慶祝 means to set off firecrackers in order to celebrate a special occasion. It is a Chinese custom to light firecrackers for almost any happy event, such as New Year's, store openings, weddings, etc.

6. 老爸, 老媽, 老哥, 老姐： here 老 does not mean "old". This form of address was formerly used only by young people, but now many people use these terms as an expression of endearment toward family members. These terms may be used both when addressing these people or when referring to them in conversation.

7. 職業棒球 means "professional baseball". The first four professional baseball teams in Taiwan were organized in November 1989.

8. 要是書念不好，會打球也不錯 means: "If one doesn't do well in his /her studies, then being good at sports isn't bad either." According to traditional Chinese values, study is of primary importance. However, when someone is not very successful in his/her studies, but excels in another activity, then family and friends strongly support that alternate career choice.

文法練習

一 要不是 if it were not for ......

⊙要不是後來犯規太多，他還可以得更多分。

If he hadn't committed so many fouls later in the game, he could have gotten even more points.

用法說明：「要不是」的後面是已經發生的事實。如果這個事實沒發生，後半句的情況就成立。說話者有惋惜或慶幸的意思。

Explanation: Following 要不是 is something which has already occurred. If it were not for this event, the situation stated in the second half of the sentence would have become true. This can express that the speaker is either pleased or displeased with the result.

練習：請用「要不是」完成下面對話。

Exercise: Please use the 要不是 pattern to complete the dialogues below.

1. 張：你們怎麼來得這麼晚？
   Chang: Why did you come so late?
   李：他起得太晚，要不是等他，我們早就到了。
   Lee: He got up too late. If we hadn't been waiting for him, we would have been here long ago.
2. 張：你不知道小王出國了嗎？
   李：沒人告訴我啊！要不是＿＿＿＿＿＿＿＿＿＿＿＿。
3. 張：你身體不錯嘛！一家都病倒了，你還好好的。
   李：是啊！要不是＿＿＿＿＿＿＿＿＿＿。
4. 張：恭喜你當選了，支持你的人真多啊！
   李：謝謝，要不是＿＿＿＿＿＿＿＿＿＿。
5. 張：難怪你願意給這個學生寫推薦信，他的成績真好。
   李：要不是＿＿＿＿＿＿＿＿＿＿。

☞ 二 就是……，也……　even if ......, then ......

⊙他拿到球，就是沒機會投籃，也不會把球傳丟了，從來沒出過錯！

When he gets the ball, even if he doesn't have a chance to make a basket, he won't lose the ball either; he never makes a mistake!

用法說明:「就是」的後面是一種假設情況，「也」後面的結論或結果不因此而改變。

Explanations: Following 就是 is a hypothetical situation which would normally adversely affect or contradict a given result. However the statement following 也 indicates that the result or theory unchanged despite the hypothetical situation. This pattern is used to emphasize the certainty of a conclusion or opinion.

練習：請用「就是……也……」完成下面對話。

Exercise: Please use the "就是……也……" pattern to complete the dialogues below.

1. 張：你為什麼不買這個東西？是不是沒錢？

   Chang: Why don't you buy that? Is it because you don't have money?

   李：這個東西好爛，我就是有錢，也不買。

   Lee: This thing is awful. Even if I had money, I wouldn't buy it.

2. 張：這個練習好難，你幫我做好不好？

   李：我也不會做啊！我就是＿＿＿＿＿＿＿＿＿＿。

3. 張：王小姐為什麼離開她男朋友了？

   李：別人的事我不太清楚，我就是＿＿＿＿＿＿＿＿＿＿。

4. 張：你明天要去上課嗎？

   李：明天期中考，就是＿＿＿＿＿＿＿＿＿＿。

5. 姐姐：你要多少錢才願意幫我帶孩子？

   妹妹：你的孩子這麼不聽話，就是＿＿＿＿＿＿＿＿＿＿。

☞ 三 讓 permit, allow, let / to make, to cause, to arouse

(I) ⊙……不知道下半場教練為什麼不讓他打了？

……I wonder why the coach didn't let him play in the second half.

用法說明：這個「讓」是「允許」、「聽任」的意思。

Explanation: This 讓 means to allow, permit, or let.

練習：請用「讓」改寫下面句子。

Exercise: Please rewrite the sentences below using 讓.

1. 他的病很重，可是這件事不能告訴他，要不然他會難過。

   His illness is very serious, but you must not tell him about it.

Otherwise, he will feel depressed.

→他的病很重，可是這件事不能讓他知道，要不然他會難過。

His illness is very serious, but you must not let him know about it. Otherwise, he will feel depressed.

2. 媽媽說我不可以跟張小明交朋友，因為他太壞了。

……………………………………………………………………………

3. 你不要替我做，我可以自己試試。

……………………………………………………………………………

4. 你坐在這裡，我過不去，你站起來，我才可以過去。

……………………………………………………………………………

5. 孩子大了，他的事情，他自己決定吧，你別管了。

……………………………………………………………………………

（Ⅱ）⊙剛剛看大家這麼興奮，讓我想到以前在臺灣看棒球賽的情形。

Seeing everyone so excited just now made me remember watching baseball games in Taiwan.

用法說明：這個「讓」是「致使」、「引起」的意思。

Explanation: This 讓 means “to make, to cause, to give rise to, to arouse”.

練習：請把「讓」放在句中合適的地方。

Exercise: Please place 讓 in the appropriate place in the following sentences.

1. 你假裝生病不去上課，爸爸很生氣。

You pretended to be sick and didn’t go to class; Dad is very angry.

→你假裝生病不去上課，讓爸爸很生氣。

You pretended to be sick and didn’t go to class; It has made Dad very angry.

2.本來是我請他吃飯，沒想到我帶的錢不夠，他替我付了帳，我真不好意思。

……………………………………………………………………………

3. 我是為了父母高興才念這個系的。

....

4. 聽到這個歌，我想起女朋友來了。

....

5. 他跟他太太那麼有默契，我們羨慕死了。

....

☞ 四 被 (passive voice)

⊙我看見九號也被他氣得要打人了。

I also saw #9 become so angered by him that he wanted to hit someone.

用法說明：用於表示被動的句子。句型如下：動作接受者＋被＋動作施行者＋動詞＋補語。動作施行者如果清楚明顯時可省略。補語表示完成或結果。「被字句」多用於描述「說話者認為不如意的事」。「被字句」可用於告誡性的句子，但不可用於「要求」或「命令」的情況。表示否定的詞應在「被」之前。

Explanation: This pattern is used to show passive voice. The sentence pattern is as follows: object of verb ＋被＋ subject of verb ＋Verb ＋ complement. If the identity of the subject is obvious, then it can be omitted. The complement shows the completion or result of an action. Most sentences using 被 describe a situation about which the speaker is displeased. This pattern can be used when one is warning or cautioning another, but cannot be used in requests or orders. The negative should be placed in front of 被.

練習：Exercises:

㈠請把下面的句子改成被動句。

Please change the sentences below to the passive voice.

1. 風把他的帽子颳跑了。

The wind blew his hat away.

→他的帽子被風颳跑了。

His hat was blown away by the wind.

2. 他打破了碗，老闆罵了他一頓。

....

3. 我還想睡，可是我室友把我叫醒了。

....

4. 孫中山先生把清朝政府推翻了。

....

5. 張小明丟的球，把我妹妹的頭打破了。

....

6. 那隻狗追得他到處跑。

....

7. 雨水把這些資料都弄濕了。

....

8. 小心，他的球會打到你。（請用「別被⋯⋯」）

....

㈡請改正下面各句，並說明原因。

Please correct each sentence below, explaining why the correction is necessary.

1. 這本書是被張教授寫的。[sic.]

→這本書是張教授寫的。因為這不是不如意的事。

This book was written by Professor Chang. [The first sentence is incorrect because this sentence does not describe a situation about which the speaker is displeased, so the use of 被 is inappropriate.]

2. 幸虧你的房租被他沒偷走。

....

3. 這份報告，下星期四一定要被交給我。

....

☞ 五 動不動就

at the drop of a hat, with very little instigation

⊙這個人很容易生氣，動不動就罵人。

This guy gets angry very easily; he curses at people at the drop of a hat.

用法說明：「就」後面的情況極容易發生，頻率非常高。多用於負面事情。

Explanation: The situation following 就 occurs very easily and very frequently. This pattern is used to describe negative situations.

練習：請根據所給情況，用「動不動就」表示某一情況發生頻率很高。

Exercise: Please use the 動不動就 pattern to indicate that the situations occur very frequently.

1. 他弟弟身體真不健康，很容易感冒。

   His little brother is very unhealthy; he catches colds very easily.

   →他弟弟身體真不健康，動不動就感冒。

   His little brother is very unhealthy; he catches colds at the drop of a hat.

2. 我們公司的老闆很容易生氣，常常給店員臉色看。

   ....

3. 我女朋友一有不如意的事就哭，真麻煩。

   ....

4. 張小明一碰到困難就說「我死定了。」

   ....

5. 我房間的電視太老，常常壞，很容易就沒聲音了。

   ....

☞ 六 說到 speaking of, now that you mention...

⊙說到打工，我得走了。

Speaking of working, I had better get going.

用法說明：「說到」的後面是剛才的話題，因為這個話題而想到別的事情，就引出後面的話。

Explanation: Following 說到 is a topic which was just mentioned. Mention of this topic reminded the speaker of something.

練習：請用「說到」完成下面對話。

Exercise: Please use 說到 to complete the dialogues below.

1. 張：沒想到東、西德這麼快就統一了。

Chang: I never imagined that East and West Germany would unite so quickly.

李：說到統一，我就想到臺灣跟中國大陸的問題。

Lee: Speaking of unification makes me think of the problem of Taiwan and mainland China.

2. 張：英國的殖民地很多都獨立了。

李：說到殖民地，＿＿＿＿＿＿＿＿＿＿＿＿＿＿＿。

3. 張：他們國家滿十八歲就有選舉權。

李：說到選舉權，＿＿＿＿＿＿＿＿＿＿＿＿＿＿＿。

4. 張：昨天那場比賽，我們的校隊最有團隊精神。

李：說到團隊精神，＿＿＿＿＿＿＿＿＿＿＿＿＿＿＿。

5. 張：我們教練的頭越來越禿了。

李：說到教練，＿＿＿＿＿＿＿＿＿＿＿＿＿＿＿。

七 V得正SV just in the midst of V SV

⊙談得正高興，你就要走了。

Just when we are talking so merrily, you have to go.

用法說明：「V得正SV」表示一個動作正進行到某種程度，就有新的狀況發生。

Explanation: "V得正SV" indicates that an action has just progressed to a certain level or degree, when a new situation arises.

練習：請根據所給情況，用「V得正SV」描述下面的事情。

Exercise: Use the"V得正SV"pattern and the information provided to describe the situations below .

1. 你正在睡覺，睡得很舒服，媽媽把你叫醒了。

You were in the midst of a comfortable sleep when Mother woke you up.

→我睡得正舒服，媽媽就把我叫醒了。

I was just in the midst of sleeping very comfortably when Mom woke me up.

2. 大家正在看電視上的球賽，都很緊張，電視台就播廣告了。

....

3. 同學們正在聽張教授講課，都很有興趣，可是下課的時間到了。

....

4. 你一個人在家念書，覺得很無聊的時候，小王正好打電話來了。

....

5. 你姐姐在房間裡哭，現在很難過，不希望別人去煩她。

....

☞ 八 一連 consecutively, successively, in a row......

⊙要是中華隊投手一連投了幾次四壞球，……

If the Chinese Team's pitcher consecutively throws several sets of 4 balls,......

用法說明：表示同一情況或動作連續不斷的發生，後面是動詞，動詞後面應有表示次數或時間的數量詞。「一」可以省略。「一連」後面的短語如否定詞「不」或「沒」，動詞應在數量詞和否定詞後面。

Explanation: This pattern shows that the same situation or action occurs repeatedly and without pause. A verb follows 一連, and after the verb should be a measure word that shows the number of times the action occurs or the time period of occurrence. 一 can be omitted. If the phrase after 一連 contains a negative, 不 or 沒, the revb should be placed after the measure word and the negative.

練習：請把「一連」放在句中合適的地方。

Exercise: Please place 一連 in the appropriate place in the sentences below.

1. 我寫了五封信給他，他都沒回。

   I wrote him five letters. He didn't write back at all.

   →我一連寫了五封信給他，他都沒回。

   I wrote him five letters in a row. He didn't write back at all.

2. 下了兩個星期的雨，今天晴了。

....

3. 上個月來了三個颱風，所以青菜都貴了。

....

4. 他打破了四個盤子，老闆就叫他走路了。

....

5. 我幾個晚上都沒睡好，所以看起來沒精神。

....

課室活動

1. 隨便談談 (Open discussion)

每個人說說自己平常做什麼運動, 為什麼喜歡這種運動？另外, 再說說自己喜歡看什麼運動比賽, 為什麼？

Supplementary words: 慢跑 (jogging), 有氧舞蹈 (yǒuyǎng wǔdào; aerobics), 舉重 (weight lifting), 拳擊 (quánjí; boxing), 騎自行車/騎腳踏車 (qí zìxíngchē/qí jiǎotàchē; bicycling), 散步 (sànbù; to take a walk, stroll), 打保齡球 (dǎ bǎolíngqiú; to go bowling), 踢足球 (tī//zúqiú; to play soccer/football), 打撞球 (dǎ zhuàngqiú; to play billiards, pool), 排球 (volleyball), 桌球/乒乓球 (pīngpāngqiú; Ping-Pong; table tennis), 曲棍球 (qūgùnqiú; hockey), 回力球 (racketball), 輸 (shū; to lose in a game).

2. 組成短文 (Piecing together a narrative)

The teacher copies the following sentences on cards, one sentence per card, then gives the cards to the students in random order, one or two per person. After the students memorize their sentence(s) the cards are again collected, and the students take turns reciting their sentence(s). After all the sentences have been heard, the students figure out the order which best forms a good narrative.

還是坐著休息最舒服。

不管是籃球，還是足球 (zúqiú; soccer, football)，

還有游泳，

都是為了一個球在球場裡跑來跑去，
可是一不小心就會喝水，
大概只有跳舞比較好了，
人人都說運動對身體、對精神都好，
他們不累嗎？
我也不懂為什麼有那麼多人喜歡看球賽。
在水裡游來游去當然不熱，
可以一邊聽好聽的歌，一邊跳；
可是我真不喜歡運動。
而且，誰贏誰輸 (shū; to lose in a game)，有什麼關係呢？
情形不好還可能會死呢！
想快就快，想慢就慢，多好啊！
可是，你想想，每次跑過、跳過以後，不都是又熱又渴嗎?!

The teacher may shorten or lengthen the contents of the narrative, depending on the number of students.

短文

系刊₁上的消息

※十一月十二日本校₂校慶₃，學校舉辦₄了很多慶祝活動，除了電影欣賞會、園遊會以外，還有運動會₅，非常熱鬧。

※本系₂，三年級學生在這次園遊會有一個擲飛鏢的攤位，生意不錯，一共賺了九十六元₆，已捐給系裡做系刊的經費。

※本系四年級攤位賣的是中國點心，因為口味新鮮，特別受歡迎，攤位前一直擠得滿滿的，系主任都一連吃了十個水餃。

※本系在這次運動會的比賽成績是全校第六名₇，二年級高偉立同學參加一百公尺賽跑，得了第一名₇，成績是十二秒₈三，打破全校記錄₉，值得慶賀₁₀。

※本校跟紐約州立大學的籃球比賽，又激烈又精彩，結束時比數是九十七比一0一，本校校隊因為默契好，犯規少，才贏了這場比賽。

※十二月三日晚上七時，李國書教授在系辦公室樓上三0八室演講，題目是：「中國的考試制度」。有興趣的同學請準時參加。

Vocabulary:

1. 系刊 (xìkān): departmental publication
2. 本校 (běn xiào): our school, this school
   本系 (běn xì): our department, this department
3. 校慶 (xiàoqìng): holiday honoring the date of a school's formation
4. 舉辦 (jǔbàn): to organize, to hold (an event)

5. 運動會 (yùndònghuì): athletic event

6. 元 (yuán): dollar (It means the same as 塊錢, but not so colloquial.)

7. 第六名 (dìliùmíng): sixth place

第一名 (dìyīmíng): first place

8. 秒 (miǎo): second (unit of time)

9. 打破記錄 (dǎpò//jìlù): to break a record

10. 慶賀 (qìnghè): to congratulate

第十三課

過節了

・龍舟賽（新聞局提供）

（陳台麗在房間裡）

台麗：喂，林建國嗎？我是陳台麗，麻煩你請高偉立聽電話[1]。

建國：好，你等一下。偉立，找你的，是陳台麗。

偉立：謝謝。（接過電話）喂，我是高偉立。

台麗：嗨，你好。我想跟你借打字機，不知道方不方便？

偉立：沒問題，你什麼時候來拿？

台麗：現在行嗎？

偉立：可以呀！你來吧！我三點**才**有課。

台麗：謝謝，我**這就**過去。

偉立：好，一會兒見。

※ ※ ※

（高偉立房間裡）

台麗：我後天要交一份報告，要用圖書館電腦的人太多，我只好來跟你借。

偉立：沒關係，**反正**我這兩天不用，就在桌上，你自己拿。

台麗：好。哇！好可愛的南瓜。我萬聖節也做了個南瓜燈。

偉立：那一定很好玩。你的感恩節是怎麼過的？

台麗：除了感恩節那天去同學家吃火雞大餐以外，我都在家看書、寫報告。

偉立：真用功。那隻火雞味道怎麼樣？

台麗：不錯，可是太大了。她媽媽烤了一隻十幾磅的大火雞，我們八、九個人都沒吃完，我看他們還要吃好幾天呢！另外還有南瓜派，我從來沒吃過，很香很好吃。

偉立：南瓜派是我媽媽最拿手的點心，可惜我吃了過敏。既然你喜歡，以後有機會我就帶一些給你嚐嚐。

台麗：謝謝。我看你們過感恩節好像跟聖誕節[2]差不多。

偉立：是差不多。感恩節是為了紀念我們的祖先，坐五月花號

・萬聖節快到了（劉咪咪攝）

・臺北燈會金雞報曉
（《中國時報》林道明攝）

來到這裡以後，因為印第安人的幫助，才能在這塊土地上過著豐衣足食的生活。

台麗：聖誕節就完全是基督教[3]的節日了，對不對？

偉立：沒錯。你們在臺灣也過聖誕節嗎？

台麗：信教的人才過。有不少人**趁著**這個機會吃喝玩樂，商人更利用這個節日作廣告，推銷他們的東西。好像**跟**宗教**沒**什麼**關係**了。

偉立：我們也覺得聖誕節一年比一年商業化了。其實聖誕節應該是全家人在一起，**歡歡喜喜**地吃飯、說笑、唱歌，享受溫暖的聖誕節氣氛。

台麗：我不信教，可是聖誕夜常去教堂做禮拜[4]，就是因為喜歡那裡的氣氛，可惜臺灣不下雪[5]，感覺就差了點。

偉立：聽說今年下雪的機會很多，你大概可以過一個銀色聖誕了。

台麗：我都等不及了。房東說今年的聖誕樹，要我跟美真幫忙裝飾。你等著看吧，那一定是全世界最漂亮的一棵。

偉立：好孩子！聖誕老人一定會送給你們一份特別的禮物！

台麗：討厭[6]！你就愛開我的玩笑[7]。小心聖誕老人今年不給你禮物了。

偉立：說到禮物，我正在頭疼不知道今年該買什麼給我老媽才好，她好像什麼都有了。

台麗：也許你可以直接問問她需要什麼。對了，我也該去買聖誕卡了，**再不**寄**就**太晚了。

偉立：聖誕節**什麼都**好，**就是**買禮物、寄聖誕卡太麻煩。

台麗：我**倒是**覺得對忙碌的現代人來說，寄聖誕卡是一個連絡感情的好辦法。

（高偉立看看錶）

台麗：對不起，你該去上課了。我也要回去打報告了。謝謝你的打字機，用完了就拿來還。

偉立：別這麼客氣，我不急著用，你慢慢打[8]。

生詞及例句

1. 過節 (guò//jié)　　*VO*: **to celebrate a festival or holiday**

　　過年過節的時候，街上都很熱鬧。

　過 (guò)　　*V*: **to pass (an occasion)**

　　去年我的生日是一個人過的。

　節日 (jié'rì)　　*N*: **festival, holiday**

　　你知道一年一共有多少個節日嗎？

　節 (jié)

　M/N: **(for section, length, node)/ holiday, festival; season**

　　他禮拜一有兩節歷史課。

　情人節 (qíngrén jié)　　*N*: **Valentine's Day**

　母親節 (mǔqīn jié)　　*N*: **Mother's Day**

　父親節 (fùqīn jié)　　*N*: **Father's Day**

2. 打字機 (dǎzìjī)　　*N*: **typewriter（M：臺）**

　打字 (dǎ//zì)　　*VO*: **to type**

　　張小姐一分鐘只能打五十幾個字。

3. 後ㄏㄡˋ天ㄊㄧㄢ (hòutiān) *TW*: **day after tomorrow**

大ㄉㄚˋ後ㄏㄡˋ天ㄊㄧㄢ (dàhòutiān) *TW*: **three days from now**

4. 反ㄈㄢˇ正ㄓㄥˋ (fǎnzhèng) A: **anyway, anyhow, in any case**

(1) 你幾點來都可以，反正我都在家。

(2) 我不想參加這次考試，反正我也考不取。

反ㄈㄢˇ (fǎn)

V/RE/AT: **to turn over, turn inside out / to be reversed**

(1) 我真受不了他，衣服穿髒了不洗，就反過來再穿。

(2) 那個孩子太小，分不清左右，又把鞋穿反了。

(3) 孩子念書，不要給他太多壓力，要不然會有反效果。

5. 可ㄎㄜˇ愛ㄞˋ (kě'ài) *SV*: **to be lovable, likeable, adorable , cute**

王老師的小女兒笑起來好甜，可愛極了。

6. 火ㄏㄨㄛˇ雞ㄐㄧ (huǒjī) *N*: **turkey**

7. 隻 (zhī)

M: **(used for one of a pair, also for boats, containers, certain animals, etc.)**

他的眼睛一隻大，一隻小。

8. 南ㄋㄢˊ瓜ㄍㄨㄚ派ㄆㄞˋ (nán'guāpài) *N*: **pumpkin pie**

南ㄋㄢˊ瓜ㄍㄨㄚ (nán'guā) *N*: **pumpkin**

派 (pài) *N*: **pie**

他最喜歡麥當勞 (McDonald) 的蘋果派。

南ㄋㄢˊ瓜ㄍㄨㄚ燈ㄉㄥ (nán'guādēng) *N*: **jack-o'-lantern**

9. 磅ㄅㄤˋ (bàng) *M*: **pound**

他比十年前胖了二十磅。

10. 拿ㄋㄚˊ手ㄕㄡˇ (náshǒu) *SV*: **to be good at, adept at, expert**

他會打很多種球，也都打得不錯。籃球是他最拿手的運動。

11. 過ㄍㄨㄛˋ敏ㄇㄧㄣˇ (guòmǐn) *V*: **to be allergic to something**

我對海鮮過敏，不能吃魚蝦。

12. 嚐ㄔㄤˊ (cháng) *V*: **to taste**

你嚐嚐這個菜夠不夠鹹？

13. 紀念 (jì'niàn)

N/V: **commemoration / to commemorate**

(1) 你把這張畫留起來做個紀念吧！

(2) 他寫這本書是為了紀念他太太。

14. 祖先 (zǔxiān)　　*N*: **ancestors**

美國人的祖先大部分是從歐洲來的。

祖父 (zǔfù)　　*N*: **grandfather, father's father**

祖母 (zǔmǔ)　　*N*: **grandmother, father's mother**

15. 土地 (tǔdì)　　*N*: **land, soil, territory**（**M**：塊／片）

他那塊土地現在值多少錢？

16. 豐衣足食 (fēng yī zú shí)

IE: **to be well-clothed and well-fed**

只要社會安定，我們就能過豐衣足食的生活。

17. 信教 (xìn//jiào)　　*VO*: **to believe in a religion**

你信什麼教？

相信 (xiāngxìn)　　*V*: **to believe, to have faith in**

他考試都考得很爛，我不相信他能得到獎學金。

18. 趁著 (chèn·zhe)

V: **take advantage of an opportunity or situation, avail oneself of**

我們趁著放假的時候，到海邊去玩了幾天。

趁 (chèn)

V: **take advantage of an opportunity or situation, avail oneself of**

趁現在時間還早，我們先去喝杯咖啡，再回來坐車。

19. 吃喝玩樂 (chī hē wán lè)

IE: **eat, drink and be merry; to idle away one's time in Epicurean, pleasure seeking pursuits**

他除了吃喝玩樂，什麼都不想做。

20. 利用 (lìyòng)

V: **to use, to take advantage of, to exploit**

他並不是喜歡我，只是想跟我練習中文會話，我覺得他是在利用我。

21. 作廣告 (zuò//guǎnggào) *VO*: **to advertise**

生意人喜歡利用美女作廣告。

廣告 (guǎnggào) *N*: **advertisement**

最近電視上有很多賣汽車的廣告。

廣 (guǎng) *SV*: **to be broad, extensive**

他的興趣很廣，慢跑、游泳、打球、看電影，什麼都喜歡。

22. 推銷 (tuīxiāo) *V*: **to promote sales**

天氣不熱，冷氣機很難推銷。

推銷員 (tuīxiāoyuán) *N*: **salesperson**

我開門一看，原來是賣洗衣粉的推銷員。

銷路 (xiāolù) *N*: **sales opportunity, market**

因為廣告作得好，所以他們的電腦銷路不錯。

23. 宗教 (zōngjiào) *N*: **religion**

24. 商業化 (shāngyèhuà)

N/V/SV: **commercialization / to commercialize / to be commercialized**

從前的情人節沒有現在的這麼商業化。

商業 (shāngyè) *N*: **commerce, trade, business**

我念大學的時候，選過幾門商業方面的課。

商人（生意人）(shāngrén) (shēngyìrén)

N: **businessman, merchant, trader**

商店 (shāngdiàn) *N*: **shop, store**（**M**：家）

25. 歡歡喜喜 (huān huān xǐ xǐ)

SV: **to be full of joy, extremely happy**

考完試，大家都歡歡喜喜地出去玩了。

26. 享受 (xiǎngshòu) *V/N*: **to enjoy / enjoyment**

(1) 這麼多好吃的東西，大家好好兒享受吧！

(2) 一天的事都忙完了，躺在床上欣賞音樂是我最大的享受。

27. 溫暖 (wēnnuǎn) *SV/N*: **to be warm/warmth**

(1)他說不管怎麼樣，他都會幫助我，讓我覺得很溫暖。

(2)這個社會上好人還是比較多，到處都有溫暖。

28. 氣氛 (qì·fēn)　*N*: **atmosphere, mood**

媽媽今天都不說話，家裡氣氛怪怪的。

29. 聖誕夜 (shèngdànyè)　*N*: **Christmas Eve**

30. 教堂 (jiàotáng)　*N*: **church, cathedral**

31. 做禮拜 (zuò//lǐbài)

VO: **to go to a church worship service**

信教的人每個星期天都要去教堂做禮拜。

禮拜 (lǐbài)　*N*: **week**

32. 感覺 (gǎnjué)

V/N: **to feel, sense, perceive / feeling, sense, perception**

(1)你感覺到今天上課的氣氛跟平常不一樣嗎？

(2)我對他那麼好，可是他一點感覺也沒有。

33. 等不及 (děng·bùjí)

RC: **cannot bear to wait, unable to wait any longer**

爸爸還沒回來，弟弟等不及，就自己先吃起來了。

34. 裝飾 (zhuāngshì)　*V*: **to decorate, to adorn**

她用花裝飾她的帽子。

35. 棵 (kē)　*M*: **(used for trees, cabbage, grass, etc.)**

36. 開玩笑 (kāi//wánxiào)

VO: **to crack a joke, to make fun of, to tease**

(1)你別生氣，我是跟你開玩笑的。

(2)這個玩笑開得太大了，難怪他那麼生氣。

37. 聖誕卡 (shèngdànkǎ)　*N*: **Christmas card**（**M**：張）

生日卡 (shēngrìkǎ)　*N*: **birthday card**

母親卡 (mǔqīnkǎ)　*N*: **Mother's Day card**

情人卡 (qíngrénkǎ)　*N*: **Valentine's Day card**

信用卡 (xìnyòngkǎ)　*N*: **credit card**

卡ㄎㄚˇ片ㄆㄧㄢˋ (kǎpiàn) *N*: **card （M：張）**

38. 忙ㄇㄤˊ碌ㄌㄨˋ (mánglù) *SV*: **to be busy, to be bustling about**

住在城市裡的人，生活一定比較忙碌。

39. 現ㄒㄧㄢˋ代ㄉㄞˋ人ㄖㄣˊ (xiàndàirén) *N*: **modern man**

現ㄒㄧㄢˋ代ㄉㄞˋ化ㄏㄨㄚˋ (xiàndàihuà)

N/V/SV: **modernization / to become modernized / to be modernized**

⑴交通建設的現代化是政府最關心的問題。

⑵那個地方離城市很遠，交通不方便，不容易現代化。

⑶這棟大樓非常現代化，裡面的東西都是電腦控制的。

現ㄒㄧㄢˋ代ㄉㄞˋ (xiàndài) *SV*: **to be modern, contemporary**

他的想法很新、很現代。

代ㄉㄞˋ (dài) *M*: **generation**

上一代的人總覺得這一代的年輕人不太懂事。

時ㄕˊ代ㄉㄞˋ (shídài) *N*: **times, age, era, epoch**

現在是電腦時代，不會用電腦，將來可能找不到工作。

40. 連ㄌㄧㄢˊ絡ㄌㄨㄛˋ（聯ㄌㄧㄢˊ絡ㄌㄨㄛˋ）(liánluò)

V/N: **to make contact with, to communicate with / contact**

好久沒跟他連絡了，你有他的消息嗎？

41. 感ㄍㄢˇ情ㄑㄧㄥˊ (gǎnqíng)

N: **emotion, sentiment, affection, feelings (between friends, relatives, etc.)**

他跟他女朋友的感情一直很好。

歎詞 Interjections

1. 喂ㄨㄟˊ（ㄨㄟˋ）(wéi, wèi) *I*: **Hello ; Hey!**

⑴（打電話的時候）

李：喂，請問張老師在家嗎？

張太太：在，請等一下。

⑵喂！那是你的東西嗎？

專有名詞 Proper Names

1. 萬聖節 (Wànshèng Jié) Halloween
2. 感恩節 (Gǎn’ēn Jié) Thanksgiving Day
3. 聖誕節 (Shèngdàn Jié) Christmas
4. 五月花號 (Wǔyuèhuā Hào)
   Mayflower, the name of a boat which carried Pilgrims to America
5. 基督教 (Jīdū Jiào) Christianity

注釋

1. “麻煩你請高偉立聽電話。” This is how a Chinese would normally ask to speak with 高偉立 on the telephone. Though it means the same as asking: “May I please speak with 高偉立?”, one should never use the expression: “我可以不可以跟高偉立說話？.” “請問×××在不在？” is another way to ask for someone on the phone. If you are the one being asked for, you should answer by saying: “我就是”, not “這就是他.”
2. 聖誕節 means Christmas. 聖 means holy, sacred. 誕 means birth. So 聖誕節 means the day of the holy birth. If someone is not a Christian, he/she might call this holiday 耶誕節. 耶 is short for 耶穌, Yēsū, the transliteration for “Jesus”.
3. 基督教：基督 means the Christ. 基督教 means Christianity. However, from common usage 基督教 frequently refers only to Protestantism, while 天主教 refers to Catholicism.
4. 做禮拜 means to participate in a worship service at a Protestant church. The term for attending a Catholic mass is called 望彌撒, wàng mísā .
5. 臺灣不下雪. Since Taiwan is in the subtropical and tropical zones, it has never snowed on most of the island. Occasionally there is snow in the high

mountains .

6. "討厭！你就愛開我玩笑！". 討厭 here does not really express annoyance or disgust. When a close male friend teases a Chinese woman and she feels uncomfortable or doesn't know how to respond, she might say 討厭 even though she is not really upset. This feminine expression has evolved into a form of teasing or flirting.
7. "你就（是）愛開我的玩笑！" Here "就（是）" is used to emphasize what follows and implies the meaning "always" or "simply". Depending on the situation and the way it is said, it can carry a tone of reproach, complaint, disagreement, flirting, or joking. Here, the tone is one of mild reproach.
8. "我不急著用，你慢慢打。" means "I am not in a hurry to use it, take your time (typing)." This is a polite remark, 客氣話. It is used to make someone feel comfortable about borrowing something and perhaps keeping it for some time.

文法練習

☞ 一 才 not...... until......

⊙我三點才有課。

I don't have class until three o'clock.

用法說明：「才」的前面是表示時間的詞或短語，強調事情發生的時間比預期的晚。（請比較第八課文法練習八）

Explanation: When 才 follows a TW or a phrase indicating time, this emphasizes the fact that the event occurs later than is desired or expected. (Please compare this with pattern 8 in Chapter 8.)

練習：請把「才」放在句中合適的地方。

Exercise : Please place 才 in the appropriate place in the following sentences.

1. 他們國家去年開始實行民主制度，比你們晚了好多年。

Their country started to implement a democratic system last year. This was many years later than your country.

→他們國家去年才開始實行民主制度，比你們晚了好多年。

Their country didn't start to implement a democratic system until last year, many years later than your country.

2. 老王四十歲上大學。

....

3. 我們八點上課，他九點來。

....

4. 我媽聖誕節前一天上街買禮物。

....

5. 今天的比賽，我打得不好，快結束的時候得了一分。

....

☞ 二 這就 right away, immediately

⊙我這就過去。

I'll be right over.

用法說明：「這」表示「現在」，「就」表示「馬上」、「立刻」。「這就」的後面是動詞，表示馬上就做該動作。

Explanation: 這 means"now", whereas 就 means "immediately, right away". A verb placed right after 這就 indicates that the action will be performed immediately.

練習：請用「這就」完成下面對話。

Exercise: Please complete the dialogues below using 這就.

1. 媽媽：建國，這個箱子我打不開，你來幫幫忙，好不好?

Mother: Jian Kuo, I can't get this box opened. Will you come help me?

建國：好，我這就來。

Jian Kuo: OK, I'll be right over.

2. 張：明天烤肉的事，你還沒打電話告訴小王啊？

李：＿＿＿＿＿＿＿＿＿＿＿＿＿＿。
3. 太太：你又忘了吃藥了！
先生：＿＿＿＿＿＿＿＿＿＿＿＿＿＿。
4. 店員：對不起，我們要休息了。
客人：＿＿＿＿＿＿＿＿＿＿＿＿＿＿。
5. 學生：助教說他一會兒就要走了，要我現在就去拿資料。
教授：那你＿＿＿＿＿＿＿＿＿＿＿＿＿＿。

☞ 三 反正 anyway......

（Ⅰ）⊙沒關係，反正我這兩天不用。

It doesn't matter; I won't use it for a couple of days anyway.

用法說明：(A) 說話者認為做某件事或發生某種狀況，都沒什麼關係或沒有什麼大影響。(B) 說話者認為不必做對話中提到的某件事或做了那件事也沒什麼用。「反正」的後面是說話者的理由。

Explanation: (A) This is a kind of downplaying. The speaker thinks that the matter just mentioned is unimportant; it does not exert any influence on the matter at hand. (B) The speaker thinks that it is not necessary to do the thing mentioned in the conversation, or to do it is meaningless. Following 反正 is the reason(s) why it does not matter or why it is not necessary.

練習：請根據所給情況用「反正」描述下面的事情。

Exercise: Please use 反正 to describe what you would say in reaction to the given situations.

(A) 1. 桌上有一塊蛋糕，你怕胖不敢吃，可是又覺得已經發胖了，再吃一塊也沒關係。你說什麼？

There's a piece of cake on the table. You are worried about gaining weight so you do not dare eat it. But on the other hand, you feel overweight already, so it would not matter if you ate just one more piece. What do you say?

→我就再吃一塊吧，反正已經胖了。

I'll just eat one more piece; I'm already overweight anyway.

2. 你今天沒課，晚一點起來沒關係。你怎麼說？

……………………………………………………………………………………

3. 朋友問你：要不要一起去看電影？你覺得已經考完試了，去看場電影沒關係。你怎麼說？

……………………………………………………………………………………

4. 你媽覺得你的成績不夠理想，可是你認為每一科都及格，能畢業就行了，你怎麼說？

……………………………………………………………………………………

5. 你打工的時候常常睡覺，你同學問你：「不怕老闆叫你走路嗎？」你覺得這個工作太無聊，你早就不想做了，你怎麼說？

……………………………………………………………………………………

(B) 1. 你有一件漂亮衣服，你室友一直很欣賞，現在你胖了，穿不下了，你要送給室友。她高興得不得了，不停地謝你，你怎麼說？

You have a pretty dress, your roomate always admires it. You have gained weight and can no longer wear it. You want to give it to your roomate. She is very happy, and continues to thank you. What would you say?

→不必謝我，反正我也穿不下這件衣服了。

You don't have to thank me. I can no longer wear it anyway.

2. 你們的籃球校隊跟別的學校比賽，小王要去給他們加油。你認為你們的實力差太多，一定贏不了對方，不必去了。你怎麼說？

……………………………………………………………………………………

3. 老李學校開園遊會，他想請你妹妹去參觀，問你覺得怎麼樣。你知道你妹妹很討厭他，一定不會去，你怎麼說？

……………………………………………………………………………………

4. 你妹妹一直在房間裡哭，因為男朋友離開她了。你覺得哭沒有用，男朋友也聽不到。你說什麼？

……………………………………………………………………………

（Ⅱ）

用法說明：跟「不管」連用，意思是因為不管怎麼樣，「反正」的後面的事實或想法都不會再改變。

Explanation: Used with 不管, meaning no matter what happens it will not change the fact or ideas following 反正.

練習：請根據所給情況用「不管……反正……」描述下面的事情。

Exercise: Please use "不管……反正……" to describe what you would say in reaction to the given situations.

1. 你有一件漂亮衣服，你一直很喜歡，可是現在你胖了，穿不下了，媽媽就把這件衣服送給別人了，你很不高興。這時候你會怎麼說？

   You had a pretty dress, you've always liked it. But you have gained weight and can no longer wear it . So your mother has given it away. You are very unhappy. What would you say in this case?

   →不管我多喜歡這件衣服，反正媽媽已經送給別人了。

   No matter how much I liked the dress, mother has given it away.

2. 你室友聽你說錢不夠用，他覺得你可以申請獎學金，叫你早一點申請，可是你覺得自己成績不好，多早申請都申請不到。你會怎麼說？

   ……………………………………………………………………………

3. 你妹妹要你快一點，因為火車就要開了。可是你看看錶，覺得已經太晚了，走多快都來不及了，你會說什麼？

   ……………………………………………………………………………

4. 你的幾個朋友今天晚上都要去跳舞，你不要去。一個朋友跟你說跳舞很有意思；一個朋友說跳舞對身體好。你真的不想去，你會說什麼？

   ……………………………………………………………………………

5. 你很愛你的女朋友，可是你爸媽不喜歡她，希望你離開她，可是你不要，你會說什麼？

……………………………………………………………………………………

☞ 四 趁（著） to take advantage of , to utilize

⊙有不少人趁著這個機會吃喝玩樂……

A lot of people use this opportunity to eat, drink, and be merry.

用法說明：「趁著」是「利用」的意思，利用某條件或機會做一件事。「趁」的後面可加名詞、SV、動詞短語 (VP) 或短句。

Explanation: 趁著 means "to use", "to utilize", "to take advantage of" some requirement or opportunity to perform some action. Following 趁著 can be a noun, SV, verb phrase, or simple sentence.

練習：如果你看到下面情況，你會怎麼說，請用「趁（著）」。

Exercise: If you encountered the situations below, what would you say? Please use "趁（著）" in your answer.

1. 王太太一直想換個衣櫃，現在搬家了，就買了一個新的。

   Mrs. Wang has wanted to change her wardrobe for a long time. Now she has moved, and so she has bought a new one.

   →王太太趁著現在搬家，換了一個新衣櫃。

   Mrs. Wang is moving to a new house, so she's taken advantage of this opportunity to buy a new wardrobe.

2. 小王上班的時候不敢打電話給女朋友，老闆不在才敢打。

   ……………………………………………………………………………………

3. 你看見同學不用功，你想告訴他：年輕的時候應該多學點東西。

   ……………………………………………………………………………………

4. 朋友要去中國留學，你羨慕他有這個機會可以多了解中國人。

   ……………………………………………………………………………………

5. 媽媽不讓弟弟出去，可是弟弟看見媽媽沒注意他，就跑出去了。

   ……………………………………………………………………………………

☞ 五 ……跟……（沒）有關係 is (not) related / connected to

⊙好像跟宗教沒什麼關係了。

It seems to have nothing to do with religion.

用法說明：說明兩者之間有關聯。「有」前面可加「很」、「非常」等程度副詞，「沒有」前面可加「都」、「完全」等程度副詞。「有」和「關係」中間可以加上修飾的成分。

Explanation: This pattern explains that two things are related. 很, 非常, or similar adverbs of degree can be added in front of 有, and 都, 完全 and similar adverbs of degree can be added in front of 沒有. Other modifiers can be added between 有 and 關係.

練習：請用「……跟……（沒）有關係」完成下面句子。

Exercise: Please use the "……跟……（沒）有關係" pattern to complete the sentences below.

1. 這篇報告跟獨立戰爭有關係，所以你得先看一些歷史方面的書。
   This report is related to the War of Independence, so you need to first look at a few history books .
2. 颱風 ____________________，所以颱風多的地方，不一定有地震。
3. 那件事我們公司管不著，因為 ____________________。
4. 為什麼你們助教對那個女孩那麼好？他 ____________________。
5. 英國政府常常支持美國政府的作法，因為 ____________________。

☞ 六 AABB（雙音節 SV 的重疊） repeating two-syllable SVs

⊙全家人在一起，歡歡喜喜地吃飯、說笑、唱歌。……

The whole family is together, joyfully eating, telling jokes, singing songs......

用法說明：雙音節的 SV 重疊時，一定是「AABB」的形式，跟雙音節動詞重疊時「ABAB」的形式不同。重疊的 SV 跟一般 SV 一樣，可以修飾名詞、動詞或做補語，但語氣較強，程度更深。在重疊的 SV 前面不可以再加副詞修飾。

Explanation: When you have the repetition of a two-syllable stative verb, it has to be in AABB format, unlike the ABAB format used for the repetition of two-syllable verbs. The functions of repeated stative verbs are the same as those of regular stative verbs – i.e., they can modify nouns or verbs, or serve as complements – but the mood is a bit stronger, the degree a bit more intense. Adverbs cannot be placed in front a repeated SV.

練習：Exercises:

㈠請把下面各句中的形容詞改成重疊的形式。

Please change the stative verbs in the following sentences to repeated stative verbs.

A. 修飾名詞 modifying nouns

1. 沒想到這麼秀氣的女孩又會罵人又會打人。

I never thought that such a refined girl would be capable of cursing at and hitting others.

→沒想到這麼秀秀氣氣的女孩又會罵人又會打人。

I never thought that such an incredibly refined girl would be capable of cursing at and hitting others.

2. 她那種大方的態度，我們都很欣賞。

....

3. 乾淨的房間，誰都喜歡住。

....

B. 修飾動詞 modifying verbs

1. 他借到錢就高興地回家了。

After he succeeded in borrowing money, he happily returned home .

→他借到錢就高高興興地回家了。

After he succeeded in borrowing money, he joyfully returned home.

2. 我母親今年六十歲，我們打算給她熱鬧地慶祝一下。

....

3. 我辛苦地準備了半天，可是客人都沒來。

....

C. 做補語 as complements

1. 錢的事情，你一定要跟他算得很清楚。

As far as money matters go, you should definitely keep things very clear with him.

→錢的事情，你一定要跟他算得清清楚楚。

As far as money matters go, you should definitely keep things extremely clear with him.

2. 她每次跟男朋友約會，都打扮得很漂亮。

....

3. 媽媽總是把家裡弄得很舒服，所以我一放假就回家。

....

㈡請改正下面各句，並說明原因。

A. Please correct the sentences below, and explain why the corrections are necessary.

1. 她的房間總是弄得乾淨乾淨的。

....

2. 昨天的「心理學」，他很輕輕鬆鬆地就考了一百分。

....

☞ 七 再不V(O)，就……
If one continues to not V(O), then......

⊙再不寄，就太晚了。

If you continue to put off mailing it, it will be too late.

用法說明：「再」是「還」的意思。「再不V(O)，就…」表示如果「再」後面的情形繼續下去，就會發生「就」後面的結果。

Explanation: "再不 V(O)，就…" indicates that if the action following 再 continues as it is, the situation (usually negative) following 就 will result.

練習：請用「再不 V(O)，就……」完成下面句子。

Exercise: Please use the "再不 V(O)，就……" pattern to complete the sentences below.

1. 已經好幾個月沒下雨了，如果再不下雨，就沒水用了。

   It hasn't rained in many months. If it continues to be dry, we won't have any water to use.

2. 你天天玩，不念書，如果你再不＿＿＿＿＿＿＿＿＿＿＿＿＿。
3. 你鬍子那麼長，再不＿＿＿＿＿＿＿＿＿＿＿＿＿。
4. 這場戰爭已經打了八年了，再不＿＿＿＿＿＿＿＿＿＿＿＿＿。
5. 我等電話等了半天了，他再不＿＿＿＿＿＿＿＿＿＿＿＿＿。

☞ 八 什麼都……，就是…… everything is......, except......

⊙聖誕節什麼都好，就是買禮物、寄聖誕卡太麻煩。

Everything about Christmas is wonderful, except buying presents and sending out Christmas cards which is too bothersome.

用法說明：「什麼都」表示所說的範圍內沒有例外，「就是」的後面是唯一的例外。「都」後面是肯定的，「就是」的後面則是否定的，反之亦然。

Explanation: 什麼都 indicates that, within the mentioned boundaries, there are no exceptions to the rule. Following 就是 is the sole exception to the rule. If the phrase following 都 is positive, then the phrase following 就是 is negative, and vice-versa.

練習：請用「什麼都……，就是……」改寫下面句子。

Exercise: Please use the "什麼都……，就是……" pattern to rewrite the following sentences.

1. 他弟弟除了玩以外，對哪件事都沒興趣。

   His little brother is not interested in anything other than having fun/ fooling around.

   →他弟弟什麼都沒興趣，就是喜歡玩。

   His little brother isn't interested in anything; he only likes to have fun.

2. 除了鴨子以外，他都吃。

   ……………………………………………………………………………

3. 我媽罵我爸爸只會吃飯，別的事情都不會。

....

4. 他很愛看球賽，可是從來不看棒球賽。

....

5. 她男朋友矮了一點，別的都很好。

....

☞ 九 倒是 but, on the contrary , however

⊙我倒是覺得對忙碌的現代人來說，寄聖誕卡是一個連絡感情的好辦法。

On the contrary, I think that sending Christmas cards is a good way for busy modern-day people to keep in contact with friends.

用法說明：「倒是」的前後是相反的（不同的）情況或意見。語氣比「可是」舒緩，但「倒是」是副詞，「可是」是連接詞。「倒是」的「是」可以省略。

Explanation: The situations or opinions preceding and following 倒是 are different from each other. In this way it is similar to 可是, however, the tone is slightly more gentle. Also, 倒是 is an adverb whereas 可是 is a conjunction. The 是 in 倒是 can be omitted.

練習：請完成下面對話，用「倒是」表示不同的意見。

Exercise: Please complete the dialogues below using 倒是 to indicate a differing opinion.

1. 張：那個男孩真帥。

   Chang: That guy is really handsome.

   李：我倒是覺得他旁邊那個更帥。

   Lee: But I think that the guy next to him is more handsome.

2. 張：這個房子冬天住好冷啊。

   李：夏天住倒是 ____________________ 。

3. 張：小王對別人很小氣，從來沒請過客。

   李：他對自己倒是 ____________________ 。

4. 張：老李這個人真奇怪，今天這麼冷，還穿短褲！
   李：就是嘛！天熱的時候他倒是 ________________。
5. 張：她們兩個，矮的那個是姐姐。
   李：沒想到妹妹倒是 ________________。

課室活動

1. 隨便談談 (Open discussion)

請說說你最喜歡的節日是哪一天，為什麼？再說說你怎麼過萬聖節、感恩節、聖誕節，你都做些什麼？有什麼特別的活動嗎？

Some useful supplementary words include: 化妝 (huà//zhuāng, put on makeup), 化裝 (disguise oneself), 化裝舞會 (costume party), 妖怪 (yāoguài; monster), 魔鬼 (móguǐ; devil), 巫婆 (wūpó; witch), 可怕的 (dreadful, terrible, fearsome, frightening), 遊行 (yóuxíng; parade), 刻 (kē; to carve), 打雪仗 (snowball fight), 堆雪人 (duī//xuěrén; make a snowman), 禱告 (dǎogào; to pray), 上帝 (Shàngdì; God), 清教徒 (qīngjiàotú; pilgrim), 基督徒 (jīdūtú, people who believe in Christianity), 天主教徒 (people who believe in Catholicism), 望彌撒 (wàng//mísā; to attend mass), 不給糖就搗蛋 (dǎodàn; this is a translation of the Western phrase "trick or treat", for which there is no traditional Chinese equivalent.)

2. 遊戲：你來猜猜

Before class the teacher copies some 生詞 the students have learned recently onto cards, one word per card. Then during class the teacher selects a card without revealing to the students what is written on it. The students try to figure out the word by asking questions such as: 是吃的東西嗎？是紙做的嗎？是東西，還是人？是不是動物 (dòngwù; animal)？會不會

動？能不能用？…… They may only ask "yes-no" or "choice type" questions, which the teacher answers. When the students think they have enough information, they guess what is written on the card. Anyone who guesses right wins a cookie or another reward provided by the teacher. Then the teacher goes to the next card, etc.

支票 (zhīpiào, check)
簽名 (qiēnmīng, to sign one'e name)

短文

中國人的節日

農曆[1]一月一日是中國新年，也叫春節[2]，是中國人最重要的節日，因為這是一年的開始。每個人不管在哪裏，除夕以前都要回家，全家一起吃年夜飯[3]，放鞭炮、拿紅包[4]。以前農業社會新年要到十五日過完元宵節[5]才結束。現在時代不同了，一般公司只放四、五天假，過年的氣氛跟以前比起來差多了。

元宵節也叫燈節，大家吃元宵[5]，孩子們還提燈籠[6]玩，因為明亮的燈籠會帶來好運。農曆五月五日端午節是為了紀念兩千多年前的愛國詩人[8]屈原[9]。除了吃粽子[10]，還有精彩的龍舟[11]比賽。

八月十五的月亮[12]又圓又亮，農人們的工作也做完了，全家人就一起賞月[13]、吃月餅[14]。慢慢就成了中秋節[15]。可惜很多賞月時說的故事[16]都在阿姆斯壯[17]上了月球[12]以後被推翻了。

Vocabulary:

1. 農曆 (nónglì): lunar calendar
2. 春節 (Chūn Jié): the lunar New Year, Spring Festival
3. 年夜飯 (niányèfàn): New Year's Eve dinner
4. 紅包 (hóngbāo): red envelope containing a gift of money
5. 元宵節 (Yuánxiāo Jié): Lantern Festival, the fifteenth day of the first month of the lunar calendar

   元宵 (yuánxiāo): a dessert of glutinous rice flour balls with a center filling in broth
6. 提燈籠 (tí//dēnglóng): to carry a lattern
7. 端午節 (Duānwǔ Jié): Dragon Boat Festival, the fifth day of the fifth month of the lunar calendar
8. 詩人 (shīrén): poet
9. 屈原 (Qū Yuán): (343 -290 B. C.) a famous poet of the Warring States period
10. 粽子 (zòng·zi): steamed food made of glutinous rice, meat, and other ingredients wrapped in bamboo leaves
11. 龍舟 (lóngzhōu): dragon boat
12. 月亮 (yuèliàng): moon

    月球 (yuèqiú): moon
13. 賞月(shǎng//yuè): to enjoy a moonlit night
14. 月餅 (yuèbǐng): mooncake
15. 中秋節 (Zhōngqiū Jié): Mid-Autumn Festival
16. 故事 (gù·shì): story, tale
17. 阿姆斯壯 (Āmǔsīzhuàng): Neil Armstrong, the first man on the moon

第十四課

放假到哪裡去

・狄士尼樂園（盧德昭攝）

（高偉立、林建國房門口，門開著）

建國：嗨！你們怎麼來了？進來坐吧！

美真：我們去四樓跟一個同學借小說，**順便**上來看看你們在不在，有些事想跟你們請教一下。

偉立：什麼事？別客氣。

台麗：快放假了，我們打算去旅行。哪些地方好玩？能不能給我們一點意見？

建國：沒問題！我想你們怕冷，去佛羅里達最好了。那裡的迪士尼世界最好玩，像雲霄飛車、鬼屋、小小世界什麼的，保證你們玩三天三夜還覺得不過癮。

偉立：佛羅里達的海灘也很棒。要是你們春假去，就可以曬太陽、游泳。

美真：我哥哥在那裡，可惜他放寒假的時候要做實驗，不能帶我去玩。我還是等他有空再去吧！

建國：加州還有一個迪士尼樂園，雖然比較小，可是也值得去看看。

美真：說來說去還是迪士尼，你真是長不大啊！

建國：**難道**你不想去**嗎**？

美真：好啦[1]！除了迪士尼，還有什麼地方**可**去？

建國：洛杉磯最有名的是好萊塢影城，可以去看看。從洛杉磯往南，還可以去聖地牙哥。那裡有一個「海洋世界」，不但可以看動物表演，而且可以得到很多有關海洋動物的知識。

偉立：往北可以去舊金山，看看金門大橋、欣賞欣賞舊金山灣的風景。有人說舊金山是全美國最羅曼蒂克[2]的城市。

台麗：真的嗎？那我可得去見識見識。

美真：我很想去大峽谷，我們自己租個車去，行不行？

・西安大雁塔
（盧德昭攝）

偉立：你們要去大峽谷，最好參加旅行團。

美真：我覺得參加旅行團只能走馬看花，每次到了一個地方，不是忙著照像，就是排隊上廁所，還能有多少時間欣賞風景呢？！

偉立：可是去大峽谷得經過一片大沙漠，參加旅行團**一方面**省事，**一方面也**安全。

台麗：那就**算了**。等以後多找些人再一起去吧！

美真：從大峽谷去黃石公園遠不遠？

偉立：遠倒是不算遠，但是黃石公園冬天只有部分開放，你等放暑假的時候再去吧！

建國：你忘了告訴她們一個有意思的地方——拉斯維加斯。

台麗：噢，賭城，聽說過。

建國：你們可以去試試運氣，**說不定**這一次的旅費都能贏回來呢！

偉立：萬一輸光了呢？你這個賭鬼！

建國：**不**賭**就不**賭，去看表演可以吧？那裡有些表演[3]一定可以讓你大開眼界。

美真：你越說越興奮，我看你就跟我們一起去吧！

建國：不行，寒假我們全家要回臺灣給我爺爺過生日[4]，飛機票都已經訂好了。

台麗：那，偉立，你呢？你要去哪裡？

偉立：我只打算跟我二哥去尼加拉瀑布，回來就得打工了。我得存點兒錢，暑假才能去大陸啊！

美真：你不是要去臺灣嗎？你還要去大陸啊？

偉立：我想先去大陸旅行一個月，然後再去臺灣。這幾天我正在打聽訂機票、辦護照跟簽證這些事。

建國：你打算去大陸哪些地方？

偉立：我一定要去看看上海、北京、西安這些大城市，另外像長江、黃河、萬里長城，我也該去見識見識。

建國：聽起來不錯，我要趕快存錢，**說不定**我們可以一起去呢！

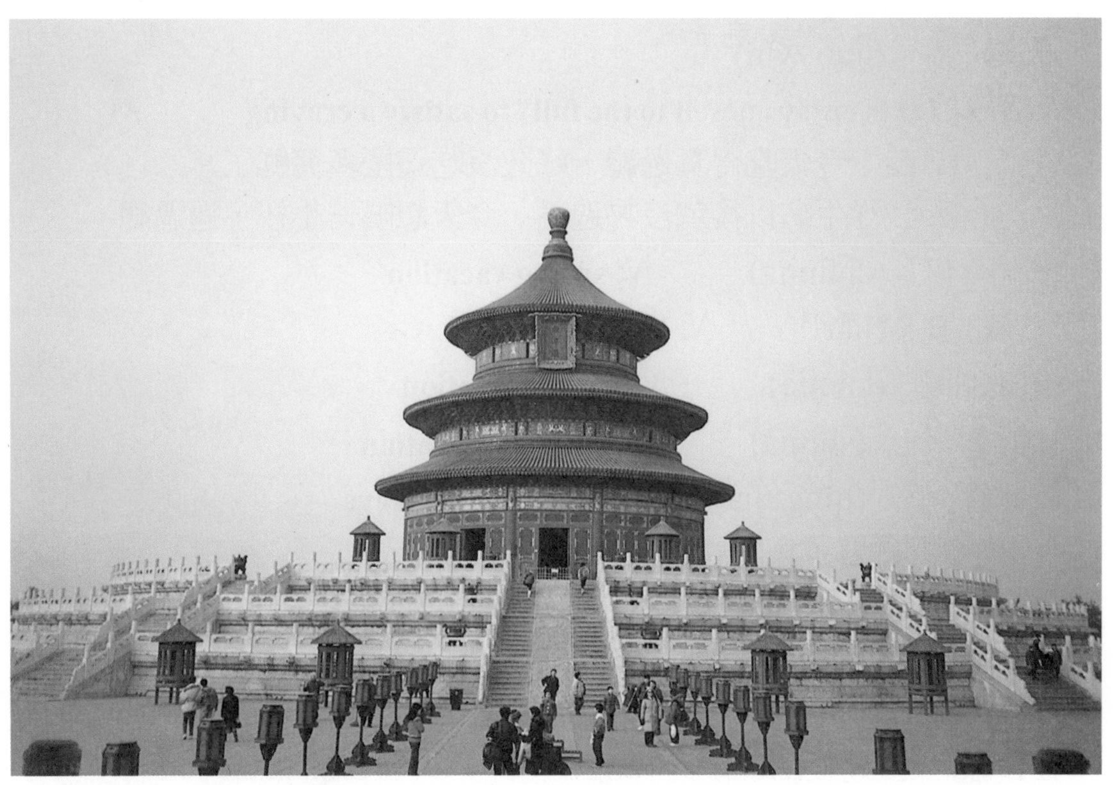

・北京天壇（盧德昭攝）

生詞及例句

1. 小說 (xiǎoshuō)　　*N*: **novel, short story**（**M**：本／篇）
2. 順便 (shùnbiàn)

   A: **incidentally; on the way, as one passes**

   你上去的時候，順便把今天的報拿給他好嗎？

3. 意見 (yìjiàn) *N*: **view, opinion, idea**

這件事該怎麼辦？各位有什麼意見就說出來，別客氣。

4. 雲霄飛車 (yúnxiāofēichē) *N*: **roller coaster**

雲 (yún) *N*: **cloud**（**M**：塊／片／朵 duǒ）

5. 鬼屋 (guǐwū) *N*: **haunted house**

6. 保證 (bǎozhèng) *V*: **to guarantee, assure, ensure**

我保證這些畫都是真的，有問題就來找我。

7. 過癮 (guò//yǐn)

SV/VO: **to enjoy oneself to the full / to satisfy a craving**

⑴哇！今天吃得真過癮，好久沒吃這麼多海鮮了。

⑵我從生病以後就沒喝過酒，今天想喝一小杯，過過癮。

8. 春假 (chūnjià) *N*: **spring vacation**

假日 (jiàrì) *N*: **holiday, dayoff**

9. 寒假 (hánjià) *N*: **winter vacation**

10. 暑假 (shǔjià) *N*: **summer vacation**

請假 (qǐng//jià) *VO*: **to ask for leave**

我感冒了，想請兩天假，在家休息。

病假 (bìngjià) *N*: **sick leave**

事假 (shìjià)

N: **a leave of absence (to attend to private affairs), personal leave**

11. 曬太陽 (shài//tài·yáng) *VO*: **to bask in the sun**

你看，很多老人坐在公園裡的椅子上曬太陽。

曬 (shài) *V*: **to dry in the sun, to bask**

太陽 (tài·yáng) *N*: **the sun**

今天太陽很大，把箱子裡的衣服拿出來曬曬吧！

月亮 (yuè·liàng) *N*: **moon**

星星 (xīng·xīng) *N*: **stars**

12. 做實驗 (zuò//shíyàn)

VO: **to perform an experiment, to make a test**

實驗 (shíyàn) *V/N*: **to experiment / experiment, test**

實驗室 (shíyànshì) *N*: **laboratory**

如果你不相信我的說法，我就用狗做實驗給你看。

13. 長不大 (zhǎng·búdà)

RC: **unable to mature, unable to become large**

我弟弟已經十七歲了，可是什麼都不懂，還像個長不大的孩子。

長 (zhǎng) *V*: **to grow up, to develop**

他長得很像他媽媽，尤其是眼睛。

14. 難道 (nándào)

A: **(used to begin an emphatic, rhetorical question) Can it be possible that......?**

(1) 你說你沒帶錢，難道連一塊錢都沒有嗎？

(2) 這件事人人都知道了，難道你還沒聽說嗎？

15. 表演 (biǎoyǎn) *N/V*: **performance / to perform**

(1) 我們這次的表演，有唱歌有跳舞，非常熱鬧。

(2) 她們的現代舞表演得很精彩，我一定要再看一次。

演 (yǎn) *V*: **to perform, to act**

那個電影明星太老了，演年輕人恐怕不合適。

16. 有關 (yǒuguān)

CV: **to have something to do with, to be related to**

有關參觀博物館的事，我們最好問問大家的意見。

跟......A......有關 (gēn......A......yǒuguān)

PT: **has to do with ......A; is related to......A**

水果長得好不好跟天氣有關。

17. 海洋動物 (hǎiyáng dòngwù) *N*: **marine life**

海洋 (hǎiyáng) *N*: **ocean, sea**

動物 (dòngwù) *N*: **animal**

動物園 (dòngwùyuán) *N*: **zoo**

18. 知識 (zhīshì) *N*: **knowledge**

只有課本上的知識是不夠的，經驗也很重要。

常識 (chángshì)　*N*: **common sense**

水當然往下流，這是常識嘛！

19. 橋 (qiáo)　*N*: **bridge（M：座 zuò）**

20. 羅曼蒂克 (luómàndìkè)　*SV*: **to be romantic**

她把房間裝飾得非常羅曼蒂克。

21. 見識 (jiànshì)

N/V: **general knowledge and experience, insight / to experience**

⑴聽他說話就知道他一點見識也沒有。

⑵他說那個地方很特別，值得去見識一下。

22. 旅行團 (lǚxíngtuán)　*N*: **tour group, touring party**

旅行社 (lǚxíngshè)　*N*: **travel agency（M：家）**

23. 走馬看花 (zǒu mǎ kàn huā)

IE: **to gain a superficial understanding through cursory observation**

那個博物館裡的東西太多，我們的時間不夠，只能走馬看花。

24. 排隊 (pái//duì)　*VO*: **to line up, to queue up**

很多人在辦公室門口排隊拿申請表。

25. 省事 (shěng//shì)

VO/SV: **to save trouble, simplify matters / to be convenient**

省錢 (shěng//qián)

VO/SV: **to save money / economical**

去飯館吃飯可以省不少事，可是不省錢。

省時間 (shěng//shíjiān)

VO/SV: **to save time / to be time-saving**

為了省時間，我們決定坐飛機去。

省油 (shěng//yóu)

VO/SV: **to save gasoline / to be gas-saving**

小車比大車省油。

省電 (shěng//diàn)

VO/SV: **to save electricity / to be electricity-saving**

省ㄕㄥˇ (shěng)　　*N*: **province**

臺灣是中國最小的一省。

26. 安ㄢ全ㄑㄩㄢˊ (ānquán)　　*N/SV*: **safety / to be safe, secure**

(1) 為了安全，你最好參加旅行團。

(2) 在紐約，晚上一個人走路安全不安全？

安ㄢ全ㄑㄩㄢˊ帽ㄇㄠˋ (ānquánmào)

N: **safety helmet（M：頂 dǐng）**

27. 算ㄙㄨㄢˋ了˙ㄌㄜ (suàn·le)　　*IE*: **Forget it!**

(1) 他不願意說就算了，我們問別人吧！

(2) 算了，別跟小孩子生氣了！

28. 開ㄎㄞ放ㄈㄤˋ (kāifàng)　　*V*: **to be open to public use**

這個圖書館假日也開放，你可以去那兒寫報告。

29. 賭ㄉㄨˇ城ㄔㄥˊ (dǔchéng)

N: **a gambling town (a city or town which has a large gambling industry, e.g. Las Vegas, Atlantic City)**

賭ㄉㄨˇ場ㄔㄤˇ (dǔchǎng)　　*N*: **casino, gambling den**

賭ㄉㄨˇ鬼ㄍㄨㄟˇ (dǔguǐ)　　*N*: **an obsessive gambler**

賭ㄉㄨˇ (dǔ)　　*V*: **to gamble, bet, wager**

他一連賭了三天三夜了，真是個賭鬼！

打ㄉㄚˇ賭ㄉㄨˇ (dǎ//dǔ)　　*VO*: **to make a bet**

我跟你打賭他一定會贏，要是我說對了，你請我吃飯！

30. 運ㄩㄣˋ氣˙ㄑㄧ (yùn·qì)　　*N*: **fortune, luck**

我的運氣真不錯，到了家才下雨。

幸ㄒㄧㄥˋ運ㄩㄣˋ (xìngyùn)　　*SV*: **to be fortunate, lucky**

我覺得我很幸運，到處都有人幫我的忙。

不ㄅㄨˊ幸ㄒㄧㄥˋ (búxìng)　　*SV*: **to be unfortunate, to be sad**

他生下來母親就死了，真不幸！

31. 說ㄕㄨㄛ不ㄅㄨˊ定ㄉㄧㄥˋ (shuō·búdìng)　　*MA/IE*: **perhaps, maybe**

李：他怎麼一直沒消息？會不會出事了？

張：別著急，說不定他已經安全回到家了呢！

32. 萬一 (wànyī) *A*: **just in case, if by any chance**

帶著你的信用卡吧，萬一錢用光了，也沒關係。

33. 輸 (shū) *V*: **to lose, to be defeated**

昨天的球賽，我們打得不好，輸了十幾分。

34. 大開眼界 (dà kāi yǎnjiè)

IE: **to broaden one's horizons**

第一次去迪士尼樂園，我們都覺得大開眼界。

開眼界 (kāi//yǎnjiè)

VO: **to expand one's experience and horizon**

她的櫃子裡有一千多雙鞋，什麼顏色的都有，真讓我開了眼界。

眼界 (yǎnjiè) *N*: **field of view, range of vision**

他的眼界很高，錢太少就不做，所以一直找不到工作。

35. 爺爺 (yé·ye)

N: **grandpa, grandfather (father's father); a respectful form of address for an old man**

奶奶 (nǎi·nai)

N: **grandma, grandmother (father's mother)**

36. 瀑布 (pùbù) *N*: **waterfall**

37. 然後 (ránhòu) *A*: **afterwards, after that**

我們先吃飯，然後去看電影，好不好？

38. 護照 (hùzhào) *N*: **passport（M：本）**

39. 簽證 (qiānzhèng) *N*: **visa**

如果你要去日本，一定要先拿到日本的簽證。

40. 趕快 (gǎnkuài) *A*: **at once, quickly, immediately**

你的病不輕，趕快去看醫生吧！

趕 (gǎn) *V/SV*: **to hurry, to rush; to catch up with**

(1) 這份資料我明天就需要用，請你幫我趕一趕。

(2) 這麼短的時間要看這麼多地方，太趕了吧！

趕上 (gǎn·shàng)

RC: **to catch up with; to be in time for**

現在已經三點了，我們趕不上三點半的飛機了。

專有名詞 Proper Names

1. 迪士尼世界 (Díshìní Shìjiè) Disneyworld
2. 迪士尼樂園 (Díshìní Lèyuán) Disneyland
3. 好萊塢影城 (Hǎoláiwù Yǐngchéng) Hollywood
4. 聖地牙哥 (Shèngdìyágē) San Diego
5. 海洋世界 (Hǎiyáng Shìjiè) Sea World
6. 舊金山 (Jiùjīnshān) San Francisco
7. 舊金山灣 (Jiùjīnshān Wān) San Francisco Bay
8. 金門大橋 (Jīnmén Dà Qiáo) Golden Gate Bridge
9. 黃石公園 (Huángshí Gōngyuán) Yellowstone National Park
10. 拉斯維加斯 (Lāsīwéijiāsī) Las Vegas
11. 尼加拉瀑布 (Níjiālā Pùbù) Niagara Falls
12. 上海 (Shànghǎi) Shanghai
13. 西安 (Xī'ān) Sian
14. 長江 (Cháng Jiāng) The Yangtze River
15. 黃河 (Huáng Hé) The Yellow River

注釋

1. "好啦！" is a contraction of 好了啊. It is used to end talk on a particular subject. It is similar to saying: "Come on !" , "Cut it out !" , "No more !" etc.. In the text 美真 does not want to admit that she wants to go to Disneyland, and so she does not wish to discuss it anymore.

2. 羅曼蒂克 is the transliteration of "romantic". The same word can also be translated as 浪漫 (làngmàn).
3. 拉斯維加斯的表演 means "the shows in Las Vegas". People in Taiwan have begun to use the transliterated word 秀 (xiù) for "show" instead of 表演. You might hear someone ask: 那個歌星在哪裡作秀？Another use of this word 秀 is in the expression 政治秀 which refers to a popularity-seeking action performed by a politician for the view of his electorate.
4. 給爺爺過生日 means "to celebrate grandfather's birthday." In Chinese society, people think every decade is a new stage of one's life, so every tenth birthday is particularly important and deserving of a celebration. Every tenth birthday over the age of 60 is especially important. This is the reason why the whole family of 林建國 is coming back to Taiwan to celebrate grandfather's birthday.

文法練習

順便

conveniently, on the way, without taking any extra trouble, at one's convenience

⊙我們去四樓跟一個同學借小說，順便上來看看你們在不在，……

We came to the fourth floor to borrow a novel from a classmate. Since we were here anyway, we came up to see if you were home.

用法說明：「順便」前面是本來要做的事，藉這個機會也可以方便地完成「順便」後面的事。

Explanation: Stated in front of 順便 is an initial action. Performance of this action creates a convenient opportunity to carry out a second action, described after 順便.

練習：下面的情形用「順便」怎麼說？

Exercise: Please use 順便 to describe what one would say in the following situations.

1. 你開車回家的時候碰到張教授，他就住在你家附近。

   While driving home you bump into Professor Chang, who happens to live near your house.

   →張教授，我可以順便送你回家。

   Professor Chang! I could give you a lift home. It's on my way.

2. 室友要去郵局寄信，你請他幫你買幾張郵票。

   ....

3. 你到紐約看表演，正好有一個朋友住在紐約，你可以去看他。

   ....

4. 你看見弟弟要出門，你想叫他出去的時候把門關上。

   ....

5. 你的車沒油了，正好也髒了，你就把車開到加油站去加油，並且把車洗乾淨。

   ....

二 難道……（嗎）？

Is it possible that......? Could it be true that......?

⊙難道你不想去嗎？

Is it possible that you don't want to go?

用法說明：「難道」的後面常用否定詞「不」或「沒」，表示懷疑或不相信的反問語氣。

Explanation: Following 難道 is a negative word like 不 or 沒, showing doubt or disbelief. The tone is that of a rebuttal or a rhetorical question.

練習：請用「難道……（嗎）？」改寫下面句子。

Exercise: Please rewrite the sentences below using the "難道……（嗎）？" pattern.

1. 這件事全校都知道了，你怎麼沒聽說？

   Everybody in the whole school knows about this. How did you not hear about it?

→這件事全校都知道了，難道你沒聽說嗎？

Everybody in the whole school knows about this. Is it possible that you didn't hear about it?

2. 你出去玩了一個月，真的還不過癮嗎？

....

3. 你真的想放棄這個好機會？

....

4. 他打了這麼多年籃球，怎麼不知道這個動作是犯規的？

....

5. 他罵得這麼難聽，你真的一點都不生氣？

....

☞ 三 可V（的） worth v-ing

⊙……還有什麼地方可去？

......What other places are worth going to?

用法說明：這個「可」是「值得」的意思。“可V（的）”可以放在名詞前，也可單獨使用，代表名詞。

Explanation: This 可 means "worth" or "worthwhile". "可V（的）" can be placed in front of a noun to describe it or the phrase can be used alone to take the place of a noun.

練習：請用「可V（的）」完成下面句子。

Exercise: Please use "可V（的）" to complete the following sentences.

1. 這件事，大家意見都不同，可討論的問題很多。

   Everybody's opinions differ on this issue. There are many points worthy of discussion.

2. 我的生活沒什麼變化，寫信的時候沒什麼可____________________。
3. 那家飯館你去過，有什麼可____________________，給我介紹一下。
4. 波士頓是個很老的城市，可____________________地方很多。
5. 你從來不聽我的話，我跟你沒話可____________________了。

☞ 四 一方面……，一方面也…… It is ..., and it is also...

⊙參加旅行團，一方面省事，一方面也安全。

When you travel with a tour group, it not only save a lot of effort, but it is also safe.

用法說明：說明做一件事的兩個原因，聽起來比較有條理。

Explanation: This explains two reasons in a particular situation. The pattern helps the speaker to present his ideas in an orderly fashion.

練習：請用「一方面……，一方面也……」改寫下面句子。

Exercise: Please rewrite the following sentences using the "一方面……，一方面也……" pattern.

1. 李小姐願意當助教，因為她可以選研究所的課，而且她對這個工作也有興趣。

   Miss Lee wants to be a teaching assistant because she can take graduate courses. Furthermore, she also has interest in the work.

   →李小姐願意當助教，一方面她可以選研究所的課，一方面她對這個工作也有興趣。

   Miss Lee wants to be a teaching assistant, on the one hand, she is interested in the work, and on the other hand, she can also take graduate courses.

2. 我不參加那個旅行團，因為那些地方我都去過，而且我也沒時間。

   ……………………………………………………………………

3. 他決定租這個公寓，因為房租便宜，交通也方便。

   ……………………………………………………………………

4. 那次革命沒成功，因為軍隊力量太弱，人民也希望安定。

   ……………………………………………………………………

5. 她能當電影明星，因為她身材好，而且也很會表演。

   ……………………………………………………………………

☞ 五 算了 forget it, never mind

⊙那就算了。

Well, then never mind.

用法説明：表示這件事情就此作罷了。（表示說話者並不滿意。）可以獨立使用，後面也可以附加說明。或是放在句尾。

Explanation: 算了 is very similar to the phrases "forget it" and "never mind", meaning that no further effort or discussion is necessary, and often indicating dissatisfaction by the speaker. One can use 算了 by itself, add other speech afterwards, or attach 算了 to the end of a sentence.

練習：請用「算了」完成下面對話。

Exercise: Please use 算了 to complete the dialogues below.

㈠獨立使用，可附加說明

used alone or with additional explanation

1. 張：他對你這麼不客氣，你應該去罵他一頓。

   Chang: He's so rude to you. You ought to go tell him off.

   李：算了，跟這種人生氣不值得。

   Lee: Forget it. It's not worth getting mad at a person like that.

2. 張：對不起，雖然你說了兩次了，可是我還是沒聽懂，請你再說一次吧！

   李：＿＿＿＿＿＿＿＿＿＿＿＿＿＿。

3. 張：唉喲！我又忘了把你的書帶來了，我這就回家拿。

   李：＿＿＿＿＿＿＿＿＿＿＿＿＿＿。

4. 張：我昨天打電話的時候跟你借的五毛錢，現在還你，謝謝！

   李：＿＿＿＿＿＿＿＿＿＿＿＿＿＿。

5. 張：我怎麼又輸了，我還要再賭一次，我不信我的運氣真的這麼壞。

   李：＿＿＿＿＿＿＿＿＿＿＿＿＿＿。

㈡放在句尾

placed at the end of the sentence

1. 張：我請他好幾次，他都不願意來。

   Chang: I invited him many times, and he never wanted to come.

   李：既然這樣，我看算了吧！

   Lee: If that's the case, I'd just say forget it !

2. 張：書店老闆說，這本漫畫書已經賣完了。

   李：那就＿＿＿＿＿＿，我們買別的吧！

3. 張：我的頭很疼，全身都不舒服。

   李：要是你真的病了，就請假＿＿＿＿＿＿。

4. 太太：你姐姐跟我們借的錢好幾年了都沒還，難道就算了嗎？

   李先生：不＿＿＿＿＿＿怎麼辦？誰叫她是我姐姐呢！

☞ 六 說不定 perhaps / maybe

⊙說不定這一次的旅費都能贏回來呢！

Who knows? Perhaps you'll win back all of the travel expenses this time!

用法說明：「說不定」的後面是短句。（如果主語清楚明顯可省略）。「說不定」、「也許」、「可能」、「大概」都表示臆測的語氣。但此四者中，越後面的詞情況發生的可能性越高。

Explanation: Following 說不定 is a clause. If the subject of the clause is clear then it can be omitted. The following four phrases indicate conjecture, listed in the order of increasing possibility: 說不定, 也許, 可能, 大概.

練習：請把「說不定」放在句中合適的地方。

Exercise: Please place 說不定 in the appropriate place in the following sentences.

1. 我很多年沒回家了，會找不到回家的路了。

   I haven't been home in many years. I won't be able to find my way.

   →我很多年沒回家了，說不定會找不到回家的路了。

   I haven't been home in many years. Maybe I won't be able to find my way.

2. 小王對政治很有興趣，將來會當參議員。

…………………………………………………………………………

3. 你把你的困難告訴房東，房租可以少算一點。

....

4. 你去學校找找，他就在圖書館裡面看書。

....

5. 換換環境，他的病會好得快一點。

....

☞ 七 不……就不……

⊙不賭就不賭，去看表演可以吧？

Okay, then I won't gamble. Do you have any objection to my seeing the shows?

用法說明：「不」的後面可以是動詞、動詞短語 (VP) 或 SV。這個句型表示勉強接受對方的說法，有妥協、無可奈何、委屈求全的語氣。後面的句子句尾常用「吧」。

Explanation: 不 can be followed by a verb, verb phrase, or SV. This sentence pattern shows that the speaker is forcing him/herself to accept what another has said. It expresses a tone of having no choice, compromising, or feeling wronged. 吧 is often placed at the end of the next sentence.

練習：請用「不……就不……」完成下面對話。

Exercise: Please use the "不……就不……" pattern to complete the dialogues below.

1. 張：你怎麼說這種話？太沒禮貌了！

   Chang: How can you say something like that? That's so rude!

   李：不說就不說。誰叫他這麼討厭?!

   Lee: So I won't say it then! But who told him to be so disagreeable?!

2. 張：還有三天就期末考了，你還要去看電影！

   李：________________________。

3. 媽媽：你不讓兒子去烤肉，他很不高興。

   爸爸：________________________，他應該在家準備考試。

4. 張：小王覺得看孩子太辛苦，不願意做。

李：＿＿＿＿＿＿＿＿＿＿＿＿＿＿，我們請別人吧！

5. 張：小陳說不能來參加你的生日舞會了。

李：＿＿＿＿＿＿＿＿＿＿＿＿＿＿，反正人已經很多了。

課室活動

1. The following assignment should be given to the students to prepare before class: The students are working for an organization which has invited some Chinese scholars to visit the United States for two weeks. The students' assignment is to plan a program for those scholars, to show them places and things that will help them better understand 美國 and 美國人. During class, they are to compare their suggestions and work out the details on the program to be offered. Some useful supplementary words include: 太空中心 (space center), 紀念碑 (jì'niànbēi; monument), 國會山莊 (Guóhuì Shānz huāng; Capital Hill), 最高法院 (Supreme Court), 科學博物館 (science museum), 憲法 (xiànfǎ; constitution), 工廠 (gōngchǎng; factory), 購物中心 (gòuwù zhōngxīn; shopping center), 百貨公司 (department store), 動物園 (zoo), 植物園 (zhíwùyuán; botanical garden), 遊樂園 (yóulèyuán; amusement park), 地下鐵 (subway).

2. Role playing:

Two students. One student plays the role of an agent in a 旅行社 (travel agency). The other is a customer. The customer is planning to take a trip to Europe for two weeks and asks for help from the agent about the travel route, airplane tickets, hotel rooms, special interest excursions, etc. The students should try to develop a lively conversation. Some useful supplementary words include: 航空公司 (hángkōng gōngsī; airlines), 轉機 (to make a flight connection), 雙人房 (double room), 單人房 (single room), 經濟艙 (jīngjìcāng; economy seating section in a plane or ship), 頭等艙

(tóuděngcāng; first class seating section in a plane or ship), 臥鋪 (wòpù; sleeping berth), 單程票 (dānchéngpiào; one way ticket), 來回票 (roundtrip ticket).

短文

在臺灣旅行

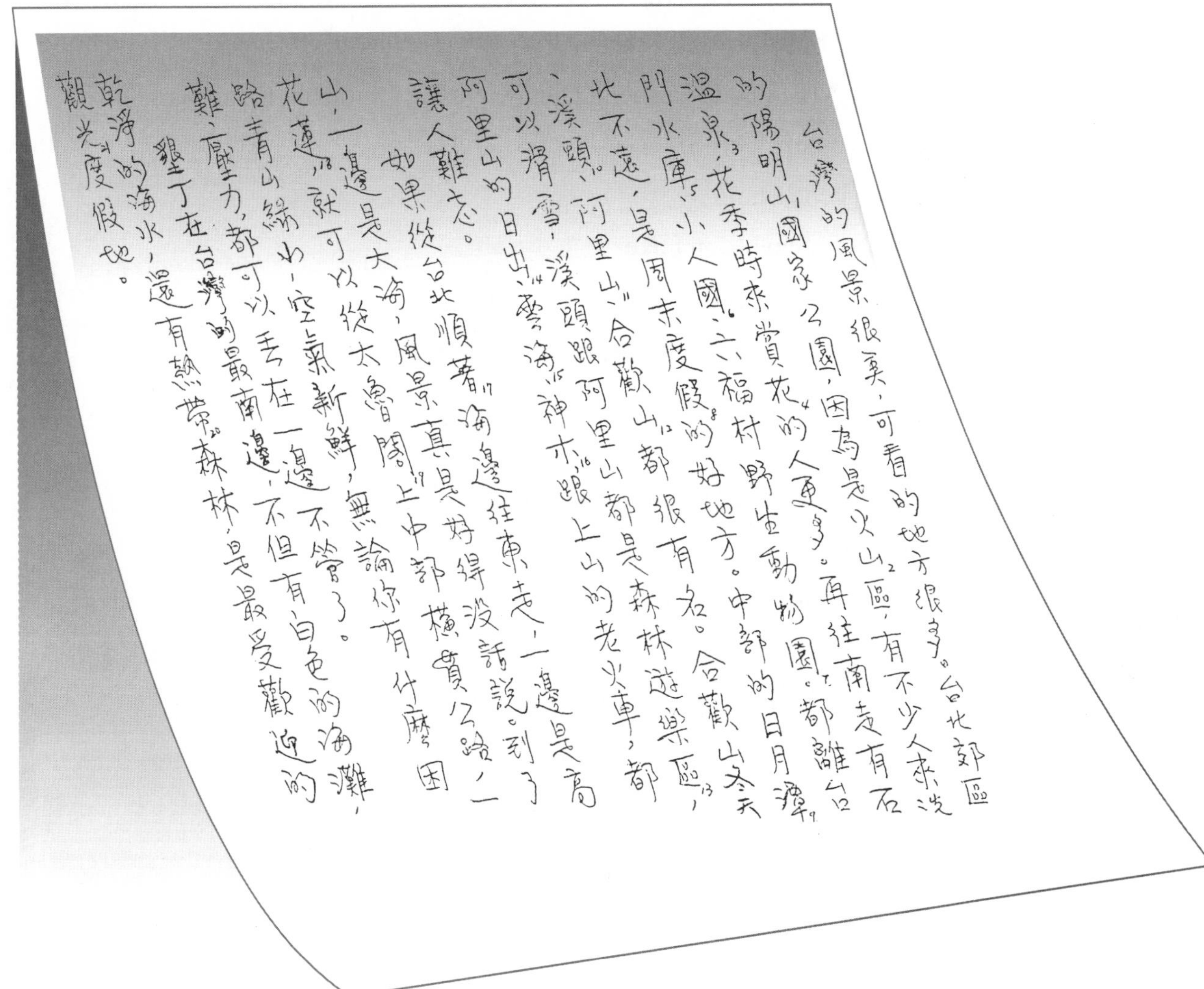

台灣的風景很美，可看的地方很多。台北郊區的陽明山[1]國家公園，因為是火山區[2]，有不少人來洗溫泉[3]，花季時來賞花[4]的人更多。再往南走有石門水庫[5]、小人國[6]、六福村野生動物園[7]，都離台北不遠，是周末度假[8]的好地方。中部的日月潭[9]、溪頭[10]、阿里山[11]、合歡山[12]都很有名。合歡山冬天可以滑雪，溪頭跟阿里山都是森林遊樂區[13]，都可以……阿里山的日出[14]、雲海[15]、神木[16]跟上山的老火車，都讓人難忘。

如果從台北順著[17]海邊往東走，一邊是高山，一邊是大海，風景真是好得沒話說。到了花蓮[18]，就可以從太魯閣[19]上中部橫貫公路。一路青山綠水，空氣新鮮，無論你有什麼困難、壓力，都可以丟在一邊不管了。

墾丁在台灣的最南邊，不但有白色的海灘，乾淨的海水，還有熱帶[20]森林，是最受歡迎的觀光[21]度假地。

Vocabulary:

1. 陽明山 (Yángmíng Shān): Yang Ming Mountain, a mountain in Taipei known for its beautiful scenery

2. 火山 (huǒshān): volcano
3. 溫泉 (wēnquán): natural hot-spring
4. 賞花 (shǎng//huā): to enjoy flowers in bloom
5. 石門水庫 (Shímén Shuǐkù): Shih-Men reservoir in 桃園 Táoyuán, south of Taipei
6. 小人國 (Xiǎorénguó): Miniatureland, a recreational area with miniature landscapes and architecture in 桃園 Táoyuán, south of Taipei
7. 六福村野生動物園 (Liùfúcūn Yěshēng Dòngwùyuán): Liufutsun Safari Park in 新竹 Xīnzhú, south of Taipei
8. 度假 (dù//jià): to spend a holiday
9. 日月潭 (Rìyuè Tán): Sun Moon Lake
10. 溪頭 (Xītóu): a botanical park in central Taiwan
11. 阿里山 (Ālǐ Shān): Ali Mountain, a recreational park in southern Taiwan
12. 合歡山 (Héhuān Shān): Hehuan Mountain, a mountain in central Taiwan, location of the only ski area in Taiwan
13. 森林遊樂區 (sēnlín yóulèqū): natural forest resort
14. 日出 (rìchū): sunrise
15. 雲海 (yúnhǎi): clouds resembling ocean waves which form around mountain peaks
16. 神木 (shénmù): extremely ancient tree
17. 順著 (shùn·zhe): to follow in the direction of
18. 花蓮 (Huālián): a port city in eastern Taiwan
19. 太魯閣 (Tàilǔgé): Taroko Gorge, a natural rock gorge in eastern Taiwan
20. 熱帶 (rèdài): tropical region
21. 觀光 (guānguāng) : to go sightseeing, to tour

出版品預行編目資料

視聽華語／國立臺灣師範大學國語教學中
-臺初版 . - - 臺北市：正中，民

公分.
957-09-1237-5(第一冊：平裝) . - -
957-09-1238-3(第二冊上：平裝) . - -
957-09-1239-1(第二冊下：平裝) . - -
957-09-1236-7(第三冊：平裝)

語言 - 讀本
88006350

實用視聽華語(二)上

主 編 者◎國立臺灣師範大學國語教學中心
編輯委員◎范慧貞・蕭美美・劉咪咪
策 劃 者◎中華民國教育部
著作財產權人◎中華民國教育部
發 行 人◎單小琳
總 編 輯◎蔡文怡
責任編輯◎黃惠娟
美術編輯◎黃馨玉

出版發行◎正中書局股份有限公司
地　址◎台北縣(231)新店市復興路43號4樓
電　話◎(02)8667-6565
傳　真◎(02)2218-5172
郵政劃撥◎0009914-5
網　址◎http://www.ccbc.com.tw
E-mail:service@ccbc.com.tw
門 市 部◎台北市(100)衡陽路20號
電　話◎(02)2382-1153・2382-1394
傳　真◎(02)2389-2523
香港分局◎集成圖書有限公司 - 香港九龍油麻地北海街七號地下
TEL：(852)23886172-3・FAX：(852)23886174
歐洲分局◎英華圖書公司 - 14,Gerrard Street,London,WIV 7LJ England
TEL：(0207)4398825・FAX：(0207)4391183
泰國分局◎集成圖書公司 - 曼谷耀華力路233號
TEL：2226573・FAX：2235483
美國辦事處◎中華書局 - 135-29 Roosevelt Ave. Flushing, NY 11354 U.S.A.
TEL：(718)3533580・FAX：(718)3533489
日本分局◎海風書店 - 東京都千代田區神田神保町一丁目五六番地
TEL：(03)32914344・FAX：(03)32914345

總 經 銷◎紅螞蟻圖書有限公司 TEL：(02)2657-0132・FAX：(02)2799-5284
行政院新聞局局版臺業字第0199號 (9754)
分類號碼◎802.00.011(版)(3000)(9.0)久裕
出版日期◎西元1999年8月臺初版
西元2001年9月第四次印行

ISBN 957-09-1238-3
定價／500元

國家圖書館出版品預行編目資料

實用視聽華語／國立臺灣師範大學國語教學中心主編．－－臺初版．－－臺北市：正中，民88

冊；　公分．

ISBN 957-09-1237-5(第一冊:平裝)．--
ISBN 957-09-1238-3(第二冊上:平裝)．--
ISBN 957-09-1239-1(第二冊下:平裝)．--
ISBN 957-09-1236-7(第三冊:平裝)

1.中國語言－讀本

802.86　　　　88006350

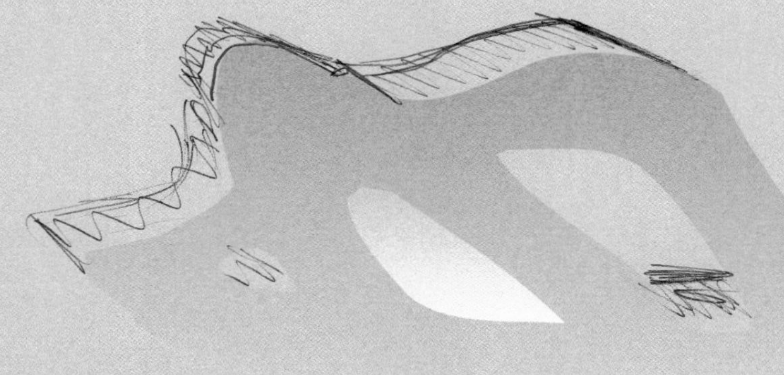
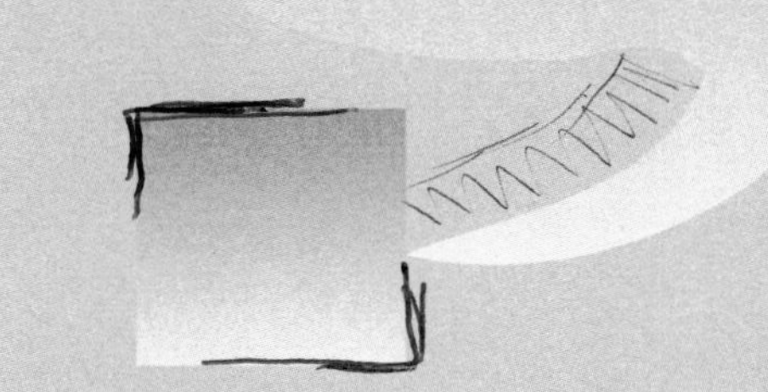

CHENG CHUNG
BOOK CO., LTD.

CHENG CHUNG
BOOK CO., LTD.

CHENG CHUNG
BOOK CO., LTD.

CHENG CHUNG
BOOK CO., LTD.